Hospital-Based
Medical Office
Buildings

Drexel Toland
with Susan Strong

American Hospital Association
840 North Lake Shore Drive
Chicago, Illinois 60611

Library of Congress Cataloging in Publication Data

Toland, Drexel.
  Hospital-based medical office buildings.

  Includes bibliographical references and index.
    1. Medical offices. 2. Medical offices—Design and
construction. 3. Hospitals—Outpatient services.
4. Health facilities—Affiliations. I. Strong, Susan.
II. Title. [DNLM: 1. Health facilities—Economics.
2. Health facility planning. 3. Medical office buildings.
WX 140 T647h]
RA974.T64   362.1′1′0682   81-10890
ISBN 0-87258-297-3   AACR2
AHA catalog no. 145138

©1981 by the
American Hospital Association
840 North Lake Shore Drive
Chicago, Illinois 60611

3M-9/81-7551

Contents

iii

List of Figures and Tables

Acknowledgments

The information in this book has been gathered over a span of a quarter of a century. For the time and experiences shared with me by my colleagues, I am grateful, for without them, this book would not have been possible.

The actual writing of this book was expertly taken from its raw form to manuscript by Susan Strong, director of communication, Drexel Toland & Associates, Inc. Only her research and ability to organize vast amounts of random data permitted this book to be completed. In addition, her intellectual integrity in constantly challenging the data and ideas contributed substantially to its quality. Besides being a professional communicator, she has been, throughout this project, a personal confidant, counselor, and friend.

In no small way, the preparation of the book was assisted by Oneta Patton, who scrutinized, questioned, and corrected the copy with the skill of a professional editor as she typed the final manuscript, and by Nell Spann, who assisted in typing earlier drafts.

Marjorie Weissman, manager, Book Department, American Hospital Association, prepared the final manuscript for publication and assisted throughout the development of the book with experience, advice, and cheerful patience. In addition, thanks are due to staff members of the American Hospital Association Division of Health Facilities and Standards and especially to Susanne Batko, formerly of the division, now assistant director, Center for Urban Hospitals, who initiated this project.

This book is dedicated to the next generation of health care administrators, with the hope that our experience will assist them in resolving some of the complex problems confronting them in the future.

Drexel Toland, F.A.C.H.A.
Drexel Toland & Associates, Inc.
Memphis
May 1981

Contributors

The following administrative and architectural staff members of Drexel Toland & Associates, Inc., Memphis, contributed substantial portions of the data and experience included in this book:

W. Robert Campbell Jr.

Debra N. Drees

Donald A. Faber

C. Larry Flowers

Arlo D. Harkleroad, A.I.A.

James A. Lawrimore

Davie L. Lloyd, P.E.

Freeman E. May, F.A.C.H.A.

Frank Ricks

Curtis C. Terry Jr.

The following persons contributed original, unpublished material and data for use in this book:

Accountants
William L. Cox, C.P.A., partner-in-charge
Ernst & Whinney
Jackson, Mississippi

Travis E. Smith, C.P.A., partner
Michael B. Taylor, C.P.A., partner
Ernst & Whinney
Memphis, Tennessee

Attorneys
Russell B. Carpenter
Farrand, Malti, Spillane, & Cooper
San Francisco, California

Lewis R. Donelson
Heiskell, Donelson, Adams, Williams, and Kirsh
Memphis, Tennessee
Commissioner of Finance and Administration
State of Tennessee

Robert J. Kilpatrick
Wise, Kilpatrick, and Clayton
Long Beach, California

Max Shelton
Harris, Shelton, Dunlap and Cobb
Memphis, Tennessee

Financiers

Robert Francoeur, president
Francoeur and Company
Encino, California

William R. Meier, senior vice-president
B. C. Ziegler and Company
West Bend, Wisconsin

Hospital Administrators

Sister M. Alfreda Bracht, O.S.F.
Saint Francis Hospital
Evanston, Illinois

Marcus E. Drewa, F.A.C.H.A.
Methodist Hospital
Jacksonville, Florida

M. J. Foerster
Holy Rosary Hospital
Ontario, Oregon

Frank S. Groner, F.A.C.H.A.
Maurice W. Elliott, F.A.C.H.A.
Baptist Memorial Hospital
Memphis, Tennessee

Pat N. Groner, F.A.C.H.A.
Baptist Hospital
Pensacola, Florida

Will J. Henderson, F.A.C.H.A.
The Queen's Medical Center
Honolulu, Hawaii

J. Craig Honaman
Tallahassee Regional Medical Center
Tallahassee, Florida

J. W. McAlvin, F.A.C.H.A.
Ronald J. Marott
Anaheim Memorial Hospital
Anaheim, California

Boone Powell, F.A.C.H.A.
Baylor University Medical Center
Dallas, Texas

Physicians

Jan Alben, M.D.
San Francisco, California

John A. Belt, M.D.
Anaheim, California

I. Hunter Crittenden, M.D.
San Bernardino, California

Richard L. DeSaussure, M.D.
Memphis, Tennessee

J. W. Douglas, M.D.
Pensacola, Florida

Andrew W. Morgan, M.D.
Honolulu, Hawaii

William E. Oldham, M.D.
Louisville, Kentucky

J. E. Robinson, D.D.S.
Anaheim, California

Frank J. Schlichter Jr., M.D.
Pensacola, Florida

Lowell L. Stokes Jr., M.D.
Louisville, Kentucky

Dan R. Sutherland, M.D.
Dallas, Texas

Benjamin C. K. Tom, M.D.
Honolulu, Hawaii

Ralph O. Wallerstein, M.D.
San Francisco, California

Hosein Yasrebi, M.D.
Jacksonville, Florida

Introduction

During the second half of the 20th century, a major trend in medical practice has been the clustering of physicians' offices around hospitals and, in particular, the increasing development of hospital-based, or on-campus, medical office buildings. Today, this trend is evidenced not only by the increased numbers of hospital-based medical office buildings that are already in existence, but also by the demand for information by the hospitals considering the development of these buildings. Not since 1959, when the American Hospital Association published Rufus Rorem's monograph *Physicians' Private Offices at Hospitals,* has a definitive book been published specifically on this subject. Since that time, hundreds of medical office buildings have opened and hundreds more are being planned.

This book examines the major areas of concern to a hospital considering or planning a medical office building and the many areas of possible improvement available to hospitals already operating such buildings. It touches on both the philosophical and practical aspects of developing and operating hospital-related medical office buildings. It is, in fact, a step-by-step approach to the information needed and the decisions to be made in the development and operation of a successful project.

Specifically, this book deals with what is called the hospital-based or on-campus medical office building. That is, it concerns itself primarily with the medical office building that is to be constructed or that has been constructed on hospital property, usually at the initiation of the hospital or its medical staff, or with the medical office building built so near to the hospital, and usually physically connected to it, that it is, in effect, part of the hospital campus. Such a building may or may not be owned by the hospital.

Although medical office buildings have clustered around hospitals for years, they have usually been developed and operated as commercial real estate ventures, based on the need for office space generated by the hospital. These buildings tend to function differently from ones developed with the goals and needs of the hospital, the medical staff, and the community in mind. This book, then, deals with those buildings based on the hospital campus and related to the hospital in concept, planning, and often even ownership, rather than those that have been developed primarily as commercial real estate. Nevertheless, the principles presented could be easily applied to any medical office building in order to make it a more effective and successful operation.

CHAPTER 1

History and Development of On-Campus MOBs

Although the trend toward hospital-based medical office buildings did not develop as an influential force in medical practice until the second half of the 20th century, the history of on-campus medical office buildings goes back many years.

One of the earliest on-campus buildings was constructed in 1928 by Baptist Memorial Hospital, Memphis. Initially, this 18,000-square-foot building was developed in response to requests from physicians on the hospital's medical staff. These physicians were also on the teaching staff of the medical school across the street and recognized the need for on-campus offices if they were to be able to go back and forth between teaching classes and attending private patients.

The hospital, on the other hand, recognized the value of and need to involve its physicians more intensely in both health care planning and the routine, day-to-day care of the hospitalized patients. The hospital also realized the economic impact of the physicians—simply, that the hospital could not survive without the physicians to admit patients. The end result was a small, hospital-owned, and hospital-operated medical office building to accommodate the increased needs of the hospital's growing medical staff.

THE BEGINNING TREND

The first indications of growing interest in hospital-based medical office buildings appeared during the Great Depression of the 1930s. At that time, interest was not directed so much toward on-campus office buildings for physicians as toward utilizing empty space in the hospital buildings themselves.

During the depression many hospitals experienced substantial reductions in patient census. Rooms were standing idle, and many hospitals were in economic trouble. Thus, in an attempt to utilize unused space, many administrators converted areas of their hospitals into physicians' offices. For the first time, substantial numbers of physicians began to locate their private offices on hospital campuses.

Then came World War II and the almost total standstill in domestic health care development by the private sector. Hospitals could not expand. Men and women were away. Physicians were away. And the health care system limped along at home.

The end of the war, however, brought rapid change. Funds and materials were once again available for the remodeling and expansion of hospitals.

Thousands of men and women returned home, and physicians who had been in the military service flooded back into private practice. Doctors were plentiful, and competition was keen. They began to set up their offices near their patients—in the newly booming suburban areas.

This system of suburban offices for physicians worked well. It was convenient for their patients. Most cities were small enough that commuting to and from the hospital was not a problem for the physicians. Time was not a major factor.

But the population began to change. The birth rate exploded. Cities grew rapidly. Neighborhoods changed, leaving the physicians no longer near their patients. The physicians who had come home from World War II began to retire. New government programs dramatically increased the utilization of the health care system. Time became a critical factor as each physician was required to handle an increasing patient load.

During this time of rapid change, almost every aspect of health care delivery was being centralized and coordinated around the hospital—every aspect except the physicians. At this point, hospital administrators and others responsible for health care delivery began to realize the importance of including the physician in the planning and centralizing process. Interest reemerged in on-campus physicians' offices. The concept was not new, but its time had finally come.

CHANGING MEDICAL CARE

Today, four developments in the delivery of health care are drawing physicians into closer working relationships with one another and with the hospitals at which they practice. They are rapidly expanding scienific knowledge and technology, greater complexity of care, greater specialization of physicians, and growing emphasis on ambulatory care rather than inpatient care.

With advancing scientific knowledge and greater availability of technological diagnostic equipment, physicians and hospitals find themselves needing, more than ever, to work closely together. The pooling of knowledge is frequently needed in order to stay abreast of current developments, and the high cost of important and highly specialized equipment requires that physicians either combine their financial resources into large group practices or look to the hospital for the provision of diagnostic outpatient services.

More complex medical care has largely been an outgrowth of this same knowledge explosion. Diseases that were heretofore mysterious and untreatable can now be diagnosed and treated, but the diagnosis and treatment depend on the increased knowledge and skill of the physician, on a substantial investment of his time in the supervision of care, and on the assistance of sophisticated and expensive equipment and a specialized allied health staff.

In addition, the knowledge explosion has also been a major contributing factor to the greater specialization of physicians. And the practice of specialization itself requires that the physicians cluster themselves together, preferably in the same building, for effective referral and consultation systems. The more highly specialized medicine becomes, the greater this need will be.

Finally, increased emphasis on ambulatory care is resulting in hospitals expanding their outpatient diagnostic and treatment services in order to make available needed equipment and resources. In turn, physicians are clustering nearer the hospital to facilitate the referral of private patients to the outpatient services, to coordinate and supervise patients' care more effectively while at the hospital, and in some cases, to become an active participant in planned ambulatory care centers and/or outpatient clinics.

CHANGING ROLE OF THE HOSPITAL

At the same time that medical care has been changing, the role of the hospital has likewise changed from that of the doctor's workshop to that of the complete medical center for the community. In the process, the hospital has taken on more responsibility for and active involvement in health care planning for the community and is now placing more emphasis on being a prime mover in meeting the community's need for physicians— for seeing that not only the number of physicians needed by the community are recruited, but also that they represent a balance of specialties needed by the population.

As the hospital assumes greater responsibility for recruiting the physicians needed by the community, the need for an on-campus medical office building usually increases.

DEMANDS ON TIME

Increased utilization of the health care system, increased congestion in cities, and greater government and consumer pressure for efficiency in medical care have significantly increased the demand on the physician's time. And from the physician's point of view, the more time he saves, the more patients he can treat. Time is a central factor in the trend toward polarization of physicians' offices around hospitals.

In addition, social and governmental pressures for high-quality care at the most reasonable prices have challenged those in private practice to develop better ways of organizing their activities. Physicians long ago gave up house calls and shifted to office-based practices in order to utilize their time more effectively. Likewise, physicians are finding that they can no longer practice in several hospitals and properly maximize their productivity. The demands are too great, and the time is too short for a doctor to spend his available office hours tied up in traffic jams between hospital and office.

Concentration of physicians' services, rather than diffusion, is more and more of an economic and physical necessity in order to realize maximum effectiveness and economy. Convenience and time saving are essential in a system that has numerous demands placed on it. A primary way that physicians have found for meeting these demands has been the location of their private offices on the hospital campus.

ACCELERATING TREND

The result of these various forces of change is a rapidly accelerating trend toward on-campus medical office buildings. Between 1929 and 1959, slightly more than 100 on-campus medical office buildings were developed. Today, conservative estimates suggest that well over 1,300 office buildings are directly on hospital campuses, with several thousand more clustered near hospitals.[1]

Current thinking recognizes that the on-campus medical office building serves to coordinate the efforts of the hospital and the physician. It brings them together for convenience and efficiency. It maximizes effective use of the health care system, saving time and waste; and it provides the physician a place in which to practice that can be physically altered without his having to uproot his practice in the event of massive changes in the health care system.

At this point, the chances for the reversal of this trend toward on- campus medical office buildings seem to be slim. All indications are that increasing numbers of hospitals will look to the on-campus medical office building as another step in improving the effectiveness of the health care system.

NOTE

1. American Hospital Association. Ambulatory Care Survey—1975. Chicago: The Association, 1976. Questions 23 and 24.

CHAPTER **2**

Concept of On-Campus MOBs Today

Although a well planned and properly implemented on-campus medical office building can result in convenience and improved effectiveness in medical practice and in improvements in patient care, specific problems or needs have often been the motivating factors that have prompted many hospitals to investigate and develop on-campus medical office buildings.

RESPONSE TO NEEDS

These motivating factors have generally been either economic or staff-related in nature. For example, the need to stabilize or increase census, the need to improve utilization or ancillary services, and the desire to improve the overall financial position of the hospital are typical economic needs that have prompted consideration and development of on-campus medical office buildings. Staffing problems might include the need to recruit additional physicians and to provide better coverage of essential services. In still a few other cases, unusual problems such as the relocation of a hospital or the consolidation of two hospitals have prompted development of medical office buildings in order to keep the medical staffs closely associated with the hospital.

As the effects of the on-campus medical office building are examined in more detail, a clearer picture emerges of how an office building can provide solutions for so many needs and problems. In fact, close examination shows that in the cases in which hospitals have properly developed their on-campus medical office buildings, many advantages have been realized that had not necessarily been anticipated originally. Because the positive effects on on-campus offices are becoming increasingly apparent, many hospitals are no longer waiting for problems to arise before considering the development of a building. The on-campus medical office building has now become established as an integral part of long-range planning in a medical complex.

ADVANTAGES TO THE PATIENT

Because the primary purpose of both the hospital and the physician is to care for the patient, patients are the most significantly affected by on-campus medical office buildings. Although physicians' offices at a central location may be somewhat less convenient for office patients, other factors and important advantages of the on-campus location generally outweigh any inconvenience.

Hospitalized Patient

First, the hospitalized patient benefits from the proximity of the physician through better supervised care. As one physician explained, "In the event that a patient develops some sort of difficulty, I am able to reach that patient in a minimum amount of time. I have the advantage of almost being in the hospital, but at the same time I have an office which is independent of the operation of the hospital."[1]

Another physician, a hemotologist, amplified that point. "We are more quickly accessible to patients and see them several times during the day. In my particular case, I can monitor the hemophilia unit, which is based at the emergency treatment department of the hospital, in a way that I couldn't if my offices were located further away."[2]

The physician's proximity to the hospital can produce a number of benefits to the patient. As described by the hematologist and confirmed by a nation-wide study of 60 hospitals with on-campus medical office buildings, physicians on campus make rounds more frequently.[3] They tend to switch from morning and evening rounds to periodic rounds throughout the day. If a patient misses an appointment, the physician often utilizes that time slot to check on a patient in the hospital.

The physician's frequent visits to the hospital may produce several effects. First, the hospital staff no longer has the tendency to put off prescribed treatments for the next shift to handle, because the physician may be back at any time to see that the procedure has been carried out. Second, because the physician can follow through with the same personnel in the same day, better communication and understanding are created between the hospital staff and the physician. Patient care staff feel more free to call the physician if they have questions or if an emergency arises, because they have better rapport with him.

Additionally, the patient's knowledge that his physician is both readily accessible and can make frequent visits to him if necessary is usually reassuring to the patient, increasing his confidence and reducing his anxiety about being hospitalized. This reduction of anxiety in itself can have a therapeutic effect, making it easier for the patient to respond to treatment.

Of particular importance to the hospitalized patient is the fact that on the average he is apt to leave the hospital one day sooner if his physician has an office on campus rather than an office away from the campus.[4] Although better supervised care and reduced anxiety contribute to this shorter stay, an even more important factor may well be simple logistics.

When two physicians consult about a patient, the primary physician may see the patient on a given morning and decide the patient is ready to be discharged as soon as the consulting physician sees him. If, however, the consulting physician is not located on campus, the time lost in contacting him, setting up a visit, and working a visit to the hospital into his schedule may result in his not being able to see the patient until that evening or even the next morning. Thus, the patient has spent a day in the hospital unnecessarily. If, on the other hand, both physicians have offices on campus, the consulting physician can usually see the patient almost immediately, and the patient may be able to go home

When the patient's stay in the hospital is shortened, the cost of that hospital confinement is reduced. In addition, another cost savings is likely in the area of testing. Frequently, when a patient is hospitalized, much of the laboratory, x-ray, and other work that has previously been done in the physician's office has to be redone upon admission, for hospital records. This unnecessary duplication of tests adds to the cost of hospitalization. When a physician is on campus, however, many of his tests are done at the hospital in the first place. In addition, most hospitals with an on-campus medical office building develop efficient systems for transporting records between the physician's office and the hospital. The information is mutually available, and expensive duplication is reduced.

One other advantage to the hospitalized patient can be the availability of the commercial services in the medical office building. The office building is an ideal place for a gift shop, snack bar, flower shop, retail pharmacy, limb and brace shop, optician, and sometimes even a barber or beauty shop and motel accommodations. Frequently, a hospital can afford to have these services in a medical office building but would not want to locate them in the hospital building itself because of the expense of hospital construction and the hospital's tax structure.

Although the family of a patient is likely to take advantage of these commercial services, the hospitalized patient receives the benefit indirectly, through gifts and flowers he may receive, through incidentals he wants that can be picked up conveniently for him, and so forth.

Office Patient

The office patient also realizes a number of advantages from his physician's practicing in an on-campus medical office building. The first is the convenience of having multiple medical and ancillary services available in one central location. An on-campus medical office building, when properly programmed (see chapter 13), provides one-stop shopping for the patient's medical needs. He sees his physician. If tests, X rays, or laboratory work are needed, he can often have them all completed in the hospital outpatient departments. If consultation or referral is needed, his physician will usually be able to set up an appointment with another physician in the same building. If he needs a prescription filled or glasses fitted, the appropriate commercial services will usually be available so that the patient can handle all of his needs before leaving the building.

Second, because of a good complement of specialties, referrals and consultations from one specialist to another, and the convenient sharing of medical knowledge that can occur within the on-campus medical office building, the patient is more likely to receive better medical care. A recent study of the medical staff of an urban Tennessee hospital showed that physicians with offices in the on-campus medical office building averaged three times more consultations per year than physicians with offices away from the hospital.[5] This study compared only physicians with similar practices, including specialty, age, length of practice, demographics, and other influencing factors.

The office patient, even more than the hospitalized patient, is often subject to duplicate tests. With physicians' offices spread out across town, laboratory and x-ray work is often repeated as the patient is referred from one physician to another. One physician kept detailed records of patients referred to him and how his time was used in treating them. On the basis of his notes, he decided that if he had had available all previous data on the patients when they were first referred to him, he could have saved from one to three hours per patient in duplication of work.[6] Referrals and consultations within a properly programmed multi-specialty medical office building (see chapters 9 and 13) may solve many of the problems of duplication, because records are nearby and can be conveniently transported from one office to another. An office building tied into a central record-keeping department in the hospital provides even greater availability of records and less duplication.

Another advantage to the on-campus office patient is that physicians are better able to run their offices on time. According to a professional practice consultant who has sat in more than 5,000 physicians' waiting rooms and talked with hundreds of patients, patients think they are kept waiting because "the doctor is badly organized" or "he's greedy and books as many patients as he can." Few patients seem aware that many delays are caused by emergencies or by patients who are late for appointments, the consultant says.[7] By being located on campus, a physician has better control over his time, with the result that the office patient is less likely to suffer from extended waiting. If an emergency arises at the hospital, the physician can leave his office, go to the hospital, handle the situation, and be back at his office in a fraction of the time necessary had he needed to drive across town.

Finally, the office patient receives a psychological benefit from the on-campus medical office building in that the professional surroundings tend to inspire confidence, giving him a more positive attitude about the care he receives.

ADVANTAGES TO THE HOSPITAL

Experience shows that the physician who rents office space in an on-campus medical office building will inevitably admit most, if not all, of his patients to the hospital where he is located. He not only admits more of his patients to that hospital, but he and his office staff usually also develop a closer working relationship with the hospital, making possible better coordination of admissions. These improvements, in turn, result in a higher and more stabilized census for the hospital, with more effective use being made of the available beds and personnel. The bottom line is increased income for the hospital.

When the hospital makes convenient and reasonably priced ancillary diagnostic and treatment services available to office patients, physicians utilize the services of the hospital, rather than seeking the same services elsewhere. Greater utilization of hospital ancillary services, in turn, creates a pressure to upgrade these services. Many services that might not have been cost efficient when made available for hospitalized patients only can become economically feasible when they serve both the hospital and the adjacent office building.

In fact, when examining the area of ancillary income, a survey shows that for each tenant physician in an on-campus medical office building, the hospitals surveyed realized an average of $4,500 per year in new net income from outpatient pharmacy, laboratory, x-ray, and other services.[8] In some cases, this increased income made the ancillary services self-supporting or profitable for the first time, because of more effective utilization of the staff and equipment that were already available. In other cases, the increased income and economy of scale allowed the hospital to reduce direct costs to the patient or to provide a wider range of more advanced technical services.

A one-day shorter stay for the patient is an advantage not only to the patient but also to the hospital. Because most tests, X rays, surgery, and other income-producing procedures occur on or near the first day of stay and because the last day usually generates little income other than room and board, the hospital gains economically by shortening the patient stay. It is able to serve more patients without increasing the number of beds or staff. This improved efficiency is also an advantage to the community, which gains by having increased capacity for handling hospitalized patients without the expense of hospital expansion.

In short, the hospital may realize economic gains from the presence of a properly functioning on-campus medical office building. Increased admissions, higher and more stabilized census, increased utilization of ancillary services, and shorter patient stays all add up to increased revenue and an overall improvement in the hospital's financial picture. In addition, the office building often contributes to improved credit, because many major lenders throughout the country realize the significant economic impact that the on-campus medical office building usually has on a hospital.

Financial gains are not, however, the only advantages to the hospital of an on-campus medical office building. An office building can also contribute significantly to the hospital's recruitment program (see chapter 10). Because physicians, particularly those just completing their training, are keenly aware of the benefits of practicing in such a building (see next section), hospitals with office buildings have a competitive edge in recruiting.

Also, the office building can contribute toward providing broader and more in-depth coverage of the emergency department and other trauma-centered services, such as intensive care, burn treatment, and alcohol treatment. Because of his location on campus, an attending physician or a needed specialist can be in the hospital in a matter of moments when a life is hanging in the balance, providing significant support for the hospital staff.

Finally, the hospital benefits from a number of other effects that take place as a result of the nearness of the physicians and their greater interaction with the hospital. On-campus physicians tend to develop a better understanding of the hospital, its functioning, and its policies, with the result that conflicts due to misunderstanding between the hospital and physicians are reduced and cooperation is better.[9] Physicians on campus tend to make themselves more available for teaching, because of both convenience and their greater involvement with the future and the goals of the hospital, attendance at staff and committee meetings improves, again because of convenience and concern, and the physicians become more conscientious about keeping their charts and medical records up to date.[10] The cumulative effect is that the medical staff and hospital administration tend to react as team members, rather than as adversaries.

The hospital, then, benefits from the on-campus medical office building both through greater financial stability and through the positive effects of a "full-time geographic staff." The end result is the centralization and streamlining of medical care, with the hospital becoming the true medical center for the community.

ADVANTAGES TO THE PHYSICIAN

Physicians currently find themselves in a difficult position. Consumer utilization of medical care has increased dramatically. Government scrutiny of costs and charges has intensified. The physician is required not only to deliver high-quality care, but also to deliver it efficiently and economically.

To most physicians, the single greatest advantage of being located in an on-campus medical office building is time savings. A physician may save, on the average, one hour a day in travel time between office and hospital by being located in an on-campus medical office building—even if he was previously located only a few blocks from the hospital. If he lives in a large metropolitan area, he will save more time. On the basis of an average of an hour per day saved in travel time, a physician can expect to increase his gross annual income by 12 percent by utilizing the time saved to see additional patients. If he has been spending more time in his automobile, he may gain even more.

"The advantages of being located in the medical office building are concerned mainly with the proximity to the hospital where I work in saving my time and not having to travel a great distance from my office to the hospital," said an orthopedic surgeon.[11] "This allows me to make frequent visits to the emergency department on short notice, and also allows me at times of waiting in the hospital to return to my office and catch up on paper work, to do other office work, and even see a few patients that I would otherwise not be able to see were I much farther away from the hospital."

Another major advantage to physicians (particularly specialists) of being located in the on-campus medical office building is the referrals that they will receive. Although virtually all physicians recognize the importance of referrals, physicians just establishing a practice in an area are particularly eager to locate in a situation that will facilitate referrals. Frequently, when patients without a family physician or needed specialist come to the emergency department or the outpatient clinic of a hospital, they will ask to be referred to a physician located in the hospital's office building when follow-up treatment is needed. Conversely, as primary care physicians in the office building need to refer their patients to specialists, they tend to refer within the building, for the convenience of both the patient and the physician and vice versa. The resulting support to a practice can be substantial.

For example, a pediatrician moved across an alleyway from a privately owned medical office building to a hospital-owned and operated one. Despite the fact that he would not be any closer to the hospital, he believed the new building would be worth the 30 percent increase in rent that it would cost him. He was right. The rental increase was more than compensated for by a 15 percent to 20 percent increase in the referrals he received.[12]

"The proximity of the hospital also provides other conveniences," explained one physician with on-campus offices. "We use the laboratory and radiological facilities of the hospital. Written reports of studies performed are available to us almost immediately."[13]

The availability of expensive technical equipment in the hospital is, however, more than just convenient for the physician in the on-campus office building. Its availability means that he can eliminate duplication of this equipment in his office, if he so chooses, as well as eliminate the need for expensive paramedical personnel to operate it. The resultant savings to the physicians in capital expenditures and salaries can be considerable. In addition, when tests and X rays are run and read in the hospital, rather than in the doctor's office, the liability for the results of those tests is shifted from the physician to the hospital, an important consideration to some physicians, because of malpractice trends.

Parking is a great source of irritation to physicians, and an on-campus office can eliminate many of its frustrations. Under normal circumstances, a physician will have to drive to the hospital in the morning to make rounds—and find a parking space. He will then drive to his office—and again need to find a parking space. If emergencies arise during the day that call him to the hospital, he will have to repeat the process. Finally, he repeats the process again when he makes evening rounds. For the physician who is located on campus, the problem is greatly simplified. In a well-managed building, parking will be readily available to him, but even if parking problems do arise, he has to face them only once a day.

Several other advantages are available to the physician because of his proximity to the hospital.

"I feel that, because of hospital administration representation at our building tenant meetings and continuing communication through our building manager, those of us in the medical building have significantly greater input of our wants and needs in the hospital than do those physicians who admit to the hospital but have their offices elsewhere," explained one tenant physician, adding, "Access to the hospital cafeteria and coffee shop makes lunch time less expensive and much less time consuming for both myself and my office staff."[14]

Other advantages include the convenience of the hospital library for research and study, mutual availability of hospital and physician medical records, and the possible availability to the physician's employees of hospital training programs and facilities.

Finally, the on-campus medical office building can provide the independent physician with many advantages of group practice without his having to become a member of a group: available specialists for consultation and referral; the possibility of physicians in his own specialty with whom he can share "on-call" duty; and opportunities for group purchasing and shared business services, such as bookkeeping, billing, medical stenography, and nursing personnel.

THE ULTIMATE BENEFIT

Bringing the physician on campus has been to the advantage of hospitals and doctors, but the real value of the concept is what it has done for patients.

Shorter patient stays, subsequent lower costs, less duplication, more consultations, better supervised care—all testify to the positive effects on the patient that result in advantages to the patient. Broader, more in-depth coverage of hospital services, improved educational programs, increased efficiency of the hospital, and greater availability of physicians and services all ultimately contribute to the care the patient receives.

So evident are the contributions of the on-campus medical office building to the patient and to the delivery of patient care that the Internal Revenue Service has ruled that an on-campus medical office building owned by a not-for-profit hospital is income-tax exempt when it houses the offices of hospital medical staff members. In issuing its ruling, the IRS stated, "While these leasing arrangements are also a convenience to the lessees, many of the benefits are passed on to the hospital and its patients in the form of greater efficiency and better overall medical care."[15]

In addition, in virtually every court decision favoring tax exemption for the medical office building from local ad valorem taxes, the deciding factor has been the substantial contribution to the delivery of patient care that the on-campus medical office building has made.

In the Genessee Hospital case in New York State, the judge said, "The evidence presented overwhelmingly emphasizes a commendable concern on the part of the hospital to maintain a first-rate hospital facility, both in terms of patient care rendered and the educational program provided. The evidence also clearly indicates that these two areas of concern are so closely akin to each other that they mutually and inevitably compliment [sic] one another in such a setting. The Doctors Office Building was an attempt to insure that both such concerns were adequately dealt with.

"In addition," he continued, "those physicians questioned upon the trial were almost unanimous in claiming that the use of the Doctors Office Building has been a success in improving both the quality of the health care provided and the level of teaching in the hospital, several noting that a very high percentage of the teaching by the 'attending staff' has been done by those physicians located in the new office building."[16]

In an article on the tax status of physicians' office buildings, the author commented on the Genessee case: "In assessing the Genessee case, one can't help but believe that it is the detailed showing by testimony of how the community's need for good hospital care was being satisfied that convinced the judge. He was able to understand clearly why the hospital needed to help its physicians to help its patients and itself."[17]

In another case, the court said in its ruling, "It is apparent that in any expansion program or new development of hospitals, a physicians' office building is now contemplated as part of the hospital complex. These buildings are designated to encourage doctors to use the hospital facilities for their patients. In turn, the hospital receives a substantial benefit from the use of its facilities by the physicians in the quality of care, educational programs, availability of a medical staff for emergencies, and other hospital-related programs."[18]

DISADVANTAGES

This chapter discusses at length the numerous advantages of a hospital-related medical office building. The better planned, programmed, and implemented such a building is, the more likely it is to live up to its full potential in contributing to the patient care goals of the hospital. However, the concept also has disadvantages.

The single greatest disadvantage of a hospital-related medical office building is that it can be constructed and put into operation without sufficient and/or appropriate planning and programming first taking place. Even though a poorly developed building can, and often does, produce positive results for a hospital, it can never live up to its potential. In addition, the problems that arise with these buildings are virtually always traceable to a failure to plan and implement properly.

The problems that can arise tend to be specific and avoidable, rather than inherent to the hospital-based building itself. They are presented in brief form here, as a red flag to the reader, but are discussed in greater depth throughout the book. The intent is to provide a hospital considering the development of on-campus offices with the information necessary to avoid the problems before they arise, so that the development of such an office building could provide the advantages without the difficulties.

Probably the one disadvantage to an on-campus medical office building that is not totally avoidable is that the central location can be less convenient for the office patient, particularly if the hospital is not conveniently located or if good public transportation is not readily available to that location. Naturally, this disadvantage varies from one community to another, depending on size and existing practice patterns of physicians. In areas where it is a problem, many hospitals are working on methods to lessen the effect through such programs as satellite clinics and shuttle buses into areas where other transportation is not readily available.

The disadvantages of the hospital-related medical office building that are in the potential problem category include parking (see chapters 14 and 15), security after hours (see chapter 11), legal entanglements with owners other than the hospital (see chapters 4, 5, and 12), leases (see chapter 12), interference in hospital operations by the physicians (see chapters 3 and 11), and possible criticism for "competing with private enterprise" (see chapter 3).

For the physician, the potential problems might best be described as apprehensions (see chapters 10 and 11). They include the fear of hospital control over his private practice, of discrimination by the hospital in admitting and scheduling, of being looked on as an employee of the hospital, of being tied to only one hospital, and of losing patients if his practice is moved. In addition, problems might arise for the physician who is an owner of the building (see chapters 4, 5, 7, and 10).

No project of this magnitude is ever likely to be totally without problems. The purpose of the remainder of this book, however, is to minimize the problems and maximize the benefits. The rest is up to the hospital.

NOTES

1. Letter to Drexel Toland & Associates from physician. Dec. 16, 1975.
2. Wallerstein, M. D., Ralph O. Letter. Dec. 16, 1975.
3. Drexel Toland & Associates, Inc. *Survey of Hospital-Owned Professional Office Buildings.* Memphis: 1974.

4. Ibid. Also, Rev. Rul. 69-463, 1969-2 C.B. 131.

5. Drexel Toland & Associates, Inc. *East Tennessee Baptist Hospital Professional Building Utilization*. Memphis: 1973, p. 25.

6. Wallerstein, M. D., Ralph O. Interview. 1970.

7. Snider, Arthur J. Scourge of doctor's waiting room is more than old magazines. Chicago Daily News Service. *Commercial Appeal*. Sec. 1, p. 23, Sept. 23, 1974.

8. Toland, *Survey*.

9. Ibid.

10. Ibid.

11. Sutherland, M.D., Dan R. Letter. Dec. 17, 1975.

12. Alben, M.D., Jan. Interview. Jan. 25, 1980.

13. Letter to Drexel Toland & Associates from physician. Jan. 31, 1976.

14. Ibid.

15. Rev. Rul. 69-464, 1969-2 C.B. 132.

16. *Genessee Hospital, Inc. v. Wager*, 350 N. Y. S. 2nd 582 (1974).

17. Horty, John F., editor. Tax status of a physician's office building. *Action Kit for Hospital Trustees* (Newsletter), p. 1, 1975.

18. Hospital taxed for medical office building. *Hospital Progress*. 56:32, Sept. 1975.

CHAPTER **3**

Role of the Governing Board

The role of the governing board of a hospital is to provide for the health care needs of the community. Theirs is a policy-making responsibility. It is important for board members to realize that their position on the board is not just honorary. They are legally responsible for what goes on in the hospital and for the quality of care rendered within the institution. On the other hand, their responsibility does not include the day-by-day management of the hospital. That authority is delegated to the administrator and his staff.

The responsibility of the governing board, then, is the overall supervision of the institution and the making of broad decisions affecting the direction of the hospital. As such, the board has traditionally made decisions concerning the provision of an adequate physical building—construction, remodeling, expansion, and other capital investments in the structure itself. The board has carried the responsibility for providing as much of the latest equipment as possible within the financial ability of the institution. The board has also been responsible for seeing that sufficient numbers of skilled employees are on hand to care for the patients, operate the equipment, maintain the building, and assist the physicians.

Only one key element of the hospital delivery system has not always been considered by the board: the physicians themselves. In past decades, the board traditionally approved granting medical staff membership to qualified physicians and agreed to removal of physicians for various disciplinary reasons. Usually, the board did not take active responsibility for seeing that sufficient numbers of physicians were on hand to serve the community and the hospital. It was not concerned to any great degree with recruitment, unless the hospital were experiencing substantial census problems. By and large, the board did not think in terms of improving patient care by helping to increase the physician's efficiency and by integrating him into the hospital complex. Much attention was given to facility master planning and very little to medical staff master planning.

In recent years, however, as the distribution of physicians has become a problem and as the time and abilities of physicians have been increasingly taxed by the expanded health care system, the hospital board has had to place a higher priority on recruiting and maintaining the medical staff. Today, in fact, the hospital is one of the few entities with sufficient financial and manpower resources to recruit successfully for a community on a continuing and comprehensive basis.

As the role of the hospital has been changing from the proverbial doctors' workshop to the community health care center, the role of the governing board has changed concomitantly to include the responsibility for providing not only a building, equipment, and the employee staff complement, but also a top-notch medical staff to serve the community and to utilize the hospital facilities. In addition, the board is responsible for maintaining the viability of that medical staff.

The result of these growing responsibilities, plus the responsibility of ensuring the provision of high-quality patient care, puts the board in the position of also being responsible for the development of the hospital-related medical office building. Likewise, medical staff master planning, particularly in relation to office facilities, is becoming increasingly important to hospitals.

INITIATING THE PROJECT

The first thought of a hospital-related medical office building may come from the board itself as it tries to remedy some of the specific problems or to achieve some of the specific goals mentioned in chapter 2. In the majority of situations, however, the hospital administrator or the medical staff members themselves will be the first to feel that a hospital-related medical office building is needed. They will, in turn, present their case to the governing board in order for the board to consider the idea.

Regardless of who initiates the idea, the board will be responsible for seeing that the concept is carefully researched and for making all major decisions concerning such an undertaking, keeping in mind the short-range goals, the long-range goals, and the needs of the hospital. Furthermore, if the project is undertaken, the board will be responsible for maintaining sufficient control to ensure that the interests of the hospital and the provision of high-quality patient care are always protected and never overshadowed by vested interests.

Although the remainder of this chapter discusses and emphasizes the role of the governing board and administrative staff in the development of a hospital-related medical office building, the reader should not interpret this to mean that medical staff involvement is not necessary. On the contrary, physician participation in the planning process is vital to the project's success. Therefore the planning role of the medical staff is discussed separately, in chapter 9. To get a complete picture of effective planning, the reader should consider this chapter and chapters 9 and 10 together, as parts of a whole.

DETERMINING MOTIVES

Sometimes members of a governing board may think of the development of an on-campus medical office building in terms of real estate, rather than patient care. However, the office building should be thought of in terms of any other department of the hospital, that is, as providing a service.

Once the office building is understood to be a functioning part of the hospital, the first step toward the development of a successful project is the establishment of clear-cut motives or objectives for developing the building. These motives should be well-planned, clearly established, and permanently adopted before the hospital proceeds. When these steps have been taken, medical office buildings have been successful. The buildings that have had problems are ones set up with the wrong motives or objectives or without the needed and appropriate policies to ensure the implementation of those objectives.

Although the hospital may have various needs or problems that the medical office building is expected to alleviate or resolve, improvement of patient care should be established early as the primary objective in developing the building, and other motives must be weeded out.

The first motive to be eliminated must be the idea that the development of a hospital-related medical office building is a real estate venture. It is not. It is *not* a means for helping physicians prosper at the expense of the patient, nor is it a means for the hospital to prosper at the expense of the physician. Furthermore, it is not a means for a third party to prosper at the expense of the hospital. An office building developed on the hospital campus that is considered primarily a real estate venture, regardless of the owner, is almost certainly doomed to be a source of problems, both internally and for the hospital.

Many board members may expect the medical office building to be an investment that will return profit dollars to the hospital to be spent on various projects as needed. The development of a medical office building *is* an investment, but not this kind of investment. The hospital will profit from increased utilization, but the hospital should not anticipate profit dollars generated by rentals to the occupants. The building is an investment in good patient care and in the long-range future of the hospital. If the hospital proposes to develop the medical office building only with rental profits in mind, then the project should be abandoned. Such an approach will create tax complications and numerous other difficulties for the hospital.

The on-campus medical office building must in no way be considered a means for the hospital to gain any kind of control over its medical staff. The medical staff is the hospital's ally, not its adversary. Only as the board looks to the medical office building as a means for making practice more convenient and more efficient for physicians will the building be able to fulfill its function of contributing to the improvement of patient care.

Step 1 to a successful medical office building: The governing board must clearly establish the improvement of patient care as the primary motive for developing the on-campus medical office building. All subsequent decisions must be based on that premise.

DELEGATING AUTHORITY

After establishing the motive for the development of an on-campus medical office building, the board must now provide for the actual research and planning to begin. Because the board's responsibility is to establish basic policy and direction, the actual implementation of the policy and the details of planning must be delegated to the administrative staff—the working arm of the board.

The administrator himself may be somewhat apprehensive about the presence of the physicians on campus, believing that they will meddle in the day-to-day operation of the hospital. Experience has shown that such meddling is not the case: physicians are too busy. However, they are likely to spend more time in the hospital and become more aware of how the hospital is being run. If the administrator runs a top-notch hospital, the result of the physicians' presence will serve only to improve relationships and solve problems more quickly.

Consequently, if the administrator wants the on-campus medical office building to help improve relationships with the medical staff, then he and/or one of his administrative staff associates must be actively involved in every step of the planning process. Only through the administrator's active involvement can he see that the principle of high-quality patient care is pervading the development of the building and can he assure the medical staff that relationships are being strengthened rather than damaged. The importance of the administrator's involvement cannot be stressed too much. An administrator should beware of any person, consultant, or firm who says, "You don't have to do a thing. We'll take care of everything for you."

In addition, for logistical reasons, the need for one central person to act as liaison during the project is great. Regardless of who will own and operate the building, the administrator or one of his immediate associates should be charged with this liaison responsibility in order to ensure hospital input into the decision-making process and to ensure smooth project development. With one person acting as liaison, the board knows where to seek answers to their questions, the doctors know with whom to discuss their problems and needs, and all consultants, architects, contractors, and other personnel know where to get major decisions cleared.

The administrator's delegated authority from the board will need to continue throughout the project. The administrator will answer to the board, but he must be given the authority to act on a day-by-day basis. When the time comes for space to be rented, the administrator will need the authority to market the building to local doctors and to recruit and negotiate with others as needed.

After the initial phase of development and marketing, however, the amount of time the administrator will need to dedicate to the building will be considerably reduced. Even if the hospital chooses to own and operate the office building itself, the administrative time needed will be minimal. Most of the work load will be absorbed into other departments of the hospital, especially housekeeping and maintenance, and the administrator essentially will deal with the building as he would any other department of the hospital.

Step 2 to a successful medical office building: The governing board must delegate responsibility and authority for project planning to the hospital administrator.

ESTABLISHING THE APPROPRIATE COMMITTEE

At the same time the board assigns responsibility and authority to the administrator, it will also need to assign the responsibility for working with the administrator to an appropriate committee within the board. If a long-range planning committee or a building committee already exists, then the project will be assigned to one of these. If, however, no standing committee exists, the board will need to constitute one.

A good building committee will be made up of two or three board members, one or more representatives of the medical staff, and the administrator. The committee should begin immediately by setting up a schedule for regular meetings, usually once a month.

The first responsibility of the committee will be to conduct a preliminary survey of the medical staff to determine members' interest in occupying offices in the building. This study should be handled by the administrative staff member of the committee, either through personal conversations with the physicians or through a very brief questionnaire. The information sought should include the following:

- The physician's interest in locating in the building, either now or over the next three years
- The present location and size of the physician's office and the expiration date of his current lease
- The size of the office he might want if he were to move into the new building

If interest on the part of the medical staff is sufficient or if the hospital's needs are great (a low occupancy rate or the need for new physicians), then the committee should proceed with further consideration of the project. The committee should note, however, that initial surveys are predictably conservative. Experience shows that for every physician initially interested, another will make himself known during construction. Many physicians do not express their interest until construction of the medical office building is certain, because of partnerships, group referral patterns, and other factors. An active recruitment program will further increase the number of physicians who will ultimately locate in the building.

Even if interest in the office building is negligible, some situations will exist in which the hospital may need to develop an office building for the sake of marketing of services, medical staff master planning, or some other reason. In such a situation, the hospital will need first to develop support from the existing staff before proceeding with the project. Offending the existing staff by proceeding without their support will only make matters difficult for new physicians recruited into the area.

At this early stage, the board already should avoid pitfalls. The first pitfall is to approach physicians about an on-campus medical office building before the objectives of the building are clearly developed. The physicians may question the hospital's motives in developing such a building if the objectives are not clearly presented at the outset. Second, the physicians should not be approached if the board has little or no interest in proceeding with the project. The hospital can do great damage to its relationship with the physicians by interesting them in an on-campus building and then not proceeding with the project.

In addition, the administrator should check quietly with key members of the medical staff to get the pulse of their thinking on the idea and to spot potential objections and problems that may develop. In any medical staff, disagreements are bound to arise and objections to be raised. The board will want to know early in the project where the potential problems and trouble spots are so that solutions can be worked out before the problems arise. Only through great sensitivity and concern for the medical staff will the board be able to develop a project smoothly. This concern is one of the primary reasons for the administrator's intimate involvement in all phases of the project. He has a vested and long-range interest, which outside parties may not have, in maintaining good relationships with his physicians.

If, after this preliminary survey of the medical staff, the board is committed to further pursuit of the project, then the next usual action of the building committee will be to call in the expert help needed to do an in-depth study of the project's feasibility. Although some large hospitals may believe they have the expertise and staff time to plan the project, because of the amount of time involved and the wide variety of disciplines that must come into play (strategic planning, medical staff master planning, marketing, research, finance, accounting, specialized architectural skills, to name a few), most hospitals will turn to outside help.

As one hospital group has pointed out, the services of a consulting firm specializing in the planning and development of hospital-related medical office buildings are useful because of the complexities unique to medical office building development, including market analysis, professional tax considerations, and the various forms of corporate structure and management. An outside consultant can more objectively relate to staff physicians, be free of hospital political concerns, and develop a realistic appraisal of the project feasibility in less time. The use of consultants by the hospital increases the credibility of the project at an early stage among the staff and at a later stage to potential lenders of necessary capital funds.[1]

Step 3 to a successful medical office building: Assign the project to the appropriate committee to conduct a preliminary survey of the medical staff and to call in expert help if the project is to be developed further.

CONDUCTING THE FEASIBILITY STUDY

Although the need and feasibility of some projects are so evident that the projects can proceed without a formal feasibility study, most projects will require in-depth scrutiny and adjustment before the board will be satisfied enough to proceed.

Basically, the study should be divided into two parts: (1) analysis of the need for the building and (2) preliminary plans for programming and implementing the building. The combined information in these two areas of the study should give the board adequate data for deciding whether to proceed with the project. When the hospital hires an outside consultant to conduct the feasibility study, it has the right to have certain subjects researched and the resultant data made available to the board.

ANALYSIS OF NEED

The subjects to be covered under the analysis of need for the on-campus medical office building will include a demographic study, a health facilities study, a medical staff profile and master plan, a study of medical staff interest, and a study on the concept of the on-campus location. If the hospital has an existing marketing plan, the feasibility study should be coordinated with it. If it does not, it may want to conduct a marketing study as part of or preliminary to conducting the medical office building feasibility study. The marketing plan will help ensure optimum utilization of the office building in relation to marketing of services by the hospital and in relation to medical staff master planning.

Demographics

The demographic information needed in a medical office building feasibility study is not nearly as detailed and comprehensive as the similar information usually gathered when making a study for the hospital itself. Nonetheless, certain information should be considered. General population trends—whether the community is growing or shrinking and to what degree—are important. Also, economic trends—whether the community is stable, depressed, or growing economically—should be considered.

The hospital should know what the future needs of the community will be. For example, to build a medical office building based on a future need to recruit 25 new physicians would be foolish if, in fact, the community were losing population and had sufficient numbers of physicians in the right age brackets and specialties to care for projected needs. On the other hand, construction of a building that would already be too small by the time it was completed would be equally shortsighted.

Health Facilities

The health facilities information that should be included in the study will also be of a general nature and should be geared toward pinpointing any problems or signs of trouble of which the hospital should be aware before proceeding. For instance, the hospital may want to know how its range of services, occupancy rate, average patient-day stay, and other general indicators compare with other hospitals in the area. This information will help the hospital determine in a broader sense how well the community's health care needs are being met and where the hospital may have weaknesses in its programs that might need to be improved simultaneously with the development of an office building.

Medical Staff Profile and Master Plan

The most important aspect of the analysis of need (and one of the least frequently done studies) is the medical staff profile and master plan. Although much of this study will be statistical in nature and can be compiled from hospital records, physician interviews are also important, because the physicians will often be able to pinpoint needs that may not surface in a purely statistical study (see chapter 9).

An effective medical staff profile should include a complete study of all members of the medical staff, categorized by active staff, associate staff, courtesy staff, and other divisions the hospital may designate. The staff should be examined by specialty to determine if the specialty composition is appropriately balanced and if any needed specialties for the area population are missing. The staff should be examined by age, particularly in relation to the specialty composition. The hospital needs to know what the average age of its staff is and how that age compares with national norms. More important, the hospital needs a profile of ages so that it can anticipate which physicians are approaching the age at which they are likely to start reducing their practice or retire. To maintain a good, balanced staff, the hospital will have to recruit specialists to replace aging physicians, but it must first know specifically which specialists will be needed.

In addition, the medical staff profile should include a profile of admissions for a five-year period. Through this profile, the hospital will be able to see which specialty areas are contributing most to admissions, which age brackets account for the largest number of admissions, which physicians on the staff are admitting the majority of patients, and which ones admit very few. By studying admissions patterns by age, specialty, and even office location, the hospital will have a clear picture of where it stands and in what direction it must go as far as encouraging loyalty on the part of existing staff members and in recruiting needed staff members.

The administrator, the governing board, and the physicians may experience surprises as a result of the medical staff profile. They may learn that the physician seen frequently in the hospital is not actually admitting as many patients as they thought. On the other hand, a physician they see only occasionally may have one of the highest admitting rates of any physician on the staff. For example, in a hospital with 100 physicians on the active staff, the board may be surprised to learn that 15 of those doctors are admitting 60 percent of all the patients and that 12 of those 15 doctors are over age 55, indicating that they may become less surpportive of the hospital if they reduce their practice in preparation for retirement. Or the medical staff profile may show that although the hospital has an adequate number of young physicians on its courtesy staff each year, very few of them join the active staff, but instead join the active staff of another hospital. In this case, the hospital usually has a problem that needs immediate attention if it is to perpetuate its medical staff.

On the basis of data assembled in the medical staff profile, the long-range medical staff master plan should be developed. This master plan is certainly as important as a facilities master plan, but is often nonexistent. The plan should include the coordination of hospital services, both existing and planned, with the specialty composition of the medical staff. On the basis of a comparison of population-to-physician ratios by specialty, the number and types of specialists needed by the community can be compared with the number and types of those practicing there.

The master plan, then, should consist of an outline of physicians, by specialty and subspecialty, needed by the community now and in the future; an outline of those specialists to be recruited in order to complete the physician complement; and those that will need to be recruited over a period of years to create a smooth transition as one physician retires and a younger one picks up the load.

The administrator, the board, and the medical staff must have a clear picture of the medical staff and its needs before proceeding with the development of an on-campus medical office building. This picture will help the hospital determine the appropriate balance of specialties to be included in the medical office building so that it can function to the maximum effectiveness, both for the hospital and for the tenants themselves. Finally, this crystallized picture of the medical staff will help the board determine just how important an on-campus medical office building will be to the hospital in regard to increased admissions and recruitment needs.

Next to be covered in the analysis of need for the on-campus medical office building is the area of physician interest. Either through personal interviews (the preferable method), questionnaires, or some other method, depending on the local situation, a consultant needs to determine which physicians might be interested in an on-campus medical office building over a three-year period. In addition, this part of the study needs to include information on present rental rates, how much space each interested doctor might need in a new building, when his present lease expires, what type of ownership he prefers for the building, and what services he would expect and want. This information is essential in determining the ultimate feasibility of the building. It would be of little value to construct a building for 25 doctors if 20 of them are locked into leases that would prevent their moving for five or six years. By the same token, a new building with rental rates totally unreasonable for the area would not be an overwhelming success. This information is necessary in order for preliminary planning to be completed for the size of the building, services to be included, and the recommended ownership and management structures.

Physician Interest

The final consideration under the analysis of need is the need for the on-campus location. Rarely does a hospital undertake the study of an on-campus medical office building without already being convinced of the advantages of the on-campus location. However, in a few cases, local circumstances or a particular situation peculiar to a certain community will require that the pros and cons of the on-campus location be considered. In this case, the feasibility study needs to clearly put forth the advantages of the on-campus location, as already outlined in this book, and compare them with the specifically stated disadvantages inherent to that particular situation. The board will decide on the basis of which side outweighs the other.

Building Location

PRELIMINARY PLANS FOR PROGRAMMING AND IMPLEMENTATION

The second half of the feasibility study needs to include the preliminary plans for the development of the building so that the board can determine how the project should be developed if it is to be feasible, or whether it will be feasible at all. Because of the complex nature of the six subject areas included in this part of the study, they are discussed only briefly in this chapter, but are presented in much greater detail in subsequent chapters. These areas include ownership possibilities, size and scope of the building, analysis of sites, preliminary design of the building, financial analysis, and developmental and operational policies.

Even before the feasibility study is initiated, board members often have a strong conviction concerning the type of ownership structure they prefer. However, many times the board will not yet have determined whether the hospital will own the building or whether a third party will own it. This decision is one of the most critical to the overall success of the project, and the hospital will need to make it no later than the time at which preliminary plans are approved. For that reason, the feasibility study may need to include a detailed evaluation of the various types of ownership—the pros and cons of each, their financial and tax ramifications, and who stands to gain what with each type of ownership.

At the threshold of board consideration may be the issue of whether permitting other than hospital ownership would amount to giving away a "corporate opportunity" in considering corporate law. Legal counsel can help in determining the application of the doctrine and any recognized exceptions to the basic principle. Conceivably, the doctrine could rule out consideration of other types of ownership. However, since practical considerations, rather than legal doctrines, may prevail, the relative merits of different types of ownership are discussed.

The development of the size and the scope of the building will follow in the feasibility study. It will be based on physician interest, the hospital's need for physicians, what is financially practical, and a number of other factors. In addition, this part of the programming and implementation section of the study should include recommended commercial establishments to be included in the building, if any, and any hospital outpatient services that will be needed in the building. The required amount of parking in relation to the size and scope of the building must also be determined.

Site selection is critical in preparing the programming and implementation plans. Therefore, long-range planning for the total medical complex should be taken into consideration. Some hospitals have rushed through an on-campus medical office building project only to learn a few years later that the location of the medical office building totally blocked further expansion of the hospital. Traffic flow and parking must also be carefully planned, and parallel plans for the expansion of hospital services should be included, where needed.

Preliminary designs for the building should also be included in the programming and implementation section of the study. These plans will show how the exterior design will look and blend with the rest of the campus. Typical floor plans will show the workability of the building. These plans are necessary to develop construction costs, rental rates, and an operating budget. In some cases, a building will be designed, only to prove itself financially unfeasible. Then, new designs may be needed in order to make the project work.

In many ways, the financial analysis is the final determination of the project's feasibility. However, it cannot be determined until all the other aspects of the feasibility study have been established. This part of the study should set forth the projected construction and operating costs. It should establish a rental rate for the building, and it should project an operating budget to indicate economic workability of the project. If a building cannot be made to work economically, it will be difficult for the board to pursue the project, regardless of the benefits to be received from it.

The feasibility study should include an established set of developmental and operating policies. This may seem to be a strange inclusion in the feasibility study, but the adoption of these policies at the same time as the adoption of the project is the insurance that guarantees the ultimate objective of the project. Through these policies, the hospital and the potential tenants meet eye-to-eye in a mutual understanding of just how the project is being developed, and the hospital ensures that improved patient care will be the ultimate goal of the building. Many decisions regarding ownership, size and scope, site planning, and financial feasibility are directly affected by the basic developmental philosophy and operating policies of the medical office building.

Step 4 to a successful medical office building: Conduct a thoroughly researched and carefully planned feasibility study.

MAKING THE DECISION

After the building committee has received and reviewed the completed feasibility study, the committee and the administrator should seek full board approval if they believe the project should receive the green light. This step in the development of an on-campus medical office building is frequently one of the most difficult to accomplish.

Because the board has both the legal and the moral responsibility for the total operation of the institution, the board members will usually be cautious in making a decision. Members must be convinced of three things.

First, through the feasibility study, they must see that the project is financially feasible. Although the project may operate at a deficit for some time, the board must understand what the overall, long-range economic effects on the hospital will be. Board members must clearly understand how much the hospital will gain through increased admissions, increased use of ancillary services, and long-range financial vitality. They must also realize that unlike some other departments of the hospital, for example, housekeeping or maintenance, the office building will be income-producing. It will ultimately pay for itself.

The second point that the board must understand is the overall effect the office building will have on patient care. Because of the many positive effects on the patient and because over the long run the building will pay for itself, the development of the on-campus medical office building is one of the few decisions the board can make to improve patient care at no long-range cost to the hospital or to the patient.

Finally, through the use of the medical staff profile, the board must be shown the physician recruitment needs of the institution in relation to the survival of the hospital and the needs of the community. When the needs are presented on the basis of a balanced specialty composition and a balance in age ranges, the board will be able to see them clearly. Not every hospital will have major recruiting needs, but most will.

After the administrator and the building committee present their case to the board, the board itself will have to weigh all the positive factors against any considerations that might hinder the development of the building. For example, the board must take into account all the needs of the hospital. In some situations the ancillary services may be in need of improvement before the hospital can proceed with the office building. In other cases, where the need for the building is great, but funds and credit are severely limited, the hospital may opt for temporary on-campus offices until a permanent office building can be constructed (see chapter 14). In still other cases, physician opposition may need to be corrected before the hospital can proceed with the building.

In the decision-making process itself, the individual board members should keep the objective of improved patient care foremost in their minds, discarding their personal business practices and interests. They have a legal and a moral obligation to decide in favor of the best interests of the community and the hospital.

The board also must be prepared to move quickly. A hospital is in trouble if its board is unable to make a decision and act upon it. Continued talk without action destroys the hospital's credibility and injures relationships with the medical staff. The physicians must make many decisions that affect their practice and their livelihood, such as whether to renew leases, whether to change partnerships, or add partners. Thus, prompt board action is essential.

Herein lies a pitfall. Frequently a board will hesitate on the decision, wanting the physicians to "sign up" in advance. The board that requires a physician to sign up before a project begins is making a serious error. Too many variables exist to expect the physician to make decisions that far into the future. The hospital's responsibility, through its careful research and planning, is to perceive and determine the need and then build for it. When this has been done, the utilization has followed.

Step 5 to a successful medical office building: Keeping all the needs of the hospital and the objective of improved patient care uppermost, make a decision *promptly*.

PROCEEDING WITH THE PROJECT

Most states now require a certificate of need before a building project can proceed. Therefore, assuming the board has made the decision to build, the next step is to get approval as soon as possible from the state planning agency. Once the project is initiated, the board will be responsible for monitoring its progress, not on a day-by-day basis, but on a broad basis. Detailed monitoring will remain the delegated responsibility of the administrator in conjunction with the building committee.

Through conscientiously carrying out each of the steps outlined in this chapter and through careful consideration of the guidelines and recommendations that follow, the governing board can be assured of being well on the way toward developing a successful and effective on-campus medical office building.

NOTE

1. In: "Guidelines for Development of Professional Office Buildings," by Ancilla Domini Health Services, Inc., Des Plaines, Illinois, a corporate structure of the Poor Handmaids of Jesus Christ that is responsible for the operation of eight Roman Catholic hospitals in Illinois and Indiana.

CHAPTER **4**

Forms
of
Ownership

Probably the single most significant decision the board must make in the development of an on-campus medical office building is the one concerning ownership. This decision will affect every phase of the planning, development, and operation of the building.

The decision-making process can be confusing and difficult. The options are numerous and varied. If a hospital wants to make a good decision—one that most adequately meets the needs of the hospital, its patients, and physicians—then first it must be aware of the choices. Second, it must be aware of and define the critical issues that most influence the long-range success and effectiveness of the building. Third, it must compare the alternatives with the issues to determine the best ownership method for its particular situation.

No pat answer exists for the question of who should own the building. The following discussion of alternatives, issues, and comparisons should successfully direct the hospital trying to make this decision into a process that will result in a good choice.

Although ownership alternatives can include many variations, combinations, and options, three basic categories include all the ownership alternatives: hospital ownership, physician ownership, and third-party ownership.

HOSPITAL OWNERSHIP

Of the three, hospital ownership is generally the simplest in legal terms. It consists of a straightforward landlord-tenant relationship. The hospital owns the building and rents or leases space to the physicians. The hospital is financially and legally liable for the building. The physician is financially responsible only for his monthly rental, which is a tax deductible item, and for the personal property within his suite. The details vary, but the basic relationships are consistent.

PHYSICIAN OWNERSHIP

Physician ownership can be considerably more complicated and varied. It may be in the form of a corporation, a condominium, or a general or limited partnership.

When a corporation is used as a vehicle for physician ownership, the physicians own the building indirectly, through stock in the corporation. The cor-

Corporation

poration itself is a separate legal entity. It is responsible for its own debts and legal obligations and is the actual owner of the building. By being stockholders, the physicians are not personally liable for the office building, its debts, or other obligations. On the other hand, any potential tax benefits resulting from ownership of the building are accrued by the corporation and not by the physicians personally.

The physician-owned corporation is rarely used as the initial ownership vehicle for developing a medical office building, primarily because of the need for a large capital outlay, the lack of tax benefits for the physicians, and the difficulty in developing a profitable building. Such a corporation is sometimes used as an exit vehicle for a physician partnership; that is, when the tax benefits of a partnership have been depleted, under some circumstances conversion of the partnership to a corporation might be financially attractive.

Condominium

The condominium as a form of physician ownership has reached various degrees of popularity in different areas of the country. In a condominium arrangement, the physician purchases his own practice suite plus the right to use the common areas—a kind of perpetual easement. Usually, a corporation is formed to own the common areas and the land and to handle such matters as management, taxes, insurance, common area utilities, maintenance, and housekeeping. The physician is a stockholder in the corporation as well as owner of his individual suite. Under this arrangement, the physician is responsible for his own financing and debt amortization and is legally liable for his own practice suite. The corporation, in turn, is financially and legally responsible for the common areas and services ascribed to it. In the condominium arrangement, interest, taxes and insurance, management expenses, other operating costs, and depreciation are all tax-deductible items for the physician.

In the development of a condominium, the hospital may be involved to varying degrees. For example, a third-party developer might put together the condominium package with virtually no involvement on the part of the hospital. The same might be said of a group of physicians developing the project. On the other hand, the hospital might choose to sell its land to the physicians or developer as part of the development process. By doing so, the hospital would have somewhat more say in who developed the project and how it was organized.

Even greater hospital involvement would occur if the hospital chose to lease, rather than sell, the land on which the building was to be developed. Through the ground lease, the hospital could exercise more influence on the condominium throughout the life of the building. Hospital ownership of the land would, however, adversely affect the initial development of the project, because financing would be more difficult to obtain and the initial down payment required by the lender would be larger—probably in the range of 40 percent.

The hospital might further involve itself in the development of the project through some form of indirect financial assistance. For example, it might construct, at the hospital's expense, parking for the building or a connecting route between the building and the hospital. The hospital's motive for providing this type of assistance would be to make the building financially more attractive and more marketable to physicians. Although hospitals have, in the past, further assisted the development of condominiums by leasing the land at a minimal rental rate, indications are that the Internal Revenue Service may now judge such assistance to jeopardize the tax-exempt status of the hospital, because the benefit is construed to accrue to the private advantage of the physician, rather than to the hospital.

The partnership is probably the most popular method of physician ownership of the hospital-related medical office building. In a partnership, two or more physicians pool their money to own the office building jointly. It differs from a corporation in that the individuals own the building themselves, rather than owning stock in a corporation that owns the building. In addition, it differs from a condominium in that the building is owned as a whole, rather than pieces of it being owned separately by individuals.

Partnership

A partnership is a flexible entity. It can be made up of any number of doctors and can include both general and limited partners. A general partner is usually defined as one who buys into the partnership with his capital, has decision-making power in the management of the partnership, and consequently takes on liability for the entire partnership. A limited partner is one who buys into the partnership, has no decision-making power, and is liable for the partnership only to the extent of his own investment.

Although numerous partnership alternatives exist, some of which might jeopardize the tax-exempt status of not-for-profit hospitals, the more frequently considered alternatives in hospital-related medical office buildings are as follows:

- General partnership of all tenant physicians
- General partnership of some tenant physicians, with other tenants renting from the partnership
- Limited partnership of physicians, with another physician(s) as general partner(s)
- Limited partnership of physicians, with the hospital as general partner
- Limited partnership of physicians with a corporation as general partner
- Limited partnership of physicians, with a developer as a general partner

A general partnership of all tenant physicians is one of the simpler forms of a partnership. The most common way of structuring it would be as an equal partnership. Each partner would purchase an equal share of the partnership, and each would have an equal vote. As general partners, the physicians would be jointly and severally liable for the entire partnership, both financially and legally. This liability means that if one partner defaults on his financial obligation to the partnership, the other partners are responsible for it. In addition, if one partner makes a financial commitment for the partnership, all the partners are liable for that commitment. Most partnership agreements contain a clause prohibiting one partner from making financial commitments for the partnership without the consent of the other partners. This clause does not, however, remove liability from the other partners in case a commitment is made; it only provides a means for the other partners to take legal action against the offending partner.

The tax deductions available to the physician through partnership ownership are essentially the same as those for a condominium, although they are computed in a different manner. In a partnership, the physician is able to deduct his share of the interest, taxes, insurance, management expenses, other operating costs, and depreciation on the building.

The general partnership of all tenant physicians might be developed in ways other than an equal partnership, although these methods are less common in hospital-related medical office buildings. For example, it might be developed as a weighted partnership, with each physician buying in according to the percentage of space he will occupy and having a vote equal to his percentage of the partnership. In fact, unless otherwise stated in the partnership agreement, all partnerships are legally weighted partnerships. Still another alternative would be for the physicians to buy in according to the space they occupy, but have an equal vote in the management of the building. This last alternative usually would not be attractive to physicians who would occupy large suites, because they would have only the same vote as physicians occupying small spaces. Numerous other alternatives exist, but would best be considered with the help of an experienced attorney.

Another form of general partnership is one that is made up of only a few of the building tenants, with the remainder of the tenants renting from the partnership. Most hospitals involved in the development of an on-campus medical office building would not choose this particular partnership form as the vehicle for ownership because few physicians would have the opportunity to own and because it is likely to generate conflict between the partners and the tenant physicians. It is more commonly used when a group of physicians develops a building on its own.

Such a general partnership is essentially the same as a general partnership of all tenants. It is subject to the same types of variations and options. It differs only in that each general partner would own a much larger share of the partnership and, consequently, would take on a much greater liability. Tax deductions would be essentially the same, but again, in proportion to the partner's larger share of the partnership.

The limited-partnership concept is more complicated than the general partnership, but it provides the advantage of limited liability, both financially and legally, for the limited partner. Every limited partnership must, however, be made up of at least one general partner, in addition to the limited partners. As in a general partnership, the general partners in the limited partnership make all management decisions and are jointly and severally liable for the partnership. The limited partners, on the other hand, do not participate in management and are not liable for the partnership. Limited partners risk only the money each puts into the partnership, but each receives the same tax advantages as the general partner (that is, in proportion to the individual's investment). Although the general partner(s) could be virtually anyone, those most commonly discussed in connection with a hospital-based medical office building are other physicians, the hospital, a corporation partially owned by the limited partners, and a developer.

An arrangement in which some physicians are general partners and others are limited partners usually arises when a group of physicians begins developing an office building on its own. The group of physicians that originates the development may need additional financial backing for the building and seek the investment of other physicians. Other physicians may be willing to invest, but insist on being only limited partners so that they do not have to share in the management and liability. Although development of a hospital-based medical office building in this manner is possible, it is not one of the more likely alternatives. Many hospitals would insist that the building be developed with all physicians on an equal basis, either as general partners or as limited partners, in order to prevent friction within the staff.

The concept of the hospital as general partner and the physicians as limited partners is one that has been discussed frequently. It does provide a means for the hospital to control the building, while providing the physicians the tax deductions of ownership. As in any limited partnership, the hospital as general partner would make all management decisions and be financially and legally liable for the project. The physician would be liable only to the extent of his investment. Although the Internal Revenue Service has not, as of this date, issued a formal ruling on this type of arrangement, indications are that it would rule that such a partnership would jeopardize the tax-exempt status of the not-for-profit hospital, because the hospital would assume the risk, whereas the tax benefits would accure to the benefit of the physicians. For that reason, this alternative is probably available only to investor-owned hospitals.

From the physician's point of view, a physician-owned corporation as general partner can be attractive. The physicians who are limited partners would also own some of the stock in the corporation that is the general partner. Thus, the limited partners would still maintain some management control through the corporation, while limiting their liability as limited partners. However, the IRS has strict regulations concerning this type of partnership structure. These regulations (see Revenue Procedure 72-13) require that the corporation have substance both in equity capital and ownership of the building. As a result, this form of ownership can be legally complicated and should be considered only after careful analysis.

Of the four general-partner alternatives listed for the limited partnership, one of the more common in hospital-related buildings is the developer as general partner and the physicians as limited partners. The key to success is finding a reputable developer or real estate development firm that can bring expertise and financial strength to the project. In this arrangement, the developer would collect a front-end fee for his contribution to the development of the project, receive an ongoing management contract on the building, and hope for appreciation of the property. As a result of those benefits, he would be willing to take on the risk as general partner in a good situation. The physician, as limited partner, would have the same status as in any other limited partnership.

As with the development of a condominium, the hospital could be involved to varying degrees with a building that is being developed as a partnership. It could let the physicians do it on their own, but more than likely the hospital would function as the organizing entity—putting together the project, hiring consultants, architects, and contractors, and helping set up the partnership alternative that best meets the needs of the hospital and the physicians. By being coordinator of the project, the hospital is able to exercise more influence over the project than if it were not involved. In addition, the hospital may financially support the project in ways similar to those already described in the discussion of condominium ownership—the provision of parking, the construction of a connecting route between the office building and the hospital, and even the provision of a loan guarantee to make the project easier to finance.

One other form of involvement the hospital might have with virtually any of the partnership arrangements (except when the hospital is general partner) is the lease-back of the entire building. The hospital would, in turn, sublease the building to the physician tenants. This procedure is another means for the hospital to lend its financial stability to the project and to maintain control of the management and occupancy of the building, at the same time giving the physicians the opportunity to receive the tax deductions. Such a procedure would, however, need to be carefully developed. The physicians would have to put up substantial amounts of money and take certain risks in order for this concept to pass IRS inspection.

THIRD-PARTY OWNERSHIP

The final category of ownership of the hospital-related medical office building is a third-party, representing neither the physicians nor the hospital. This third-party owner might be an individual, a group of individuals, a corporation, a real estate development firm, or even some type of trust. As an outright owner of the project, the third party would usually rent space to the physicians on a typical landlord/tenant relationship. The third-party owner would be financially and legally liable for the project, and the physicians' liability would be the same as if he were renting from the hospital. His rent would be his tax-deductible item.

Another type of arrangement might arise if the hospital contracted with the third party to develop the project, with the understanding that the hospital would lease the entire building from the owner and sublease space to the physicians. This type of arrangement puts financial and legal liability on the third party, with an indirect financial responsibility on the hospital through its lease agreement. It provides the hospital with control over the building management and occupancy without actual ownership. Again, the physician would be a rental tenant.

Already mentioned is the alternative of the third party actually being the general partner in a limited partnership of physicians. Under this arrangement, rental might be handled directly with the physicians or the hospital could lease the entire building and sublease space to the physician tenants.

As with physician ownership, the options for varying degrees of hospital involvement and assistance are considerable. The hospital might lease the land at a fair market rental rate. It might provide parking or a connector to the hospital. It might work out the initial contractual agreement with the third party to develop the building, paying the fee itself or including the fee in the overall financial structure of the building. Actual hospital development of the project, sale to the third party, and hospital lease-back is also an alternative; although, as with some other options, a revenue ruling should be sought concerning it.

CHAPTER **5**

Deciding on Ownership

Once the hospital knows what its various ownership alternatives are, it must then address the issue of how to determine which of these alternatives to select. In deciding ownership, the hospital must ask and answer three key questions: What form of ownership will contribute most to the hospital and its goals? What form of ownership is most marketable to the physicians? What form of ownership best satisfies the financial requirements of the situation? By examining all the elements that these questions imply and by answering the questions thoroughly and objectively, the hospital can find its way through the maze of alternatives to the form of ownership best suited to its particular needs.

Answering these questions is, however, more far-reaching than a first glance would indicate. Numerous factors must be considered to arrive at a judgment.

> *Question:* What form of ownership will contribute most to the hospital and its goals?
>
> *Answer:* The form of ownership is one that best ensures the planning, implementation, and maintenance of a medical office building with the following qualities:

1. A building that is programmed in conjunction with the long-range master plan and marketing plan of the hospital.

For a building truly to serve the hospital and its patients, its planning must be coordinated with the planning of the hospital itself. The actual type, size, and location of the facility not only should relate physically to the master plan of the hospital, but also to the marketing goals—to the services that will be developed and emphasized in the future. Occupancy of the building must relate in a similar manner. For the hospital to develop a specialized service such as cardiac care and not to plan its office building with the facilities to recruit and serve cardiologists would be shortsighted. By the same token, if the hospital plans to emphasize outpatient treatment, the physical facilities as well as the physician specialists to be located in the building need to relate to this plan.

2. A building that is all medical or health care related.

An office building that is occupied by physicians, dentists, and medically related commercial establishments becomes a functioning part of the total medical complex. The physicians support the hospital by admitting patients and prescribing tests and treatments performed in the hospital's ancillary departments. The commercial establishments provide needed services and products for both the physicians and the patients who utilize the building. The patient has the advantages of being able to receive complete medical and dental care and related services at a single location. In contrast, a building occupied by lawyers, architects, and other professionals and/or unrelated commercial enterprises, such as finance companies and travel agencies, would contribute nothing to the medical complex, patient care, the hospital, or the physicians. In fact, such a building would waste valuable space near the hospital and detract from the central function of the medical center.

3. A building in which all tenants are medical staff members (except for commercial establishments).

The tenants of the building not only must be physicians (except for persons operating commercial businesses), but also members of the hospital's medical staff. The whole concept of the on-campus medical office building revolves around closer, more cooperative relationships between hospital and physicians and around the concept of the physician being near his hospitalized patients. If a physician is not a medical staff member, these objectives are defeated. In addition, medical staff membership as a prerequisite to tenancy guarantees a high level of professionalism among the building tenants. By the same token, if a physician is removed from the medical staff of the hospital for disciplinary reasons, his removal from the office building is also desirable — both to maintain the level of professionalism and to remove a potential source of discord.

4. A building that has a planned specialty composition of physicians, geared to the needs of the community and the hospital.

A planned specialty composition helps guarantee the effective functioning of the office building. First, the specialty composition must relate to the services provided by the hospital so that the building and the hospital function as an integrated whole. Second, the specialty composition must be balanced between primary care physicians and needed specialists. Third, the building should include physicians of all ages, so that the hospital will not be faced with a medical staff that is retiring over a short period of time. The planned specialty composition guarantees a good balance of services to the patients. It means that competition among the physicians will be at appropriate levels — no overstaffing in one area or a total absence of a needed specialist in another. It means good referral patterns for the physicians and good consultation patterns for the patients. The need to plan and sustain the specialty composition throughout the life of the building is central to its effectiveness (see chapters 9 and 10).

5. A building in which no commercial services will compete directly with or syphon off sources of income from the hospital, unless developed in conjunction with the hospital.

One factor that makes the development of an on-campus medical office building financially feasible from the hospital's point of view is the increased revenue anticipated from greater utilization of hospital ancillary services.

Because laboratory and x-ray services are major revenue producers and the hospital already has outpatient laboratory and x-ray facilities, it usually wants any new business generated by the office building channeled into its existing departments, both as an additional source of income and as a means of improving overall efficiency through better utilization of existing staff and equipment. In some cases, the office building will be large enough to support laboratory and x-ray facilities located within the medical office building, and the hospital may want to operate these branch facilities. In still other cases, the hospital may want to lease the operation of these services to private individuals or companies. The key issue is that the hospital have some control over the establishment of these and other commercial services that would compete directly with existing hospital departments. The hospital wants to avoid the situation in which it develops the building for the physicians or other owners, only to have them turn around and use the advantage of their location to develop services that would syphon off hospital income. Control over establishing these services should not be confused with any effort to require the physicians to use the services. The physician should still be completely free to utilize the hospital outpatient facilities, private laboratories and x-ray services provided elsewhere, or use equipment in his own office. Special legal consultation should be obtained to ensure that leasing provisions do not constitute anticompetitive measures among tenants that would raise federal antitrust issues.

6. A building that has recruitment capability—specifically, space held for recruitment.

When a medical office building is developed in conjunction with a thorough study of the hospital's medical staff, programmed in conjunction with the long-range plans of the hospital, and developed with a balanced specialty composition, recruitment needs will invariably surface. Physicians in specialties not represented on the staff, additional physicians in specialties that are underrepresented, and young physicians who can begin picking up the load from aging physicians may all be needed. A critical factor in the development of a successful recruitment effort is the availability of desirable office space for the physicians being recruited. Consequently, the most effective office building will not only accommodate existing staff members who want to occupy the building, but also have space available for physicians to be recruited over a three-to-five year period (including construction time, and depending on the specifics of the situation). Such a building provides for the future as well as the present needs of the community and the hospital. It is a building that will not already be outdated and oversubscribed by the time construction is complete.

7. A building that provides flexibility of space utilization for the hospital.

Increasingly restrictive regulations on the hospital and its facilities make the need for flexibility of space utilization more and more desirable. An office building in which the hospital has the option of locating certain functions can be a tremendous asset. For example, the hospital may want to move administrative offices, classrooms, or some hospital departments such as public relations or even medical records to the office building. By doing so, the hospital is able to locate these offices conveniently, but in a building of less expensive construction and safety requirements than the hospital. Thus, expensive hospital space is freed for greater utilization by patient care departments and ancillary services. The flexibility to utilize space, to increase or decrease the amount of space used, or even make use of space on a temporary basis while physicians are being recruited to fill it can increase significantly the building's contribution to the total medical complex.

8. A building that is efficient in both design and function.

To the investor renting space to physicians, design efficiency means producing a building with maximum rentable space and minimum core space (space used for stairways, corridors, elevators, public rest rooms, and such). Most investor-owned buildings will be designed with deep rentable spaces (the distance from the public corridor to the exterior wall). Depths of 35 feet to 40 feet throughout the building give the owner an optimum ratio of rentable space to core space. For most physicians, however, a 35-foot to 40-foot depth does not work well for suite design (see chapter 15). For example, a physician who might need 1,000 square feet of space in a building designed with 28-foot depths might have to rent 1,200 square feet of space in a building with only 40-foot depths available. That costs him more in rent, but to the investor landlord more rent from fewer tenants is desirable. The hospital's perspective on efficiency is, however, somewhat different. For the hospital, each physician on campus means additional dollar revenue for hospital services used. Consequently, from the hospital's point of view, a building that is functionally efficient, which houses more physicians renting less space, is more desirable than a building that involves fewer tenants renting more space. The result is that the best on-campus medical office buildings are those that combine both types of efficiency. An effective building is functionally efficient—one designed to accommodate the maximum number of physicians renting or owning the minimum amount of space needed to meet their practice needs. It is also a building that sacrifices as little as possible in the rentable space-to-core-space ratio.

9. A building that is built with high-quality construction methods and materials.

High-quality construction methods and materials are desirable for several reasons. First, the hospital is an enduring institution, and the office building is also likely to be in service for some time. Because the medical office building is on the hospital campus and affiliated with the hospital, it reflects on the hospital. A well constructed, high-quality building will reflect well on the hospital. Poor-quality construction and materials can only detract from the hospital campus and hurt the public attitude toward the institution. Perhaps even more important is the attitude of the tenant physicians. Regardless of who owns and constructs the building, if the building is of poor quality, develops problems and begins to deteriorate, or is inferior in any way, the physicians who occupy it will become unhappy, and will ultimately blame the hospital for not seeing that the project was done right in the first place. The hospital wants the building to develop support among the physicians, to enhance physician/hospital relations, and, indirectly, produce improved patient care. The hospital cannot afford to have an inferior-quality building on its campus that is a source of irritation to its medical staff and injures the very relationships the hospital wishes to enhance.

10. A building that has ongoing high-quality maintenance and housekeeping.

High-quality maintenance and housekeeping is only an extension of initial high-quality construction. It is essential for the same reasons. Only a building that is in good repair, that functions properly, and is clean and well cared for can reflect appropriately on the hospital with which it is associated and keep its physician tenants happy.

11. A building that has sensitive management to enhance the hospital/physician relationship.

Sensitive management is a subjective quality, and yet it is important to a building that is functioning well. Management of the office building needs to understand the specific needs of physicians and the particular problems they face in their daily practice. It needs to be supportive and helpful, responding quickly to problems and even anticipating them before they arise. Management needs to be fair, working with the physicians in policy matters and problems, rather than simply dictating to them. In short, management that is truly concerned about keeping the physician happy is an important factor in helping the building function smoothly as a part of the total medical complex.

12. A building that is physically connected to the hospital.

In virtually every part of the country, a physical connection between the office building and the hospital is essential. In very cold climates, a tunnel or an enclosed and heated walkway of some kind is essential if the building is to function optimally. Physicians need to be able to carry on a "shirt-sleeve" practice—to be able to go from their offices to the hospital and back without having to go out into the weather or to waste time putting on and taking off coats and rain gear. By the same token, outpatients need to be able to have convenient access to ancillary services in the hospital, again without having to brave the elements. Even in areas of tropical weather year around, a minimum of a covered and side-protected walkway is desirable to shield users from wind and rain. The best way for the office building and the hospital to function as a whole is with convenient, protected access between them.

Question: What form of ownership is most marketable to physicians?

Answer: The form of ownership that best provides the following qualities will be the most marketable to physicians.

1. A financially attractive opportunity.

Although not every physician decides to own or rent on the basis of a good financial alternative, a building that is a financially good opportunity for the physician is considerably easier to market. In some cases renting may actually cost the physician less than owning, but in other cases the situation may be reversed. If the building offers a rental situation, then the rent must be competitive or even less expensive than the comparable going rate for a facility of similar quality. If the building offers a purchase situation for the physician, then it needs to be a good investment over the long run, not just for the first few years. In any purchase situation the financial figures should be extended to the point at which the tax advantages reverse and should include the exit options and what they will cost the physician (see chapter 7).

2. A psychologically acceptable alternative.

Physicians have many viewpoints, and the strengths of their varying convictions may be a major factor in which forms of ownership are viable. Here the following questions must be answered:

- Are the physicians emphatic about ownership?
- Is the hospital an acceptable landlord?
- Is another physician an acceptable landlord?
- Is a third party an acceptable landlord?

3. An alternative that provides the physician with maximum input and minimum liability.

Physicians want to express their opinions on how the building is developed, what services it will include, what kind of policies will govern it, how their suites will be designed, and so on. Rarely, however, is a physician eager to take on greater liabilities than he already has as a physician. Thus, an ownership option that will give him a maximum input while limiting his liability and responsibility is a very marketable entity.

4. An alternative that guarantees good management of the building.

Physicians are concerned about how the building will be run. A marketable building is one in which a plan for good, ongoing management has been developed and is guaranteed as a part of the ownership structure.

5. An alternative that will provide long-term security in regard to how the building will be run and how well the landlord can be trusted.

Physicians are concerned about the long haul. Moving a practice into an office building is an expensive operation. Before a physician wants to commit himself to occupancy—whether as an owner or a tenant—he wants some feeling of security about the building over the long run. He wants to know that the building ownership and management will be stable and that he will be able to practice there without periodic hassles over the building.

6. An alternative that gives the physician flexibility.

Physicians' practices are rarely static over a long period. Physicians add partners, partners retire, partnerships are dissolved, and group practices are formed. Consequently, the physician wants a building that provides him with as much flexibility as possible. He wants the ability to move his practice, expand it, or make it smaller with a minimum of inconvenience. Although he may not openly talk about it in regard to his office, he is concerned with government regulations and what they may bring. The building that is designed with the capacity for part of it to be converted into a large group practice is desirable. In short, a building that provides the physician with maximum flexibility is a marketable building.

7. An alternative that is likely to result in a minimum of legal problems for the physician.

An ownership vehicle that ensures a minimum of legal problems and a minimum of the physician's time being taken up with these problems is a marketable entity.

8. An alternative that is likely to result in a minimum of management problems for the physician.

Physicians want to practice medicine. They do not want to manage office buildings. An ownership vehicle that requires the least amount of the physician's time in management and is likely to confront him with the fewest problems is desirable from his point of view.

9. Many of the qualities that enable a building to meet the goals and objectives of the hospital are also qualities that enhance its marketability to physicians.

Those qualities already named that are of particular importance to the physicians include the following:

- All medical building
- Planned specialty composition
- Design and functional efficiency
- High-quality construction
- High-quality maintenance
- Physical connection

Question: What form of ownership best satisfies the financial requirements of the situation?

Answer: The answer hinges on whether the hospital wishes to own the office building. If the hospital is interested in owning the building, then it must determine by use of the three major criteria listed here if ownership is financially feasible. If the hospital does not wish to own the building, or ownership is not financially feasible, four different criteria, also listed here, will help determine the form of ownership that will be the most attractive financial alternative.

Criteria for financial requirements of hospital ownership

1. The hospital must be able to afford to own the building. Does it have the capital and/or credit available to undertake ownership?

In many cases, if the hospital does not have sufficient capital on hand, up to 100 percent financing can be arranged. However, the hospital may have previous bond issues outstanding or stipulations related to major gifts received that limit the indebtedness the hospital can carry. Consequently, in some cases, even if capital and financing are available, the hospital may not be able to carry the additional debt. Thus, the hospital must explore its total financial picture and debt structure to determine if, in fact, it can afford to own the building.

2. Building ownership must fit within the financial priorities of the hospital. Does the hospital have other priorities for which its available capital/credit must be expended?

Many times the need for an office building is not the only need facing the hospital. Ancillary services or other departments may require upgrading and/or expansion. Patient rooms may need renovation. New services may need to be developed. In such cases, the hospital must determine all its needs, examine its financial ability to provide for them, and if unable to provide for all of them, establish its priorities.

3. The projected construction costs and operating budget for the proposed medical office building must project a financial picture acceptable to the hospital.

If money and priorities do not present a major obstacle to hospital ownership, the hospital will have to look at the project in greater depth. On the basis of a building programmed to meet the needs of the medical complex, construction costs will have to be projected and an operating budget estimated. If operating deficits are projected for a year or two, the hospital must determine whether it can afford to carry those deficits until the building is operating in the black. The hospital may also need to ask, Is the building too large or too expensive for the hospital's financial capability? Can a less expensive or smaller building be constructed without sacrificing important quality and the needs of the hospital? These and other factors that involve the long-range picture must be considered as a judgment is made (see chapter 7).

Criteria for financial requirements of alternative ownership
1. It must be possible to finance the project.

Ownership options vary considerably in their ability to be financed. Consequently, in deciding on an alternative, the hospital must examine carefully which alternatives can be financed at good interest rates and under agreeable terms.

2. It must be a financially marketable project.

Already covered under the discussion of marketing to physicians is the need for the ownership to provide an alternative that is a good financial opportunity. Generally, the better the financial opportunity, the easier the project is to finance.

3. It must be a financially stable project, projected over the long run.

Ownership options also vary widely in their overall financial stability. The stronger the owner or owners or the broader the base of owners who are liable, the greater the financial stability is likely to be and the less likely the project is to fail.

4. Its financial success must depend on the input of hospital capital only to the extent that is compatible with the hospital's financial priorities.

The ownership option that can stand on its own financially is certainly the ideal in this regard; however, almost every project, whether investor-owned or physician-owned, will depend to some degree on the injection of hospital capital. For that reason the hospital must consider carefully what form the financial assistance will take and to what extent it can afford that assistance. If the hospital's financial situation is difficult, the issue of capital outlay can be a key factor.

COMPARING THE OPTIONS

Once the key issues and the alternatives of ownership by the hospital, physician, or third-party are established, the decision-making process becomes a matter of comparing the alternatives with the issues. Certainly, no one form of ownership is appropriate in every situation; however, some general statements can be made about the innate strengths and weaknesses of the various options. The comparisons that follow will present those general characteristics, as well as potential problems that will need to be resolved with the different alternatives of ownership (see chapter 4).

Twelve criteria have been listed in order to determine how well the alternatives may contribute to the goals of the hospital. Here is how the types of ownership possible compare with regard to those criteria.

Contribution to Hospital Goals

1. A building that is programmed in conjunction with the long-range master plan and marketing plan of the hospital.

Hospital ownership is the vehicle that most readily facilitates coordination of planning. No conflict of interest exists, and a single ownership structure is responsible for making decisions for both the hospital and the office building. Hospital ownership guarantees a building that is not only planned with community and hospital needs in mind, but also is implemented and has the potential of being maintained in a manner responsive to those needs.

In a condominium arrangement, a coordination of planning could be reasonably carried out initially, particularly if the hospital were the organizing force in the development process. By its very nature, a condominium is, however, a fairly rigid entity over the long run, limiting its long-range responsiveness to community and physician needs.

With the various partnership agreements, initial coordination of planning can be expected, again, particularly when the hospital is involved as the organizing force. In addition, provisions in a land lease or a lease-back agreement are two mechanisms by which the hospital can maintain some continued coordination of building tenancy and utilization with hospital and community needs. Without the land lease or the lease-back agreement, the hospital has no way of ensuring the continued coordination of the medical office building with the hospital.

Basically, the same controls that are available with a physician partnership are available with third-party ownership. The hospital could have some input into the initial planning, if it were an organizing force. In the long run, however, the only way the hospital could ensure continued coordination of the building is through provisions in a land lease or through a lease-back agreement.

2. A building that is all medical or health care related.

Again, hospital ownership provides the simplest and most complete control. If the hospital owns the building, it can lease to whomever it pleases, guaranteeing that all tenants are either physicians or medically related businesses.

Some loss of control occurs with every other ownership form; however, steps are available to minimize that loss. In a condominium, the hospital can be the moving force that gets it organized, and, as such, it can provide considerable input into the drafting of the rules and regulations of the condominium. In addition, land-lease provisions might specify the maintenance of an all-medical building.

In the various partnership agreements, a clause relating to the all-medical nature of the building might be included. The best insurance, however, is either a provision in the land lease or a lease-back agreement. With a third-party owner, a lease-back agreement is the best mechanism for maintaining the all-medical building. Land-lease provisions are also good, but the third party may be less willing to accept that arrangement.

3. A building in which all tenants are medical staff members (except for commercial establishments).

The discussion above for an all-medical building applies equally well for the criterion of medical staff membership, with the exception of situations in which a physician is removed or resigns from the medical staff. In a hospital-owned building the rental agreement would normally include a clause stating that in the event the physician was no longer a medical staff member, he would have to vacate his office (see discussion of related tax issues in chapter 6). The same could be included in the lease of a third-party owner; however, through the hospital's land lease, it would have to require such a clause in the physician lease and would probably have to provide compensation for the vacated space to the third-party owner, in order to obtain his agreement to such a plan.

The requirement of a physician owner to vacate his space would be considerably more complicated. In a condominium, the rules and regulations would have to require his vacating the suite and his selling it through a prearranged means. The means might be for the hospital to have first right of refusal on the purchase of the suite at a price determined through appraisals.

Although the partnership situation would be structured somewhat differently, the same problems would arise. The individual physician's lease with the partnership would need to include a clause requiring that he vacate in the event he were no longer a staff member, and the partnership agreement would need to provide for a means for the physician to sell his partnership interest. Sale of the partnership interest would probably be handled in a manner similar to a condominium.

Regardless of how it is planned, maintaining the medical staff requirement in a physician-owned building is cumbersome, legally complicated, and potentially costly for the hospital.

4. A building that has a planned specialty composition of physicians, geared to the needs of the community and the hospital.

Hospital ownership provides the simplest and most thorough means for establishing and maintaining a building's planned specialty composition.

Maintenance of a specialty composition could be difficult with a condominium. Initially, the suites could be sold according to a predetermined composition of specialists, but maintaining the complement over the long run would be considerably more difficult. A land lease might be able to specify that a doctor selling his suite must sell it to a physician in the same specialty. However, such a clause would not provide for adjusting to changing staffing needs. The other possibility would be for the land lease to state that the hospital had the first right of refusal on the purchase of any suite, thus allowing the hospital to buy the suite and sell it to the specialist needed at the time. All of these options are considerably more complicated and costly than hospital ownership. Without the hospital as general partner, about the only way a hospital could satisfactorily maintain the planned specialty composition of a building owned through a partnership would be if it leased the entire building itself and subleased to the physicians. The same is also true of third-party ownership.

5. A building in which no commercial services will compete directly with or syphon off sources of income from the hospital, unless developed in conjunction with the hospital.

As with any type of control the hospital wishes to have, control of commercial services is simplest under hospital ownership. This type of control over what services go into the building is not, however, a particularly difficult legal problem with other forms of ownership, as long as the hospital is involved and plans ahead.

In a condominium arrangement, the rules and regulations could cover this point; however the hospital would have to be an organizing force so that it had the input into drafting those rules. The partnership agreement could also contain a clause covering this point, again assuming that the hospital was involved enough in the planning of the project to insist on this clause.

The fact that not every type of control can be guaranteed through the rules and regulations of a condominium or a partnership agreement should be emphasized, however. Once the hospital is out of the picture, the owners can change the rules or the agreement. By and large, however, making changes is difficult in areas that do not directly affect the owner's ability to sell his interest. For that reason, control of the commercial services is one area that can be adequately handled through this procedure. A problem that might arise would be if services provided by the hospital and not allowed in the building became noncompetitive in cost or service offered. In such a case, the physician owners would probably take legal action to amend the rules of the condominium or the partnership agreement, and the court would probably uphold the change.

The best way to control the commercial services with third-party ownership is through a lease-back agreement. Although some provisions could be made in the land lease, a third-party owner is not likely to accept that type of agreement.

6. A building that has recruitment capability—specifically, space held for recruitment.

For the hospital to require that space be held vacant until the right specialists are recruited, it will have to bear the cost in one way or another. If the hospital owns the building, holding the space open is a simple matter that involves the loss of revenue until the space is filled, and this loss is more apparent than real, for it is primarily a loss "on paper" that is compensated for by other factors (see chapter 7).

In a condominium arrangement, the hospital will probably have to pay rent on a vacant condominium until it is sold. Depending on the agreement, this rental could be reasonable or quite expensive.

With a partnership or a third party-owner, the simplest way to hold the space vacant is for the hospital to lease the entire building. In addition, the hospital could probably work out an agreement to pay rent on space being held vacant. However the hospital arranges, holding space for recruitment is likely to be more costly when the hospital does not own the building.

7. A building that provides flexibility of space utilization for the hospital.

When the hospital is owner, it can plan the utilization of space within the medical office building. It can set aside spaces for short-range or long-range occupancy on the part of the hospital. It can move some hospital offices and administrative functions to the office building to free additional space within the hospital, either temporarily or permanently. Over the life of the building, the hospital has the flexibility to vacate space at any time and rent that space to physicians; however, if the hospital wanted to occupy larger portions of the building, it would need to wait for vacancies to occur before doing so.

Other forms of ownership provide varying degrees of flexibility. A condominium is the poorest because of its rigid ownership structure. Through a lease-back agreement with a partnership or third-party owner, the hospital could maintain flexibility almost equal to that provided by hospital ownership, but at a slightly higher price. Without the lease-back agreement, any degree of flexibility that the hospital would be able to maintain would be considerably more costly and complicated.

8. A building that is efficient in both design and function.

The issue of design efficiency versus functional efficiency involves a basic conflict of interest between landlord and tenant in every case except hospital ownership. When the hospital owns, it can have control over the design of the office building to see that it is both functionally and design efficient. The hospital and the tenant physician both stand to gain—the hospital, through more physicians on campus, the physician by being able to rent the minimum amount of space he needs.

In a condominium, the individual owners may or may not be interested in design and functional efficiency, because no rental is involved. If the hospital is involved in the planning stages of the condominium, it may influence the design of the building so that functional, as well as design, efficiency is considered.

Whenever a partnership is involved that will include renting to other physicians, or whenever a third-party owner is involved, the conflict of interest surfaces. Whether the investor is a physician or a third party, he will be more interested in design efficiency than functional efficiency because that means dollars in his pockets. Particularly, the third party has no innate interest in the convenience of the individual doctor, how well his suite design works, whether the hospital is getting maximum utilization from the building, or whether the doctor has to rent more space than he actually needs. In fact, the investor would likely prefer the physician to have to rent more space than he needs. In these situations, the only way the hospital could exercise control over the design of the building would be if it signed a lease-back agreement with the partnership or third-party owner before the building was constructed.

9. A building that is built with high-quality construction methods and materials.

Although hospital ownership is no guarantee that high-quality construction methods and materials will be used, the hospital does have much to gain by their use. Unfortunately, even hospitals make sacrifices in these areas on some projects, reducing the long-range effectiveness of the building.

In a condominium, hospital involvement during the early planning stages can influence the quality of the building. A few minimum specifications might even be included in the land lease.

With other forms of ownership—namely, partnerships or third-party ownership—the best alternative is for the hospital to be involved early, to have a lease-back agreement with the owner or owners, and to have some minimum specifications written into the land lease. Through this combination, the hospital can usually exert enough influence to produce a high-quality building.

The involvement of a developer as a general partner or as an outright owner can produce varying results in relation to quality. Because of their financial strength, some developers might be able to actually build in more quality than the hospital or physicians could. However, finding the right developer is essential, for just the opposite is often true. Unfortunately, many developers are not interested in the long-range future of the hospital and construct buildings as cheaply as possible, cutting corners and creating problems that emerge as the building ages. The hospital should be aware that both extremes are possible with a third party and be sufficiently involved to protect itself where necessary.

10. A building that has ongoing high-quality maintenance and housekeeping.

The hospital can control the quality of housekeeping and maintenance if it owns the building. If the building is a condominium, it might be able to control the matter to some extent if it had a contract to manage the building. With a partnership or third-party owner the hospital would either have to lease back the building or sign a maintenance and housekeeping contract with the owners. Beyond these methods, any control over this important aspect of the ongoing quality of the building is, at best, difficult.

11. A building whose sensitive management enhances the hospital/physician relationship.

The hospital has much to gain by providing sensitive management for the office building, and, when it owns the building, it can provide that type of high-quality management. Hospital ownership, however, does not guarantee sensitive management, for unfortunately, some administrative staffs either do not have the skill or the desire to operate a building with physician satisfaction in mind.

Nonetheless, just as sensitive management is most likely under hospital ownership, it is least likely under third-party ownership. A third-party owner is most likely to do the minimum and let everything else slide, and a third party certainly has little to gain by promoting good relations with the hospital. Even so, excellent management can be provided through a third-party owner, if the right owner is selected.

With the various forms of physician ownership, the quality of management can vary considerably. If the physicians try to manage the building themselves, there will likely be bickering and grumbling. On the other hand, if they hire a good manager and specify the high quality that they want, the building has a better chance of being managed well.

With any kind of ownership other than hospital, the hospital can exercise virtually no control over that quality of management unless it leases back the building. He who controls the purse strings, in essence, controls the management.

12. A building that is physically connected to the hospital.

Legally speaking, hospital ownership is the simplest when the connection of the two buildings (hospital and medical office building) is concerned. If the hospital owns both buildings, the situation is simple. If, however, separate ownership of the office building is involved, no great problem arises, only the need for careful legal documents to delineate ownership, areas of responsibility and liability, and other factors in regard to the office building, the connecting structure, and the hospital.

Summary of Issues for the Hospital

Consideration of all the forms of ownership indicates that the hospital cannot remove itself from the planning, development, and operation of the on-campus medical office building without jeopardizing the long-range effectiveness of the building in relation to the hospital's goals and objectives.

The hospital can maintain this involvement through various ownership alternatives, but hospital ownership is the first choice in regard to this key issue. An arrangement in which the hospital leases back the entire building from a physician partnership or a third party also provides a building in accord with the hospital and its goals, assuming IRS approval can be secured. However, when the hospital gives up ownership, it does give up considerable control.

Probably the poorest alternatives in relation to this key issue are a condominium or an unrestricted third-party owner. In addition, physician partnerships over which the hospital has little control (no lease-back agreement, few restrictions in the land lease) are, at best, chancy, but might work under some circumstances.

The second key issue to be considered in the decision-making process is the form of ownership most marketable to the physicians. The initial discussion of this issue presented nine criteria for determining marketability. Here is how the various forms of ownership stack up with regard to those criteria.

1. A financially attractive opportunity.

The financial attractiveness of a particular ownership vehicle depends largely on the situation. It depends on such variables as the rent charged by the hospital or other landlord, the down payment needed for the physician to purchase a piece of the ownership, the overall cost of the building, the extent to which the hospital financially supports the building, and the type (if any) of exit vehicle available to the physician owner when he has depleted all tax advantages—just to name a few.

Detailed financial comparisons of the various types of ownership are presented in chapter 7. They compare a hypothetical, though realistic, building and the financial implications of each type of ownership.

On a financial basis, these figures indicate that over a 10-year period a physician-owned partnership is a slightly more attractive financial vehicle for the physician than hospital ownership. That edge assumes that an appropriate exit vehicle from the partnership was established in the beginning so that the physician could sell his interest at the end of 10 years, before his tax advantage turned into a tax liability. However, the exit vehicle value cannot be guaranteed in the beginning or the risk factor is removed and tax benefits are lessened. The attractiveness of ownership decreases with each subsequent year.

Condominium ownership also ran only slightly ahead of rental from the hospital over the 10 year period, again assuming the physicians were able to sell the condominium at the end of 10 years, before it became a tax liability. Rental from a third-party investor proved to be the poorest financial alternative for the physician, including renting from other physicians.

Although these general comparisons can be made, each individual situation will vary widely. In some circumstances, rental from the hospital will clearly be the best financial opportunity for the physician, in other situations the partnership will be. Only rarely would the condominium or rental from a third party be the first choice. One important point must be kept in mind, however. Any ownership the physician goes into will involve a certain amount of financial risk and increased financial liability. For example, the physician has no guarantee that the building will be a financial success or that he can sell his interest when and at the price he wants. He may even have to assume responsibility for a greater portion of the debt than his percentage of ownership. Consequently, the physician will need to consider carefully the risk and liability assumed versus the potential financial gain of a particular ownership.

Which Form of
Ownership Suits
Physicians?

2. A psychologically acceptable alternative.

Physician attitudes vary widely. For example, some physicians want to own their offices as a matter of pride. They may not care whether it is a good investment or not. Other physicians may have a strong desire to own, based on an impression that it is an outstanding financial investment abounding in tax shelters, accruing property value, and with few problems. Consequently, the hospital must discern physicians' attitudes about owning and why they feel that way. If a large number of physicians want to own regardless of the cost, then physician ownership may be the only alternative. The problem then becomes to select the best form of physician ownership under the circumstances. If, on the other hand, the physicians want to own because they are convinced it is an excellent investment in general (even before they know the facts), then the hospital will be free to explore the financial figures for the specific project with the physicians to help them determine whether or not physician ownership is a desirable investment.

The hospital also will have to consider the doctors' attitudes toward hospital ownership. Some physicians will be strongly in favor of it because they believe the hospital will be fair and lend stability to the project. Others will be highly suspicious of the hospital, fearing manipulation and interference. The hospital must determine which feelings are predominant and, if negative feelings are strong, whether the hospital will be able to change them (see chapters 9, 10, and 11).

Finally, the hospital will need to determine how the physicians view other physicians as landlords or view a third party as landlord. Frequently, physicians will refuse to accept another physician as a landlord, but will accept a third party.

No pat answer can be given to this criterion for ownership. Only careful examination of the individual situation will show what alternatives are or can be acceptable to the physicians.

3. An alternative that provides the physicians with maximum input and minimum liability.

Hospital ownership offers an option with virtually no liability for the physician and varying degrees of input, depending on the situation. A hospital dedicated to the integration of the office building into the total medical complex can develop the office building in such a way that the physician has considerable input (see chapters 9, 10, and 11). On the other hand, some hospitals may have a less sensitive administration that is not interested in working closely with the physicians. In those cases, physician input would be considerably more limited.

The condominium provides the physician with maximum input accompanied by maximum liability. The general partnership provides the same maximum input and liability.

The limited partnership provides the physician minimum liability, but his ability to have any say in the project depends largely on the general partner. If the general partner is a corporation in which the physicians own some of the stock, then they will have a proportionate amount of input into the project. With any other general partner, the input will depend on how much the partner is willing to work with the limited partners. Usually, because of the financial partnership, the interests of the physicians will be given consideration.

With a third-party owner, the physician will have virtually no liability, but he will also have little or no input.

If the physician protects himself by restricting his liability, then he usually gives up a certain amount of input in the development of the project. Probably, the best situation would be hospital ownership, but only if the hospital is willing to work closely with the physicians. A partially physician-owned corporation as general partner in a limited partnership is also a good alternative with regard to this criterion.

4. An alternative that guarantees good management of the building.

Realistically speaking, no form of ownership guarantees good management. Some have a better chance than others, however. The possibility of good management under hospital ownership is considerable, for the hospital has much to gain by operating the building properly. Nonetheless, poor management is possible under hospital ownership, particularly if hospital administration is either insensitive or inexperienced.

One statement could be made emphatically. If the physicians decide to manage the building themselves—whether it be a condominium or a partnership—the building will be run poorly. Physicians themselves tend to be poor managers, and the physician who is a good manager must usually reduce time spent in patient care. Most doctors simply do not have the time to do both. Consequently, the quality of management depends largely on whom the physicians hire to operate the building and, as owners, how well they can agree on major operational decisions.

When management is considered, the third party as general partner would not differ substantially from simple third-party ownership. The third party may be a real professional, able to offer excellent management, or he may not be. He may provide excellent management from the economic point of view, but that may involve compromises not necessarily good for the physician tenant.

The key to good management is careful planning before the building goes into operation. If the hospital can and wants to handle management, it may be the best alternative, but good, qualified professional management from outside may also be a good alternative under the various forms of ownership.

5. An alternative that will provide long-term security in regard to how the building will be run and how well the landlord can be trusted.

Hospital ownership undoubtedly provides the best possibility of long-term stability because the hospital, by the nature of its business, tends to be a stable institution. The hospital will usually continue to own the building for years to come. Nonetheless, extreme administrative staff changes could cause major changes in how the building is operated over the long run. Thus, although the hospital is most likely to provide long-range stability, it is not guaranteed.

The various forms of physician ownership are going to result in ownership changes and resulting operational changes. The condominium and the general partnership depend so much on the agreement of so many physicians that long-range operational stability would be difficult to project. As suites are sold and needs change, management decisions will change. In addition, any partnership will usually want to sell the building after 10 to 12 years, before it becomes a tax liability. Unless the building is sold to the hospital, ownership is likely to continue to change periodically.

Third-party ownership will not provide long-range continuity. An investor will own the building only long enough to take out the maximum tax benefits, then he will "roll" the project. Thus, the physicians could anticipate periodic changes in ownership and assignment of leases, with unpredictable changes in building management, maintenance, and policies.

6. An alternative that gives the physician flexibility.

Hospital ownership provides excellent flexibility for the physician. Because he is a renter and because IRS guidelines stipulate the hospital-owned medical office building is to be rented to medical staff members, even with a strong lease the physician is usually able to break the lease and move out of the building simply by resigning from the medical staff. Such a dramatic step would normally not even be necessary, because the hospital has little or nothing to gain by keeping an unhappy physician in its office building. In regard to changing space needs, the hospital is likely to be the most understanding landlord around. The hospital needs a satisfied medical staff. Consequently, the hospital is most likely to work closely with the physicians in making expansion of their suites possible, in helping them move from one suite to another within the building, or in allowing them to reduce the size of their suites.

The opposite extreme of hospital ownership flexibility would be the condominium. It provides the physician with almost no flexibility. Because he owns his suite, he is tied to it. Expansion is almost impossible, unless he decides to buy an entire additional suite. The legal problems of a suite being divided and resold to two neighboring suites for the sake of expansion are not entirely, but almost, insurmountable. In short, what the physician buys in the first place is what he is going to have, until he sells out.

If partners are committed to flexibility, then a partnership can provide flexibility for the physician. Although some arrangements would need to be worked out for a partner to sell and the other partners or a new partner to buy his interest in case he wants to move out, that legal problem can generally be handled. (The physician should be aware, however, of the lowered attractiveness to a new investor of buying into a partnership that owns a building already substantially depreciated. The physician will usually have to sell his share in the partnership at a discounted price in order to compensate the buyer for the lost tax advantages.) Particularly, if the partners own a share in the building that does not relate exactly to the square footage they occupy, then problems of expansion or moving within the building are held to a minimum.

Third-party ownership can also be flexible, although a third-party owner is not likely to be as understanding and want to work as closely with the physicians as the hospital would. In addition, with a third-party owner, the physician would normally have a long lease with little means for getting out of it if he decides to move. One other disadvantage would be that the cost of expanding or changing a suite might be somewhat greater with the third-party owner.

In short, careful planning can provide reasonable flexibility with most forms of ownership. The real exception is the condominium, which is, by its nature, inflexible. In regard to this criterion, hospital ownership would probably rank highest, followed by some physician partnerships, and then third-party ownership.

7. An alternative that is likely to result in a minimum of legal problems for the physician.

The hospital and a third party as owners are the best alternatives, for the physicians are not involved in ownership or major liability for the building. The most difficult legal problems the physicians are likely to become involved with under these forms of ownership would have to do with lease agreements or some type of damage done to the suite.

The condominium, on the other hand, is generally the worst alternative legally for the physician. Condominiums, by their nature, involve very complex legal documents, and experience has shown they are a continuing source of legal problems.

Although the limited partnership provides the physician with limited liability, it is more likely to be the source of legal problems than the general partnership because of its more complex nature. Of the forms of physician ownership, the general partnership is more straightforward and less likely to involve the physician in legal hassles.

8. An alternative that is likely to result in a minimum of management problems for the physician.

The hospital and the third-party owner run neck and neck in regard to management problems and the time factor. Because the physician is not involved in ownership, he will not have to be involved in management. Thus, a minimum of his time will be consumed.

The second best alternative in regard to this criterion is the limited partnership. Here the physician is involved in the ownership, but the general partner will be carrying the burden of decision making and management. Other than an occasional meeting, the physician would probably not have to spend any more time with his form of ownership than if he only rented.

The condominium and the general partnership bring up the rear. Both require frequent decision making on the part of the owners. In addition, because so many individuals are involved in trying to agree on how the building should be run, squabbles are common, resulting in still more time being needed to iron out difficulties. Experience has shown that the problems and resulting time involved in owning and managing a condominium or a general partnership are almost always greater than the physicians anticipate initially.

9. In addition, many of the qualities that enable a building to meet the goals and objectives of the hospital are also qualities that enhance its marketability to physicians.

All the points of interest were discussed in regard to the first key issue — the building's contribution to the hospital.

Summary of Ownership Issues for Physicians

No clearcut alternative emerges as the single most marketable form of ownership to the physician. Much depends on the attitudes of the physicians themselves and the manner in which the project is developed. Hospital ownership or a physician partnership are the most likely to emerge in first place, with the limited partnership ranking above the general partnership. The condominium would fall at the bottom of the list if all facts were considered openly. Third-party ownership, which would also normally fall at the bottom, could even emerge as the choice by the physicians, if they did not want the liability and hassles of ownership, but also did not want to rent from the hospital.

Only careful examination of the local situation, the physician's attitudes, the legal and tax implications within a particular location, and other details of a proposed project would indicate the form of ownership most marketable to the physicians.

Satisfying the Financial Requirements

The final key issue to be considered in making the decision on ownership deals with satisfying the financial requirements of the situation. Either the hospital will want to own and therefore need to determine whether it can afford to, or it will be interested in determining which other ownership options are most feasible. With regard to the hospital's ability to own, little more can be said than has already been stated under the discussion of the criteria in the previous section. The hospital must simply examine its credit, its priorities, and the projected financial figures for the project to make a decision. Whether or not it can afford to own is totally a matter of the individual situation (see chapter 7).

With regard to the other ownership options, some general statements can be made. Here is how the other alternatives stack up against the four criteria already listed in this chapter.

1. It must be possible to finance the project.

Although this discussion is primarily concerned with ownership other than hospital ownership, it should begin with the statement that hospital ownership is usually the easiest form to finance.

A limited partnership with a strong developer as general partner would also be relatively easy to finance. The limited partnership with a corporation as general partner would be one of the most difficult to finance. Also, the limited partnership with a physician(s) as general partner(s) would be more difficult, unless the physician general partner(s) was extremely strong financially. A limited partnership would be made more easy to finance if the limited partners were willing to sign personally for the note; however their doing so removes much of the protection normally sought in a limited partnership.

The general partnership of all physicians would usually be a little easier to finance than the limited partnership, depending on several variables. Usually, the general partners would have to guarantee more of the loan than their actual percentage of ownership. Consequently, a lender feels secure because he has more than 100 percent coverage over his loan. That coverage in a general partnership would have to be weighed against the strength of the general partner in the limited partnership to determine which would be more easily financed. If the limited partners each had to sign notes to secure part of the loan, then that would give the limited partnership the edge. Financing any type of physician partnership is usually further complicated by the difficulty of finding enough physicians to put up sufficient front-end money.

The condominium is one of the more difficult forms of ownership to finance because most lenders do not want to commit themselves to carry the permanent loans for each individual doctor and because office condominiums do not have a particularly good track record financially. In addition, if the physician defaults, ownership of a practice suite is not nearly so desirable to a lender as ownership of all of a building.

Financing the project owned by a third party would depend entirely on the third party and his financial strength.

Financing a building owned by a partnership or a third party would be easier if the hospital had already signed a lease-back agreement for the entire building. In effect, the hospital's strength would then guarantee the loan indirectly. In addition, the hospital could actually guarantee the loan directly, if it felt that procedure would be to its advantage.

2. It must be a financially marketable project.

The determination of financial marketability depends to some extent on what the physician desires. Does he want to minimize his expenses or does he want a good investment? Chapter 7 looks at some comparative figures for rental from a hospital, rental from a third party, condominium ownership, and partnership ownership.

On the basis of those figures, over a 10-year period, the physician comes out slightly ahead through partnership ownership or condominium ownership. However, the financial advantage over renting from the hospital is very small. Third-party ownership brings up the rear. (These figures reflect such considerations as equity build up under physician ownership, see chapter 7 for details.)

Consideration of the financial marketability must consist of more than just a comparison of the bottom line figures, because much more is involved. In judging any investment, an individual must consider risk versus return and capital outlay versus return.

Although on the basis of these theoretical figures, a physician would come out $1,826 ahead over a 10-year period if he were a partner rather than a renter from the hospital, he would also assume a risk as a partner and have to put up an initial capital outlay. As a renter he would have neither risk nor outlay. If he were a general partner, he would risk the loss of his investment plus, usually, assume liability for a greater percentage of the debt than his percentage of ownership. The risk coupled with the responsibilities, problems, and time involved in ownership might not make the "investment" worthwhile, especially since investments with less risk and better return are often available to a physician. On the other hand, if the physician were a limited partner, if he were not required to sign a note for any part of the loan, and if the general partner were financially strong, the physician might be willing to risk his initial investment in relation to the possible gain.

Much the same could be said about the condominium as an investment. The lack of substantial financial advantage, coupled with the risk of owning, the legal complications of a condominium, the management problems, and general inflexibility make it a rather unmarketable entity to the wise physician. Third-party ownership is the most expensive for the physician on a straightforward financial basis. It does, however, provide the advantage of no risk and no capital outlay, because the physician is a renter.

Obviously, each individual project will differ; the financial figures will change, and various options may become more or less attractive. Nonetheless, because of the one-purpose building, because medical office buildings are considerably more expensive to build than regular office buildings but tend to rent for the same rates, and because of the risk involved, many accountants and lawyers will steer their physician clients away from investment in medical office buildings. If a physician wants to minimize his expenses, ownership in a medical office building may provide a good vehicle. If on the other hand, he wants a good investment with low risk and an expected high return on his capital outlay, he should look elsewhere.

3. It must be a financially stable project, projected over the long run.

Several factors would contribute to the financial stability of the various ownership options. For example, if the hospital owned the building or were leasing back the entire building, that would tend to produce a more stable project. If the physicians were tied to long-term leases, some stability would be gained from the guaranteed income from those leases.

Specifically, the condominium is only as stable as each individual physician. Because each doctor carries his own financing and is independent, just one or two defaults could create problems for the operation of the building as a whole, particularly with regard to common areas and legal entanglements.

Of the various partnership options, a strong developer as a general partner would normally be very stable, especially if the hospital leased back the whole building. The corporation as general partner could not guarantee a stable entity because in the event of financial difficulty, no one would be responsible for stepping forward and salvaging the situation. Physicians as general partners in the limited partnership would provide stability only to the extent of the combined wealth of the physicians.

A general partnership of all physician tenants would certainly provide more stability than the latter two limited partnerships just mentioned. In the general partnership, each physician would be required to guarantee a larger share of the loan than his share of ownership. Consequently, if one or two physicians get into financial trouble, the other physician partners will be responsible for picking up that additional share of the financial responsibility.

The long-range financial stability of the third-party owner would depend entirely on the owner. A developer with good financial strength coupled with a lease-back agreement with the hospital could provide a stable project.

4. Its financial success must depend on the input of hospital capital only to the extent that is compatible with the hospital's financial priorities.

Medical office building construction is expensive when compared with other types of office buildings: It requires more walls, more plumbing, better heating and cooling—all of which add considerably to the cost. Consequently, most on-campus medical office buildings constructed today will require some form of financial assistance. It can come from the tenants, from the hospital, or from the owner.

Sometimes the tenants are willing to "subsidize" the building through premium rents or ownership costs in order to have a high-quality facility in a prime location. Third-party owners or a small group of physician owners would rarely be willing to "subsidize" the building. More than likely, the financial support will come from the hospital because the hospital gains from the presence of the building.

Financial support can take many forms. If the hospital owns the building, it might rent space at reduced rental rates, using the outpatient ancillary income generated by the building to supplement the rent. If another owner is involved, the hospital might bear the cost of parking, the connection between the hospital and the office building, or other facilities in order to provide assistance. The hospital might bear some of the cost of planning and development in order to maintain some controls. It might even be willing to guarantee a loan, which is also a form of financial support.

Basically, the condominium will be the form of ownership requiring the least amount of additional financial support, because the physicians take all the risk. Because ownership of the individual suites is involved, any financial assistance from the hospital other than an initial parking lot, for example, would be difficult.

A third-party owner also would be less likely to receive financial assistance from the hospital, because his is strictly a profit motive. The various forms of partnerships are most likely to get the hospital involved in providing facilities, guaranteeing loans, or providing other assistance. Each individual situation is different, however, and the extent to which the hospital would involve itself financially would depend entirely on that situation.

Financially speaking, projects are individual enough that general statements on what is most likely to work are hard to make. Hospital ownership and partnerships are the most likely choices, and condominiums and third-party owners, least likely. Nonetheless, examination of all the facts and figures related to a particular project is the only way to determine adequately what form of ownership is most desirable with regard to this key issue.

Summary of Financial Requirements

MAKING THE DECISION

Once the alternatives are known, once the key issues and their related criteria are considered, and once the alternatives and issues are compared, the only thing remaining is the decision itself. Prejudices must be set aside. Issues must be considered carefully. Only with honesty and serious deliberation will the hospital be able to determine what is best in its particular situation. In general, the hospital is an excellent owner. The right kind of physician partnership can also be a desirable ownership vehicle. The third-party owner or condominium are less desirable, but should not be discounted. Much depends on the requirements of the individual situation. As stated at the beginning of chapter 4, no pat answer exists.

CHAPTER 6

Tax Ramifications

When the governing board of a not-for-profit hospital considers the issue of hospital ownership of the on-campus medical office building, one of the most frequently asked questions is what will hospital ownership of the office building do to the hospital's tax-exempt status? Because this question is a critical one for the hospital, accuracy of information and impartiality of point of view are vital.

For that reason and because tax laws tend to be complicated, this separate chapter is presented here to attempt to answer that question in accordance with current federal income tax law and its interpretation by the Internal Revenue Service. In addition, information is presented on trends in ad valorem taxation of hospital-owned on-campus medical office buildings.

Tax laws are constantly changing, what prevailed at the time of publication may need updating by the time a particular hospital is facing the question. For that reason, a hospital will undoubtedly want to seek special counsel at the time a project is being developed. The hospital would be wise to seek only the most knowledgeable help in this area.

FEDERAL TAX CONSIDERATIONS

Before federal income tax exempt status can be extended to include the ownership of an on-campus medical office building, the hospital itself must qualify as a true "charity":

> "In the general law of charity, the promotion of health is considered to be a charitable purpose . . . . A nonprofit organization whose purpose and activity are providing hospital care is promoting health and may, therefore, qualify as organized and operated in furtherance of a charitable purpose. If it meets the other requirements of section 501(c) (3) of the Code, it will qualify for exemption from federal income tax under section 501(a)."[1]

Furthermore, the following types of facts are evidence that a hospital is operated to serve public rather than private interests:

- No member of the medical staff has ever had any proprietary interest in the hospital.
- Legal control of the hospital rests with a board composed of independent business and civic leaders.

- There is no de facto control of the hospital by members of its medical staff.
- Membership on the medical staff is open to all qualified physicians.
- Services rendered to indigent patients are not inconsequential.
- The hospital operates an active and generally accessible emergency department.

These are some of the objective factors that have been considered by the IRS and the courts in deciding whether a hospital is entitled to exemption from federal income tax under section 501(c) (3). [2]

When a hospital is exempt from federal income tax, then the issue becomes whether this exemption will encompass the operation of a medical office building or whether the office building will, in fact, jeopardize the tax-exempt status of the entire hospital. The fear expressed by some hospital board members is that exempt status of the hospital will be lost because the office building might be construed to serve the private interest of the physicians, rather than the public, charitable purpose of the hospital. However, no single factor controls the retention or loss of exemption. In considering whether a not-for-profit hospital claiming such exemption is operated to serve a private benefit, the IRS weighs all the relevant facts and circumstances of each case. The determination does not necessarily depend on the absence or presence of any of the particular factors described. [3]

It seems clear that where the benefited party (the physician renting from the hospital, for example) controls the organization (the hospital), the IRS and the courts will scrutinize all aspects of the exempt status very closely. The cases of *Sonora, Maynard,* and *Harding* all involved hospitals founded by physicians who continued to exercise de jure or de facto control over their operations. [4] Because the hospitals were subservient to the founding physicians, they were not dealing at arm's length when setting fees, rent, and such. Each hospital lost its exempt status because, among other things, it was found to operate for the personal benefit of the controlling physicians.

When the exempt organization is independent of the benefited party, a much different situation exists. This point is best illustrated by Revenue Ruling 73-313, which dealt with a community organization formed to provide a doctor with a medical building and facilities in a remote area: [5]

> "The rental agreed to was less than what would be necessary to provide a normal return on the investment in the building and other facilities, but it nevertheless was negotiated in good faith....
>
> "None of the parties involved in founding the organization, in the negotiations with the doctor, or in the periodic review of the arrangements are related or associated in any way with the doctor involved....
>
> "The terms of the arrangement entered into to induce the doctor to locate his practice in the locality bear a reasonable relationship to promotion and protection of the health of the

community. The arrangements in question were completely at arm's length . . . .

"In these circumstances, *any personal benefit derived by the doctor (the use of the building in which to practice his profession) does not detract from the public purpose of the organization* [authors' italics] nor lessen the public benefit flowing from its activities and is not considered to be the type of private interest prohibited by the regulations . . . ."

It thus appears that the inurement of a private benefit, standing alone, will not result in loss of exemption where (1) the parties are independent, (2) the agreement is made at arm's length and in good faith, and (3) the transaction does not detract from the public purpose of the organization. In other words, an overriding public benefit may make an ancillary private benefit permissible.

This rationale was also illustrated in Revenue Ruling 69-464, which concerned a community hospital leasing space in its adjacent office building to members of its medical staff:[6]

"A community hospital exempt from federal income tax under section 501 (c) (3) of the Code built an adjacent office building for doctors in order to encourage members of its medical staff to maintain their private medical practices near the hospital . . . .

"The hospital has established that (1) as a result of having members of its medical staff practicing medicine in offices adjacent to the hospital, greater use is made of the hospital's diagnostic facilities and patient admissions are easier, and (2) the physical presence of members of the medical staff on the hospital's grounds makes the services of these doctors more readily available for outpatient and inpatient emergencies, facilitates carrying out their everyday medical duties in the hospital, makes their attendance at staff meetings easier, and serves to increase their participation in the hospital's medical education and research programs. *While these leasing arrangements are also a convenience to the lessees* [authors' italics], many of the benefits are passed on to the hospital and its patients in the form of greater efficiency and better overall medical care."

The IRS concluded that the leases did not generate unrelated business taxable income because they were "substantially related to the performance of hospital functions." Essentially, the same criterion is applied in determining whether the leases jeopardize exempt status. It is noteworthy that Revenue Ruling 69-464 was not conditioned upon charging fair rental value.

In a companion ruling, the IRS approved the leasing of an entire office building to a medical group for which the hospital would also provide substantial services:[7]

". . . In order to improve the hospital's ability to deliver a full range of health services to the community, the board of trustees decided to enter into negotiations with a medical group to induce them to carry on their professional activities on the hospital premises. . . .

"As a result of arm's length negotiations, the hospital leased its adjacent office building to the group. . . .

"The hospital maintains all medical records of the group as part of its central record-keeping system. . . .

"Under the terms of the contract, the hospital provides the group with the nursing, secretarial, billing, collection, and record-keeping services needed to carry on its medical practice. In consideration for the office space and services provided, the group is required to pay the hospital a fixed percentage of its gross billings for services rendered to both hospital and private patients. . . .

"It is held that the group practice described above contributes importantly to the hospital's operations and is therefore substantially related to the carrying on of hospital functions. Accordingly, the leasing activity described above is not unrelated trade or business under section 513 of the Code."

The current IRS position may thus be summarized as follows: when an exempt hospital deals at arm's length with noncontrolling parties for purposes substantially related to the hospital's exempt functions, exempt status will not be lost. The rulings mentioned show that leasing space in an adjacent office building to staff physicians is substantially related to a hospital's exempt functions. (The phrase *at arm's length* should not be interpreted to imply that the hospital cannot negotiate rental agreements directly with its medical staff members. Not only can hospitals deal directly with the physicians, but most do.)

To date, the inclusion of related commercial services within the medical office building has not jeopardized the tax-exempt status of the building or the hospital. However, the hospital considering the inclusion of these services should be careful in the selection and marketing of them. Just which services are acceptable for inclusion in the building tends to vary from one IRS district to the next. The main rule of thumb the hospital would want to follow in this regard is to make sure that each commercial establishment located in the building is "substantially related" to the building's function. For example, a pharmacy, a laboratory, an x-ray facility, an optical shop, and an orthopedic brace shop are types of commercial enterprises that might be justified for the building. A travel agency, insurance agency, and finance company may be somewhat harder to justify.

Another key factor is that the commercial establishments should be set up to serve the patients of the office building and not to solicit business from beyond the hospital campus. For that reason, exterior doors into the shops, exterior signs, and other forms of advertising are best avoided. Where commercial establishments have fallen within these guidelines, they have not been challenged by the IRS in regard to jeopardizing the tax-exempt status of the building and the hospital.

The IRS has ruled, however, that when the hospital operates the pharmacy in the building and sells to patients of physicians in the building, the revenue generated is considered unrelated business income and the profits are subject to income tax for that portion of the business generated by outpatients.[8] To date, only private rulings have been made on hospital operated laboratories and x-ray facilities within the building, and these rulings have varied according to local circumstances.

STATE AND LOCAL TAX CONSIDERATIONS

State and local ad valorem tax laws vary widely throughout the country. Some states require exclusive charitable use of the property and building in order for the office building to be exempt. Other states require only that the property belong to a charity and the earnings from it be used by the charity for charitable purposes.

Even in states where "exclusive use" of the property is required, the interpretation of the law varies greatly according to the wording of the law and facts of the situation. Consequently, in some states tax exemption has been granted to hospital-owned medical office buildings based on the same type of reasoning used by the IRS. In other states, however, the contribution of the medical office building to patient care is not considered sufficient for ad valorem tax exemption.

Simply stated, most states and local governments require the paying of ad valorem taxes on a hospital-owned medical office building. However, the law has not been tested in many areas, and where it has been tested, some hospitals have won exemption.

Baptist Memorial Hospital, Jacksonville, Florida, won property tax exemption by convincing the court of its need for the on-campus medical office building. In that case the court said the hospital has the right to say what is necessary to the basic function of the institution.[9] In one New York case, Genessee Hospital, Rochester, was granted ad valorem tax exemption based on its proof of the contributions made by the medical office building to patient care and the educational programs of the hospital.[10] In still another New York case, the supreme court of Onodaga County ruled that the office building owned by Community General Hospital, Syracuse, would be taxed only partly—in relation to the number of patients treated who needed no hospitalization. A fair percentage was to be developed between the hospital and the local tax authorities.[11] In Texas a county hospital was judged to have the right to own an office building, but the decision clearly stated that all government hospitals would have to be judged individually according to local law.[12]

Because of lack of precedent in most states, the best approach for a hospital trying to obtain exemption from ad valorem taxes is usually to prove the value of the building to the basic functioning of the hospital, rather than to cite previous cases. In addition, the hospital would be wise to plan ahead for any tax requirements it may be necessary to meet. "Those of us planning such new medical office facilities on hospital premises should carefully examine the tax implication of such construction. Some state and local tax laws may provide specific conditions relative to tax exemption. Proper planning and utilization may result in tax exemption for all or a substantial part of such a building."[13]

NOTES

1. Rev. Rul. 69-545, 1969-2 C.B. 117.
2. See Rev. Rul. 69-545 *supra;* Rev. Rul. 56-185; *Harding Hospital, Inc. v. United States* 505 F2d 1068, 74-2 USTC ¶9816 (6th Cir. 1974); *Maynard Hospital, Inc.* 52 T.C. 1006 (1969) and *Sonora Community Hospital* 46 T.C. 519 (1966) *aff'd per curium* 397 F2d 814 (9th Cir. 1968).
3. Rev. Rul. 69-545, *supra.*
4. See footnote 2.
5. Rev. Rul. 73-313, 1973-2 C.B. 174.
6. Rev. Rul. 69-464, 1969-2 C.B. 132.
7. Rev. Rul. 69-463, 1969-2 C.B. 131.
8. Rev. Rul. 68-375, 1968-2 C.B. 245.
9. Florida hospital wins property tax exemption. *Modern Hospital.* 110:44, May 1968.
10. *Genessee Hospital, Inc. v. Wagner,* 350 N.Y.S. 2nd 582 (1974).
11. Hospital taxed for medical office building. *Hospital Progress.* 56:32, Sept. 1975.
12. Davis, C. Dean. Legal angle: ancillary medical clinics. *Texas Hospitals.* 31:32, Aug. 1975.
13. Regan, W. A. Hospital taxed for medical office building: Community-General Hospital of Greater Syracuse. *Hosp. Prog.* 56:28, Sept. 1975.

CHAPTER 7

Determining Financial Feasibility

The financial feasibility of a project is not so much a matter to be determined as to be developed. In actuality, it is worked out simultaneously with many other aspects of the project. The ownership structure, the program of the building, the size of the building, and its many design features are just some of the aspects that influence the financial feasibility.

Ideally, when a project is needed, it is carefully planned, programmed, and designed to meet the needs of the situation, and the financial aspects fall into place. However, most situations are not ideal. Once the financial figures are projected on the "ideal" building, the rental rate needed to amortize the loan and make the project break even might be too high to be competitive. Or, in a project developed for physician ownership, the initial down payment the physicians would need to make might be too large to be practical. These and other difficulties do not necessarily mean that the project is not financially feasible, but only that it must be reexamined because the right combination has not yet been reached. The building might need to be developed with a different ownership structure, need to be redesigned, or need some optional features deleted to make it work financially. The project's program might need to be adjusted.

The important issue is that financial feasibility is not so much a yes or no issue as it is a matter of determining all the right elements and putting them together to create the most effective project to meet the financial circumstances. It is, indeed, a flexible entity.

PROJECTING AN OPERATING BUDGET

Although ballpark figures might be used at an early stage of planning in order to shed some light on how the building might shape up financially, a true picture cannot be developed until the building is programmed and preliminary designs are completed. Once the building has been programmed and sized, the site examined, preliminary designs completed, and typical floor plans developed (density studies), projecting construction and operating costs becomes a realistic proposition. Also, at this point of preliminary design, adjustments can be made if the building appears to be too expensive to meet financial requirements of the situation.

For the sake of discussion in this chapter, a hypothetical (though realistic) building is used as an example for developing financial figures. This building has 50,000 gross square feet and 40,000 net rentable square feet: 35,000 for offices and 5,000 for commercial establishments. Such a building would normally provide offices for 35 to 40 physicians.

The first step in developing a pro-forma operating budget for a proposed medical office building is to project building and land costs based on the preliminary designs. The major figures that must be included are the cost of the building structure; the cost of improvements to the building; site improvements; architectural and consulting fees, construction financing, points, and closing costs; and the cost of land. Typical building and land costs for a hypothetical building could run something like this:

Building structure	$1,500,000
Building improvements	750,000
Site improvements	60,000
Architectural and consulting fees, construction financing, points, and closing costs	450,000
Land	120,000
Total project cost	$2,880,000

On the basis of the $2,880,000 cost and the square footage of the building, the total project cost is $57.60 per gross square foot and $72 per net rentable square foot. Obviously, on a specific project each of the figures above would need to be developed on the basis of the peculiarities of the project and the locale. Variations in the figures are inevitable, with the cost per square foot differing from one project to the next and from one area of the country to another. In fact, because of rapidly escalating construction costs, the figures quoted above may appear low to the reader. That fact, however, will not affect the conclusions reached in this chapter, because the comparisons are relative.

The next step in developing the operating budget is the projection of operating expenses. In projecting these expenses, the hospital would be well advised to consult with the best source of current information on operating expenses: *Downtown and Suburban Office Building Experience Exchange Report*, published annually by the Building Owners and Managers Association International (BOMA). On the basis of information from BOMA International and current experience, the annual operating expenses for the hypothetical building could be projected as follows:

Taxes, per gross square foot		$0.71
Insurance, per gross square foot		$0.067
Management fee:		
Hospital owned, flat annual fee	$15,000	
Private ownership	5% of rental income	
Maintenance and other operating expenses:		
Hospital owned, per gross square foot		$2.40
Private ownership, per gross square foot		$2.67

The slightly lower operating expenses experienced by the hospital are the result of the hospital's ability to absorb the operation of the building into already existing management, housekeeping, and maintenance operations.

The result is somewhat greater efficiency of operation that produces somewhat reduced costs.

The one missing element is rental rate. One method for determining rental rate is to project all the costs of the building and the operating expenses and then to work back to establish a rental rate to cover all those costs and expenses. If, after that is done, the rental rate is not workable—too high or not competitive with the market—then the building must be reexamined to determine whether adjustments can be made in order for the rent to be salable. This particular method for establishing rental rate is used in the pro forma operating budgets that follow.

On the basis of the foregoing construction costs and operating expenses, pro formas can now be prepared showing projections for the various types of ownership. For the sake of discussion, the financial picture is projected for a 10-year period.

Table 1, page 70, shows how the pro forma for that hypothetical building would look if it were hospital-owned and hospital-operated.

Hospital-Owned Building

This budget indicates that an average occupancy of 65 percent was projected for the building for the first year. The second year, the occupancy was projected to be at 85 percent. By the third year and every year thereafter, the building is projected to be operating at 96 percent of capacity, taking into account a 4 percent vacancy factor for tenants moving in and out.

In table 1, revenues are broken down into two categories with corresponding columns of figures. Column A indicates revenues to be received through rental income. The figures are based on an office rental rate of $8 per square foot per year and commercial rental rates of a minimum annual rate of $12 per square foot plus a percentage (of gross revenue) rental projected at $9 per square foot (see chapter 12).

Column B figures reflect projected income from new business generated by the physician tenants in the office building and performed in the outpatient laboratory and x-ray department, either in the hospital facilities located in the office building or within the hospital itself. A 1974 study indicated that the new net ancillary income generated by each physician in the office building averaged more than $4,500 per year.[1] At this time, that figure is considerably higher. A portion of that income—in this case, $3,000 per physician—is utilized to supplement the rent in the office building.

The hospital's rationale in inserting this income into the office building budget is that this income is new and is generated as a result of the physicians being in the office building. Without the office building, this new income would not be produced. If the building were privately owned or were owned by the physicians, the owners or physicians would likely be receiving the benefit of this income through establishment of their own laboratory and x-ray services placed on the hospital campus in direct competition with the hospital.

Whereas under hospital ownership competitive laboratory and x-ray services are not allowed in the office building, except in an individual physician's office for his own use, and whereas the increased utilization of existing hospital services increases both their efficiency and profitability, the hospital

Table 1. Projected Pro Forma for Hospital-Owned Medical Office Building

Year	Avg. Occupancy, %	Revenue, $000		Expense, $000		E
		A	B	C	D	
		Rentals	Lab and X Ray	Cash Operating Expense	Interest and Principal	Cash Flow (Deficit)
1	65	$251	$ 68	$160	$284	($125)
2	85	328	89	170	284	(37)
3 and after	96	369	101	174	284	12

considers it appropriate to return some of that income generated by the physicians in the building to the debt reduction of the building, and this results in a reduced rental rate.

Inclusion of this income in the operating budget of the medical office building is certainly optional, however, and some hospitals do not do it. It is also a flexible entity in that if the $3,000 figure used in this pro forma were increased, the rental rates for the hypothetical building could be adjusted downward. And if it were decreased, the rental rates would need to be increased.

For reimbursement purposes, when this income is to be included in the medical office building budget, separate records should be kept for the branch laboratory and x-ray services in the office building or for the referrals that come from the building into the hospital's existing outpatient ancillary departments.

Column C in table 1 is based on the percentage of occupancy of the building and on the operating expenses projected in the original assumptions. No inflationary increase in these expenses is projected, because the assumption is made that as actual operating expenses increase, the rental rate will be increased equally to cover those expenses. Consequently, such an increase would not affect the overall financial projection.

Column D shows what the hospital will be paying annually in interest and principal to amortize the loan on the building. The figures are based on a $2,760,000 loan for 25 years at 9.25 percent interest. These figures represent a 96 percent loan and assume that the hospital already owns the land or has made a down payment of $120,000. Also, these figures reflect an early beginning to the repayment of principal, based on the fact that hospitals tend to close on permanent financing much sooner than private owners. The difference is because most hospitals are not-for-profit and therefore are not concerned about taking an interest deduction on their tax returns, as private owners are.

Column E shows what the actual cash flow for the building will be. It is based on revenues less operating expenses, interest, and principal. At the end of the first year, the building will have a deficit of $125,000. The second year deficit will be $37,000. And by the third year the building will be showing a positive cash flow of $12,000 per year.

Once the building is filled and operating at stable occupancy, the figures level off and remain relatively constant. Consequently, only three years are shown on the pro forma. Figures for the 4th through the 10th years will be essentially the same as for the 3rd year, with inflationary increases in expenses balanced by increases in rent.

In this particular pro forma, all aspects fall into place. The rental rate is an acceptable one. The two years of cash flow deficit will quickly be recovered by the addition of new physicians to the staff, who will generate new income for the hospital. The first two years of operating deficit result from the "over-building" of space for recruitment purposes. Most hospitals that plan ahead in this manner consider the initial cash flow deficit to be a form of investment in the recruitment program and the long-range goals and viability of the hospital.

If, however, this pro forma had indicated serious financial problems, such as rental rates that were too high to be competitive, then the whole picture would have had to be reexamined. The hospital would begin by examining the points of flexibility in the program and design of the building to see if sufficient, appropriate adjustments could be made in order for the project to work.

The hospital should determine whether the building is sized realistically or just idealistically, whether too many expensive or elaborate services are designed into the building, and whether there are too many architectural frills. The hospital should also consider whether or not it should inject more of the projected new outpatient or ancillary income generated by the building tenants into the building budget. It should reexamine the amount of space allowed for recruitment and the projected length of time to fill it. Through the thoughtful reexamination of these factors, the hospital can usually make appropriate changes to improve the financial picture, if needed.

Privately Owned Building

Development of a pro forma for a private owner or owners of the medical office building is somewhat more complicated. First, the private owner will need to make a profit, not just break even. In addition, the private owner will be able to take advantage of certain tax deductions, such as interest and depreciation. Because of the need for a good return on investment for the owner, and because of the slightly higher operating costs incurred by a private owner, the rental rate that emerges on the hypothetical medical office building is higher than for hospital ownership.

Using the same costs and building dimensions used in the hospital-owned projection, a pro forma statement of operations for a privately owned medical office building follows in table 2, page 73.

The occupancy for this building is projected in the same manner as for the hospital-owned building: 65 percent the first year, 85 percent the second year, and essentially full, 96 percent, from there on out.

Column A figures represent the revenue anticipated from the building with an office rental rate of $10.25 per square foot per year. Commercial rental is based on an average minimum rental rate plus a percentage of gross profit on the individual business, with the average total assumed to be $24 per square foot per year. The higher office and commercial rental rates reflect the profit motive, that is, rental rates high enough to produce an acceptable return on investment.

Just as with hospital ownership, no rental increases due to inflation are included in the figures. The assumption is made that as actual cash operating expenses increase, the rent will be increased to cover those costs. Such an increase would not change the overall financial picture. In addition, the owner may well increase rents in excess of the actual increases in costs—if the inflationary spiral is sufficient and if the market in the particular area will bear the increases. No rental increases are included in the projections because of the unpredictability of such increases. However, the ramifications of such increases are considered at the end of this discussion.

Column B figures represent the cash operating expenses of the building, based on the original assumptions made concerning the hypothetical office building and based on the rate of occupancy. As stated, the cash operating ex-

Table 2. Projected Pro Forma for Privately Owned Medical Office Building

Year	Avg. Occupancy, %	Revenue, $000	Expense, $000					Cash Flow, $000	
		A Revenue	B Cash Operating Expense	C Interest	D Depreciation and Amortization	E Taxable Income (Loss)	F Principal	G Without Tax Benefit	H With Tax Benefit
1	65	$311	$165	$204	$134	($192)		($58)	$38
2	85	407	183	222	157	(155)		2	79
3	96	460	195	204	147	(86)	$22	39	82
4	96	460	195	202	138	(75)	25	38	74
5	96	460	195	200	129	(64)	27	38	70
6	96	460	195	197	122	(54)	30	38	65
7	96	460	195	194	118	(47)	33	38	61
8	96	460	195	191	117	(43)	36	38	59
9	96	460	195	187	115	(37)	39	39	57
10	96	460	195	183	114	(32)	43	39	55

penses will increase with inflation; however, rental rates will be increased correspondingly to cover the costs — a move that does not affect the total financial picture appreciably.

Column C reflects the interest the owner of the building will be paying annually. The first two years are based on an interim loan, which assumes a higher interest rate than for the permanent financing. In addition, not all of the construction money will be needed until the second year, because tenant improvements are not made until the tenants are ready to move in. The third year and thereafter the amount of interest is based on a permanent loan of $2,160,000 at 9.5 percent interest for a 25-year period. Such a loan assumes a 25 percent down payment on the part of the private owner. The interest paid decreases steadily each year during the life of the loan.

Column D shows that depreciation and amortization are of primary importance to a private owner. In this example, the depreciation is calculated by using the 150 percent declining balance method, a 45-year life for the building structure, and a 15-year life for the improvements. The 45-year life is conservative, though realistic. If, however, the Internal Revenue Service would approve a shorter life, then additional cash flow would result. Accelerated methods are used so that the owner receives the maximum tax benefits as quickly as possible, and thus maximizes cash flow. This column of figures also represents the amortization of construction-period interest over a 10-year period.

Column E figures represent the projected taxable income (loss) arising from ownership of the building. Real estate investments typically yielding the highest return on investment generally show a taxable loss and have a positive cash flow during the intitial years, as this investment does. In this example, losses are derived by subtracting the cash operating expenses, the interest paid, and the depreciation and amortization from the gross revenues on the building.

It is important to understand that, although operating expenses and interest are actually cash expenditures that have to be paid from revenues generated by the building, depreciation and amortization are deductible items that require no current cash outlay. They are referred to as an expense "on paper." As in any good real estate investment, the cash flow and the taxable loss decrease each year due to the decrease in interest and depreciation and the increase in principal. In this example, the tax shelter effect ends in the 11th year. Because the taxable income will continue to increase each year, the net cash flow and return on investment will continue to decline each year thereafter.

Column F shows that by taking into consideration the amount of principal being paid off on the loan each year, the projected cash flow on the building can be determined. Note that for the first two years the owner is paying only interest and no principal on the loan. Then, as interest payments decrease, principal payments increase throughout the life of the loan.

Column G, together with column H, reflects the actual cash flow on the project, before taxes and after taxes. Column G, reflecting cash flow before the tax benefit is taken, is derived by subtracting the cash operating expenses, the interest, and the principal payments (all requiring cash) from the gross revenues. In the first year, the building shows a negative cash flow of $58,000 before tax considerations. In the second year, the pretax cash flow becomes positive. And in the third year, due to an increase in occupancy, it increases by a substantial amount.

Column H shows what the cash flow on the building will be once the owner includes the tax benefit. Because the taxable income actually shows a loss, the owner saves half of the amount of the taxable loss (assuming a 50 percent tax bracket). That amount added to the cash flow results in a positive cash flow. Thus, a building that is shown as operating at a loss as far as income taxes are concerned is actually producing a positive cash flow to the owner.

An important point to understand concerning the "after-tax" cash flow is that the tax benefit received is in money saved, not in new dollars coming in. Also, the potential owner must understand that although the end result of the first year's operation is a positive cash flow, he will have to fund the operating deficits during the first year with tax dollars otherwise spent. That is, he probably will have to inject additional capital into the project during the first year to cover "without tax benefit" cash flow deficits until he can recoup that money at the end of the first year. Unless the owner is aware of and prepared for this lapse, cash flow problems could arise during the first year.

As previously mentioned, during the 11th year the taxable income will no longer show a loss, but a profit. That profit is taxable at the same rate as above, 50 percent (assuming that to be the tax bracket of the owner.) When that turnaround occurs, the return on investment becomes less and less, and most private owners will "roll the project"; that is, they will sell the building and reinvest in a new project where the depreciation can start all over again. For these reasons, private owners, whether physicians or third-party owners, will usually not want to own a medical office building for more than 10 to 12 years. If they do not sell or are unable to sell at the appropriate time, the rapidly increasing income taxes will soon overtake the tax savings realized during the first years of ownership.

Effects of Inflation

At this point, the ramifications of inflationary increases in rental rates need to be considered. The value of commercial rental property is directly tied to the cash flow produced by the property. Consequently, regardless of what the inflationary rate is, the value of the property usually does not go up appreciably unless the cash flow produced by the building goes up.

In a building in which the rental rate is kept stable or only increases enough to cover increased operating expenses, little or no appreciation would normally occur. In a building in which rental rates rise in amounts larger than the amount of increase in expenses, the building would appreciate in proportion to the increased cash flow. Thus, if a private owner continually increases rental rates, the property will usually appreciate in value. That factor is a positive one for the owner, and a negative one for the physician tenant who is paying a constantly increasing rent.

Another relevant factor is that the faster the rental rates increase, the faster the taxable income loss becomes a profit and the sooner the owner needs to roll the project in order to maximize the return on his investment.

Because of the special-purpose nature of the building and because inflationary factors vary so widely according to current trends, the local market, the status of the hospital, and other conditions, no attempt was made to develop additional pro formas with these trends assimilated. At best, a hospital or a private owner can guess at what will happen in this regard in the future. To assume current inflation rates over a 10-year period could prove to be risky. The investor is usually wise to project conservatively.

The bottom line: As far as the physician tenant is concerned, these two pro formas show that renting from a hospital versus a private owner costs substantially less—in these examples, $2.25 per square foot less.

The hospital considering financial feasibility, assuming it has credit available, will usually elect hospital ownership over third-party private ownership. Not only is it more attractive to the tenant physicians, but it carries the many tangible and intangible benefits discussed in chapter 5.

HOSPITAL OWNERSHIP VERSUS PHYSICIAN PARTNERSHIP

Ownership by a physician partnership is very similar to private ownership, except that the physician is typically a tenant as well as an equity owner. The partnership can consist of some of the physician tenants or all of them.

From the point of view of the hospital, the following factors must be kept in mind when examining the financial feasibility of such an ownership structure. First, can the physicians actually put up the money for the project or will the hospital have to initiate the project with its own money and sell to the physicians one at a time or as a group? In most cases, the project will not get off the ground or fully meet the needs of the hospital unless the hospital initiates the building with its own money and credit. Second, the hospital must consider whether it will be required to guarantee the loan on the building for the partnership. Again, the hospital usually will have to do so. If the hospital's motive for considering the physician partnership is its own desire or need to remain financially uninvolved, the partnership may not be the answer. In physician partnerships the hospital generally assumes most of the financial risks for the project while giving up the advantages of ownership.

In many instances, however, the major motivating factor for the hospital to consider the physician partnership is not so much its own needs or desires to stay uninvolved as it is pressure from the medical staff members who believe they will reap tremendous profits and tax shelters from ownership. Because of this widespread belief among physicians, and because the quality of the investment is an essential aspect of whether the physician partnership is financially feasible, comparative figures are presented here concerning the physician partnership in relation to hospital ownership.

The financial comparison in table 3, page 77, based on the hypothetical building pro formas in tables 1 and 2, shows the actual costs to the physician of renting from the hospital versus owning 1/35 of a partnership and renting space from the partnership. The figure of 1/35 is based on the building's ability to provide offices for 35 physicians. With each physician owning 1/35 of the partnership, the physicians own not only the rough equivalent of their office space, but also the common and commercial areas.

In table 3, column A, figures represent what the physician pays in rent to

Table 3. After-Tax Comparison of Cost to Physician of Renting from Hospital versus Cost of 1/35th Partnership Interest and Renting from Partnership

| Year | $ Cost as Renter from Hospital (0 investment required) | | | $ Cost as Renter and 1/35 Owner in MOB ($20,571 investment required) | | |
| | A | B | C | D | E | F |
	Rent Paid, Net of Tax	Investment Earnings	Total	Rent Paid, Net of Tax	1/35 of Cash Flow from Private Ownership	Total
1	$ 4,000	$(1,029)	$2,971	$ 5,125	$(1,086)	$ 4,039
2	4,160	(1,080)	3,080	5,330	(2,257)	3,073
3	4,326	(1,134)	3,192	5,543	(2,343)	3,200
4	4,500	(1,191)	3,309	5,765	(2,114)	3,651
5	4,679	(1,250)	3,429	5,995	(2,000)	3,995
6	4,867	(1,313)	3,554	6,235	(1,857)	4,378
7	5,061	(1,378)	3,683	6,484	(1,743)	4,741
8	5,263	(1,447)	3,816	6,744	(1,686)	5,058
9	5,474	(1,520)	3,954	7,014	(1,629)	5,383
10	5,693	(1,596)	4,097	7,294	(1,571)	5,723
	$48,023	$(12,938)		$61,529	$(18,286)	$43,243
						$(9,984)[a]
		Comparative cost $35,085				$33,259

[a]Estimated proceeds, assuming buildings were sold at end of 10th year, less the initial investment of $20,571

the hospital each year, net of tax. That amount is based on the $8 per square foot rental rate used in the hospital ownership pro forma statement (see table 1, page 70) and on the assumptions that the physician is renting 1,000 square feet of space and is in the 50 percent tax bracket. In addition, the rent (after taxes) is assumed to increase 4 percent each year to cover increasing operating costs. The total, then, that a physician spends on rent, net of tax, over a 10-year period is $48,023.

Column B figures are some of the most readily overlooked but, nonetheless, essential aspects of a comparison of renting versus owning. They take into account the cash down payment of $20,571 required by the owner/renter. As a renter, he would not have to put that money into the building, but could invest it in other ventures. The second column is a conservative estimate of the income he could expect from investing the $20,571. The income is based on a 5 percent return on his money, after taxes (that would be 10 percent return before taxes), and assumes the reinvestment of the earnings. The total earnings over the 10-year period would be $12,938.

Column C represents the total cost to the physician of renting from the hospital for the 10 years, as compared to renting and owning a 1/35 interest. The numbers are derived by subtracting the amount of the physician's investment earnings from the amount of rent he pays each year. By so doing, a figure is obtained that will compare realistically to the cost of owning. When the total cost of renting, net of tax, is reduced by the total amount of the investment earnings over the 10-year period, the comparative cost of renting from the hospital is $35,085.

Column D shows the comparable information for the physician as a partner, owning 1/35 of the building. This column indicates the amount of rent, net of tax, that he would pay to the partnership for each of the 10 years and the total of that rent. The rental rate used is the $10.25 per square foot per year rate used in the private ownership pro forma. All the other assumptions are the same as for hospital ownership. The physician rents 1,000 square feet of space, and the rental rate escalates at the rate of 4 percent per year. The physician is assumed to be in the 50 percent bracket. The total, then, for his renting space from the partnership is $61,529 for the 10-year period.

Column E figures reflect the positive cash flow, after taxes, that the physician will receive from his partnership interest. These figures are derived by dividing the "Cash Flow with Tax Benefit" figures on the private ownership pro forma (table 2) by 35. The total cash flow the physician will receive from his ownership in the partnership will be $18,286 for the 10-year period. Keep in mind, however, that the cash flow does not necessarily represent new dollars made, but, rather, frequently reflects the tax dollars saved.

Column F represents the total cost to the physician of renting from the partnership for each of the 10 years. These figures are derived by reducing his rent paid (net of tax) by the amount of cash flow benefit (net of tax) received through his partnership interest. The cumulative total of rent paid, less cash flow, for the 10-year period is $43,243. Because of his ownership interest, however, this rental figure cannot be compared with the figure representing rental from the hospital. It must be reduced further by his accrued equity in the building, that is, by the benefit he would receive if he sold his interest in the partnership or if the whole building were sold by the partnership at the end of the 10th year.

The $9,984 figure used in the comparison indicates the estimated cash value of the physician's share of the partnership, based on the sale of the building at the end of the 10th year.[2] This figure is net of taxes, real estate commissions, recaptured depreciation, other expenses, and the original investment of $20,571. Thus, when the physician's cost of renting from the partnership is reduced by his equity value in the partnership, his comparative cost of practicing in a suite rented from the partnership in which he owns 1/35 interest becomes $33,259 for the 10-year period.

The bottom line: The result of these accounting gymnastics is that the physician in this example can rent 1,000 square feet from the hospital for 10 years at the total comparative cost of $35,085. The same space rented from a partnership in which the physician owns 1/35 interest will cost him $33,259 for the 10-year period. Over the 10 years, then, the physician can save $1,826 ($182 a year) by owning, based on the hypothetical pro formas. Thus, as a physician considers whether he prefers to rent from the hospital versus owning through this type of partnership, he can consider not only the many tangible and intangible pros and cons discussed in chapter 5, but also whether the tangible dollar savings of $182 per year is worth his investment of over $20,000 in cash and a substantial amount of his time in handling the ownership responsibilities.

RESALE VALUE

Because a resale value had to be assigned to the hypothetical medical office building before the foregoing financial comparisons could be completed, a discussion of how that value was determined is presented at this point.

Traditionally, the resale value of real estate is determined in any one or combination of three ways: comparable sales, replacement cost, and cash flow. Because of the one-purpose nature of a medical office building, and particularly because of its on-campus location, comparable sales are usually a negligible or nonexistent factor in determining resale value for this type of building. Replacement cost can be considered, but again, because of the one-purpose nature of the building, replacement cost is considered only in relation to the building structure and core, but not the internal improvements and finishes. The best and most widely used means for determining resale value of commercial real estate is cash flow.

The computation of the individual physician's proceeds received at the time of sale of the medical office building assumes that the price of the building on the commercial market would be primarily determined by its cash flow. A real estate investor would look at the building from the point of view of return on investment. If the cash flow were not sufficient to provide an acceptable return, he would normally look elsewhere for a better investment. However, if he believed that the building has potential, he might further examine the cash flow to see if it could be improved; that is, he would examine the possibility of raising the rent sufficiently to produce the cash flow needed to make it an attractive investment.

In determining the sale price of this hypothetical building, standard valuation techniques were used—capitalized cash flow, application of an appropriate discount rate (10 percent), assumption of a building life in excess of 20 years, and so forth.[2] Because the rental rates have escalated only enough to cover the cost of increased operating expenses, the value of the building on the commercial market would have actually decreased, rather than increased, over the 10-year period. The cash flow (before principal and interest payment) produced by this building at the end of 10 years would indicate a sale price of only $2,650,000, as compared with an original cost of $2,880,000. Such a low sale price would seem incredible in view of current real estate trends. Nonetheless, to an investor looking at the building from a strictly commercial, cash-flow point of view, the $2,650,000 sale price is all the building could support at its current rental rates (which have reached $14.58 per square foot by the end of the 10th year).

To the commercial investor, then, this building would be of interest only if it could be purchased for less than its original cost or if the rental rates could be increased dramatically in order to produce an acceptable return on investment. The physician owner finds himself in the position of either having to sell the building at a loss, having his rent take a large jump, or holding onto the building that will soon begin costing him accelerating amounts in tax dollars.

Despite the fact that the resale value of the building, as projected through an examination of projected cash flow, is a realistic figure based on sound principles, it was assumed that the building would probably be of greater value to the hospital than these figures indicate. As a result, a sale price of $3,700,000 was used in computing each physician's proceeds from the sale. This figure is based on the assumption that the hospital might be willing to pay more than a strictly commercial price for the building in order to keep it as an integral part of the total medical complex.

However, caution should be exercised in making such an assumption, for the hospital is certainly limited, financially and ethically (not to mention by certificate-of-need restrictions), in how far it could go in paying an "above the market" price for a building owned by members of its medical staff. Even if the hospital did not want to purchase the building, however, the assumption was made that the physicians might be willing to have their rental rate raised sufficiently to merit the $3,700,000 sale price.

For the skeptic who believes that the building will appreciate at a highly inflated rate, regardless of how the figures develop, one other point must be kept in mind. These figures are comparative. That is, if the reader wants to apply any annual inflation rate of appreciation to the building that he chooses, he can do so at his own risk. But in order for the comparison to be valid still, he must remember that the physician who rents has that $20,571 down payment that he can invest elsewhere as well as or better than in the office building.

Instead of assuming that the physician renting from the hospital will buy bonds or certificates of deposit at a 10 percent annual return, before taxes, with no appreciation of the principal (the conservative investment indicated in the financial figures), the reader would need to assume that the physician could invest that money in some other real estate investment with at least a similar rate of appreciation to that provided by investing in the medical office building. If the physician is guided into one of the better types of real estate investments, his investment is likely to appreciate not only as much as the on-campus medical office building, but probably at a faster rate, because it is a more marketable property. When the same principles are applied to both sides of the comparison, the relative figures do not change much. In fact, the financial attractiveness for renting and investing elsewhere is likely to improve.

Many different figures might be used and justified as the sale price of the building, but an attempt has been made here to be realistic, without being either overly conservative or optimistic. The variables are numerous in making such computations, and in a specific situation, the physician would be wise to seek a competent, independent accountant to help analyze the variables and their relationship to the *long-range* financial picture.

What is vitally important to the physician is that he understand that a medical office building is not comparable to the home real-estate market with which he is usually most familiar. The value of a piece of property does not go up just because of inflation. Its value is tied to the competitive market within a city and the return on investment necessary to make the building an attractive investment. Most important, it is tied permanently to a hospital, making it vulnerable to changes in hospital management and quality of care and making it primarily a one-purpose building. These risks affect the value of the building.

This discussion is not to imply that the physician should not invest in office building ownership, but he should not assume that just because his house had doubled in value over the past five years that his office building will do so — without regard to the realities of financial investment. The physician must simply be cautious in looking at such opportunities, making sure he grasps the long-range as well as short-range financial picture.

For the accounting-minded, the computation showing the sale price of the hypothetical building, capital gains taxes, sales commissions, and recaptured depreciation and amortization on the sale of this property are presented in the second entry under Notes at the end of this chapter.

HOSPITAL OWNERSHIP VERSUS PHYSICIAN-OWNED CONDOMINIUM

Another alternative for medical office building ownership by physicians is the condominium. Although it differs substantially from a partnership in structure, accounting techniques, and risk, its bottom line financial figures are basically the same. The primary differences rest in the fact that the condominium is generally less flexible for the physician and can be harder to sell than a partnership. Nonetheless, for the sake of thoroughness, table 4, page 82, shows how the condominium compares financially with renting from the hospital.

These figures are based on a 1,000 square foot condominium purchased by the physician for $79,000. The sale price was determined by adding a 10 percent profit to the developer's cost in constructing the building. Condominium ownership is based on 40 owner/tenants (or 40 increments of 1,000 square feet), rather than the 35 used in the partnership, because typically the commercial space would be owned by its occupants in a condominium. In a building owned by a physician partnership, the partnership typically owns the commercial areas; thus only 35 owners are involved.

Table 4. After-Tax Comparison of Cost to Physician of Renting from Hospital versus Cost of Condominium Ownership ($19,000 investment required)

Year	A Cash Operating Expense	Expense, $ B Interest	C Depreciation	D Tax-Deductible Expense	E Principal	F After Tax Cash Disbursed
1	$ 4,875	$ 5,674	$ 4,266	$ 14,815	$ 617	$ 3,758
2	5,070	5,613	4,212	14,895	678	3,913
3	5,273	5,545	4,160	14,978	746	4,075
4	5,484	5,471	4,110	15,065	820	4,242
5	5,703	5,390	4,061	15,154	901	4,417
6	5,931	5,301	4,014	15,246	990	4,599
7	6,169	5,202	3,969	15,340	1,089	4,790
8	6,416	5,094	3,925	15,435	1,197	4,989
9	6,672	4,976	3,882	15,530	1,315	5,198
10	6,939	4,845	3,841	15,625	1,446	5,417
	$58,532	$53,111	$40,440	$152,083	$9,799	$45,309
						($11,441)[a]

10-year cost of condominium $33,868

Comparable renting costs, less investment earnings $36,073

Condominium savings $ 2,205

[a] Estimated proceeds, assuming condominiums were sold at end of 10th year, less initial investment of $19,000.

Column A itemizes the cash operating expenses the physician must pay each year for the operation of the condominium. The numbers are based on 1/40, or 2½ percent, of the operating expenses shown on the private ownership pro forma for the first year of full occupancy (see table 2). The figures include common area expenses and are escalated 4 percent each year.

Column B details the amount of interest the physician will pay on the mortgage each year. The total for the 10-year period is $53,111. The interest is computed on the basis of a $60,000 mortgage (implying a $19,000 down payment) for 25 years at 9.5 percent interest, with monthly payments.

Column C indicates the depreciation the physician can take on the property. It is based on a 45-year life for the structure and a 10-year life on the improvements and is computed on an accelerated basis. The total depreciation for the 10 years is $40,440.

Column D is the total of columns A, B, and C. It reflects each year the total deductions the physician can take on his taxes as a result of owning his condominium suite. For the 10-year period, he can take a total of $152,083 in tax deductions.

Column E is the annual amount of principal the physician pays out. It increases annually, just as the amount of interest paid decreases annually. At the end of 10 years, the physician has paid $9,799 in principal. The computation of the amount of principal is based on the same assumptions mentioned in the discussion of interest — a $60,000 mortgage for 25 years at 9.5 percent interest.

Column F indicates the actual amount of cash the physician pays out each year for his condominium after all tax benefits are taken into consideration. The numbers in this column are derived by adding together the actual cash the physician spends — cash operating expenses, interest, and principal — and subtracting 50 percent of the tax deductible expenses. The 50-percent figure is derived from the assumption that the physician is in the 50-percent tax bracket so that every dollar he can deduct from his income tax saves him 50 cents in taxes. The cash outlay made by the physician over the 10-year period, exclusive of the cost of his $19,000 investment, comes to $45,309.

To make the comparison between renting and condominium ownership comparable, that $45,309 figure is reduced by the amount the physician would gain if he sold his suite at the end of 10 years. His initial down payment of $19,000 has been subtracted from his proceeds so that the net proceeds from the sale would amount to $11,441[3]. Thus, his 10-year comparative cost of owning the condominium is $33,868.

That cost can be compared to the cost of renting a similar space for 10 years ($48,023 — see the partnership pro forma, table 3) reduced by the amount of interest he could gain if the $19,000 down payment were invested conservatively at 10 percent interest (5 percent after taxes or $11,950). The comparative cost of renting is then $36,073.

In the case of a condominium, cash flow is not the factor used to determine resale value. Comparable sales and replacement value may be applied to some limited degree, but the reader must keep in mind that a physician's practice suite is limited in marketability. The buyer usually must not only be another physician, but also he must frequently be a physician in the same specialty. Because of this limited market and because selling to anyone outside this market would usually require extensive renovation of the suite, resale values tend to appreciate very slowly for physician practice suites.

Again, the reader is free to add any rate of appreciation of the property to the figures that he chooses, but he should keep in mind the limitations of the condominium. Also, to keep such a comparison valid, he would have to apply a similar appreciation rate to the investment made by the renter.

The bottom line: In this example, the physician saves $2,205 over a 10-year period by owning his condominium suite. These figures are based on the assumptions that no dramatic plunge in the market takes place, that the maintenance of the building has been good, and that the physician is able to sell his condominium when he wants to. The computations for the proceeds the physician receives at the time of sale of his suite are presented in note 3 and are developed in primarily the same manner as those for the partnership.

CONCLUSIONS

An accountant or a statistician can prove virtually anything with numbers, and the author is well aware of this pitfall. For that reason the reader is cautioned more than once always to look carefully at any ownership situation, to seek competent, independent accounting help, and to look at long-range as well as short-range ramifications of each of the ownership alternatives.

On the basis of the information presented in this chapter and the experiences of chief executive officers (CEOs) and investment counselors across the country, a few conclusions can be reached concerning the financial feasibility of a project:

- Most hospital-owned projects can be made financially feasible.
- The rental rate for the physician is almost always lower when the hospital owns the project than when someone else does.
- The third-party private developer's project will usually result in the highest rental rates and/or higher suite improvement costs for the physician.
- Ownership of a condominium suite or a partnership interest based on the space the physician occupies usually does not present sufficient savings to the physician to merit his investment of money and time. However, situations vary, as do the attitudes of medical staff members. The specifics of a situation may override the normally negligible benefits of this type of ownership.

With these general conclusions, the hospital considering the development of a medical office building should be better equipped to analyze its own situation. The combined consideration of the tangible and intangible aspects of each form of ownership presented in chapters 4 and 5, the general financial ramifications of each type of ownership as presented in this chapter, the goals of the hospital, and the attitudes of the physicians will generally lead the hospital toward making the decision concerning what form of ownership will produce the most effective project in its given set of circumstances.

NOTES

1. Drexel Toland & Associates, Inc. *Survey of Hospital-Owned Professional Office Buildings.* Memphis: 1974.

2. The computations for the proceeds the physician partner receives at the time of sale of the building:

Estimated sale price of medical office building		$3,700,000
Building cost	$2,880,000	
Depreciation and amortization	(1,291,041)	
Sales commission — 6%	222,000	(1,810,959)
Taxable Gain		$1,889,041
Depreciation recapture — depreciation in excess of straight-line:		(125,276)
Capital Gain		$1,763,765
		x25%
		$ 440,941
Ordinary gain on depreciation recapture (125,276 x 50%):		62,638
Total Tax		$ 503,579

Summary:

Proceeds from sale	$3,700,000	
Less: Mortgage balance	($1,905,000)	
Tax above	(503,579)	
Commission	(222,000)	
	$1,069,421 ÷ 35 = $30,555	

3. The computations for the proceeds the physician receives at the time of sale of his condominium suite:

Estimated sale price of condominium suite:		$102,700
Suite cost	$ 79,000	
Depreciation	(40,440)	
Sales commission — 6%	6,162	($ 44,722)
Taxable Gain		$ 57,978
Depreciation recapture — depreciation in excess of straight-line:		(5,604)
Capital Gain		$ 52,374
		x 25%
		$ 13,094
Ordinary gain on depreciation recapture (5,604 x 50%)		$ 2,802
Total Tax		$ 15,896

Summary:

Sale price	$102,700	
Less: Mortgage balance	(50,201)	
Tax above	(15,896)	
Commission	(6,162)	
	$ 30,441	

CHAPTER **8**

Financing the Project

Consideration of how the medical office building will be financed should come early in the process of developing an office building. It is closely tied to the ownership decision and financial feasibility. Chapter 5 already touched upon the ease or difficulty of financing various types of ownership structures. This chapter discusses some important considerations in financing, the basic methods available, and a method for financing hospital-owned buildings that can save both time and money.

In general, financing the hospital-related medical office building has become easier over the years, as the buildings have grown in number, have developed positive track records, and have grown in acceptance among the nation's many lending institutions. Specifically, however, the current money market is such that all financing is somewhat difficult to obtain, with considerable competition for the available money. Consequently, astute, creative, and alert purchasing is required in order for the hospital or other owner to obtain financing on the most attractive terms.

KEY FACTORS OF FINANCING

Before any move is made toward financing a project, the hospital must first evaluate outstanding loans, examine any restrictive covenants in those loans that may impede new financing packages, and determine its financial priorities (see chapter 5).

Next, the hospital must evaluate the financing alternatives available to it. Basically, three factors are central to an attractive financing package. They are availability, flexibility, and cost. The hospital or other owner of any medical office building project should seek these three qualities in the best possible combination.

Availability is a prerequisite to other loan considerations, particularly in a tight money market. "Financing is available today, but is not easy," one speaker explained at an AHA seminar on hospital-based medical office buildings. Although his comments were made several years ago, they are even more pertinent today than they were then. He continued, "Condominium financing is very difficult to obtain, and the terms are harsh. There is a greater availability of funds if you have a hospital-owned building, and the money market, to a large degree, may tell you what form of ownership you are going to take. I would think that in this money market, the hospital-owned building, or at least the type of building where the hospital fully guarantees it, is about the only method."[1]

Although availability is a prerequisite of any financing package, flexibility is the single most important element. The hospital wants to secure the best possible terms for its particular needs, whether the loan is for a short or long term. It wants to be able to prepay the loan with unborrowed funds, without having harsh prepayment penalties standing in its way. In addition, the hospital wants the ability to refinance, both in relation to future projects or if interest rates drop significantly. It wants to make sure that it does not tie itself up with financing today that will prohibit potential projects in the future, and it does not want its normal operations restricted by excessive protective covenants. Both long-range financial planning and careful loan negotiation are aspects of flexibility.

Finally, the cost of the loan is a consideration. Surprisingly, cost often runs third in relation to the two previous factors. The availability of money at the right time may well be more important than a slightly higher cost of one type of financing over another. During periods of rapid inflation, delays in obtaining a loan or loans that require a lengthier process to obtain, even with lower interest rates or fees, may end up costing more in terms of the increases in construction costs that occur while the loan application materials are prepared and the loan negotiated. Over the long run, flexibility to refinance, to secure other loans, and to expand operations may be more important to the hospital than obtaining the cheapest possible loan cost. In perspective, then, the hospital wants to obtain the lowest possible loan cost, but not necessarily at the expense of flexibility or availability. A delicate balancing act of the key factors may be required.

FINANCING ALTERNATIVES

Many sources (including the American Hospital Association's book *Capital Financing for Hospitals*[2]) are available to provide an in-depth discussion of types of financing, application procedures, relative merits and costs, and other related characteristics. For this reason, detailed information on each type of financing are not presented here. Rather, the financing alternatives available for medical office buildings are presented briefly, with information related to the type of projects for which they might be used.

Basically, the financing alternatives available are conventional financing, taxable securities, tax-exempt bonds, and a few miscellaneous methods, including government programs.

Conventional Financing

Conventional financing is the most widely used method of financing hospital-related medical office buildings. It can be arranged by the owner directly with a lending institution, or it can take the form of a private placement through a mortgage banker or investment counselor. Generally, when the owner arranges the loan himself, it is a first mortgage loan with a local bank, with a savings and loan institution, or, occasionally, if the borrower is large and well-known, with an insurance company. Conventional financing arranged through a mortgage banker or investment counselor also takes the form of a first mortgage loan, but these loans are usually placed with large insurance companies, pension funds, or other lenders who are not directly accessible to the borrower.

One reason conventional financing is so widely used for medical office buildings is that it is available for hospital-owned buildings, investor-owned buildings, and physician-owned buildings alike. No other form of financing is so widely available for different ownership structures.

Currently, the ownership structure most difficult, and almost impossible, to finance is the condominium, because of its negative track record with lenders. At this time, about the only way to finance a condominium is through a local bank or savings and loan institution, which might be willing to finance the project in the hope of obtaining the other banking business of physicians involved. Even then, financing is difficult to obtain and the project size limited.

Another reason that conventional financing is so popular for hospital-related medical office buildings is that it is relatively quick and simple to arrange, is reasonably flexible, has low front-end fees, and is a good long-term vehicle (20 to 30 years). However, its major drawbacks are that it is usually available only for small loans ($3 million and under), has higher interest rates than other methods available to the hospital, and usually has more restrictive covenants than some other forms of financing, so that substantial prepayment penalties are standard.

Taxable Securities

Other financing alternatives are available primarily to hospital-owned medical office buildings. The most widely used, particularly in a tight money market, are taxable securities—bonds or notes. Because of the various legal details, this type of financing is almost always arranged through a mortgage banker or investment counselor. The bonds may be issued through private placement or through public offerings. Under most circumstances, for-profit organizations must register with the Securities and Exchange Commission in order to sell securities publicly—a process that is usually too costly and cumbersome to be practical. For this reason, office buildings in the form of partnerships or with doctors involved in the ownership are almost impossible to finance this way.

Taxable securities are a reasonably simple form of financing to arrange, are easier to prepay than conventional mortgages, and have fewer restrictive covenants than tax-exempt bonds. This form of financing is particularly effective for small projects under $3 million, but can be utilized for projects up to $10 million. Taxable securities are also quite adaptable for short-term financing in the range of 10 years, but can be arranged for loans up to 20 years.

The primary disadvantages of financing a medical office building with taxable securities is that they have higher interest rates than tax-exempt securities, the long-term market is limited, the hospital cannot arrange for financing without professional help, and more time is usually needed for securing this type of financing than for conventional loans.

Tax-Exempt Bonds

Tax-exempt bonds are the second most widely used financing alternative available primarily to hospital-owned medical office buildings. Individual state laws determine what type of bonds can be issued. Two of the most prevalent are bonds issued through a Health Care Financing Authority or through a local government unit. Although tax-exempt bonds may be available for physicians or other private owners, they are infrequently used.

Tax-exempt bonds have the lowest interest rates of any form of financing. They are an especially good vehicle for large projects over $3 million and for long-term loans of 20 to 40 years.

The drawbacks of using tax-exempt bonds are that they have more restrictive covenants than other forms of financing (for instance, no prepayment for 10 years); have high front-end costs; are often sold to individuals, making them extremely difficult to amend or alter;[3] are usually secured by a gross revenue pledge, which can be financially restrictive to the hospital; and, finally, require going through political bodies, increasing the red tape, and lengthening the time required to secure the financing.

Other Alternatives

A few other alternatives exist for financing hospital-owned medical office buildings but, for various reasons, they are infrequently used. For instance, mortgage loans insured by the Federal Housing Administration are sometimes available. They are moderately expensive, long-term loan vehicles. However, the additional time required to obtain these loans and the inconvenience of government bureaucracy generally make them unattractive to most hospitals. The Farmers Home Administration also provides loan guarantees for projects in communities of under 50,000 population and low-interest loans for communities under 20,000 population.

Whereas the use of community fund drives or hospital endowment funds for construction of hospital-owned medical office buildings was once unheard of, community attitudes are changing and these are now possible alternatives. Particularly in small communities that desperately need physicians, community fund drives are used more and more often. However, endowment funds are a special legal entity and may or may not be used, according to their restrictions. Any hospital considering the use of endowment funds must be sure that the office building facility is consistent with the hospital's charter, that the funds used are not restricted in such a way as to prevent their use for such a project, and that the project could be proved to be a prudent investment if challenged in court. Community attitudes are important here, as are the legal ramifications. A hospital should use endowment funds cautiously and only after thorough legal consultation.

Finally, some hospitals today find themselves able to use available hospital cash for part or all of the construction of the medical office building.

EFFECTIVE FINANCING FOR THE BOLD BORROWER

The traditional approach to financing includes doing a feasibility study, completing design drawings, obtaining bids on the construction, obtaining formal commitments from tenants, projecting financial figures, arranging permanent financing with the lender, getting a commitment in writing, and then taking that commitment to another lender and arranging for a construction loan. This loan process frequently takes six months to complete, and a six-month delay in the start of construction can add 5 percent to the cost of the building (based on an annual inflation rate of 10 percent).

Certainly, a hospital planning a hospital-related medical office building will want to consider all the financing options available to it, and it may well decide to go with the traditional approach of securing permanent financing before proceeding with the project. For the aggressive hospital that is financially sound, another option is available for consideration; it is faster, less expensive, more flexible, and takes advantage of the changing money market. This other alternative in financing consists of a six-step process:

1. The hospital completes a feasibility study to determine approximate costs of the medical office building and the total time needed to construct and fill the building. For example, a typical project might be projected to cost $3 million, take 18 months to construct, and need approximately two years to fill with tenants. Consequently, the hospital can anticipate a building completed and running at full occupancy at the end of 3½ to 4 years.

2. At the same time the feasibility study is being completed, the hospital analyzes its financial situation and organizes its collateral, including real estate, deposits, endowment funds, and so forth. The hospital should be careful to use a recent market appraisal to value its property, not the book value.

3. With collateral "in hand," the hospital goes to a local lending institution—a bank or a savings and loans institution—and applies for a loan against its available collateral, not against the proposed office building. Banks are limited to five years on such loans, but that will provide the hospital sufficient time. The loans will usually be secured by a wrap-around loan, similar to a second mortgage on hospital property. Other collateral such as endowment funds can also be used to secure the loan. In some cases, one local lender may not have sufficient money available to meet the needs of the hospital but will handle the loan with several local banks or savings and loans institutions providing the money.

4. The hospital proceeds immediately with construction of the office building.

5. As soon as the hospital obtains its short-term financing, it begins to watch the money market and to shop for permanent financing.

6. The final step is to secure the permanent financing for the project, at any advantageous point during the five-year period.

The prerequisites for financing a project in this manner are that the hospital be financially sound with sufficient collateral to secure the wrap-around loan, that the hospital be sufficiently bold to begin a project before permanent financing is arranged, and that it be willing to assume the risk inherent in fluctuating interest rates. If the hospital can meet these three criteria, then it may benefit in many ways from this financing approach.

On the front end, the hospital gains time, which converts to money. Because it does not have to wait until drawings are complete, bids are in, and leases are signed by doctors in order to begin the financing process, and because dealing with local banks or savings and loans institutions is one of the fastest financing methods, the hospital is usually able to initiate construction three to six months sooner than with more traditional financing methods. This earlier start-up will provide substantial savings in construction costs and will allow the building to be completed and rented sooner, with physicians admitting patients and utilizing ancillary services and thus creating new revenues. The front-end time savings and resultant financial benefits are reason enough to pursue this financing method.

Further, the hospital stands to gain other advantages. It gains flexibility—the ability to change the project, to add to it or to delete from it—because the financing is not attached to the building. It also gains a valuable edge in the money market as it negotiates for permanent financing, because it is not locked into current money market conditions at the time the project begins. The hospital has five years to obtain permanent financing, and it can watch the fluctuations in the market so as to obtain the financing during a down cycle in interest rates.

Particularly if the hospital waits until the building is completed and occupied, it can obtain a negotiating edge in the money market, for it will then be negotiating for an existing building filled with tenants, not for a building that exists only on paper. In a tight money market, buildings already constructed get preferred consideration by lenders over buildings not yet constructed. In addition, lenders indicate that a hospital stands to save one percentage point in the interest rate when it finances a building already constructed, as opposed to one to be built. In effect, what the hospital does by waiting to secure permanent-financing is to change the money market for its particular project from a seller's market to a buyer's market. Not only is the hospital able to negotiate better interest rates, but it also is able to negotiate better or more customized terms for its particular needs.

For the hospital able to meet the basic criteria for this type of financing, it is certainly a vehicle to give priority consideration. Experience has proven its advantage and workability.

NOTES

1. Francoeur, Robert. American Hospital Association seminar, Los Angeles, May 13, 1974.
2. American Hospital Association. *Capital Financing for Hospitals,* cat. no. 1175. Chicago: The Association, 1974.
3. Although taxable securities theoretically can be sold to individuals also, with the same problems of inflexibility arising, they are rarely attractive investments to individual purchasers, who are usually more interested in the tax sheltering qualities of tax-exempt bonds. Most taxable securities are purchased by large trusts, partnerships, and institutions that have their income sheltered through other means and, consequently, do not suffer from this problem.

CHAPTER 9

Working with the Medical Staff

One premise is fundamental to the successful development of a hospital-based medical office building: the physician is the hospital's "customer." He is the only person who can admit patients and prescribe hospital services and treatment. As such, he is the key market for the hospital.

Although the hospital wants to be respected by the public within its geographic community, it will not have patients unless it has the respect of the medical community. The hospital develops a medical office building in order to improve and sustain the quality and quantity of patient care. However, neither of these goals can be met without the support, loyalty, and involvement of the medical staff. Consequently, the development of good working relationships with the medical staff during planning and construction of the office building is vital. Although the hospital will best be able to develop these relationships when it controls the project (see chapter 5), even when other ownership options have been selected, the following steps for working with the medical staff should be taken.

First, and most important, the medical staff should be involved in all phases of the project—early, in the planning stages. They should be a part of the development process; their needs should be heard and their wants and problems responded to.

As soon as the on-campus medical office building becomes a consideration, the leaders of the medical staff should be consulted in an informal manner. They should be given the opportunity to express their interests and concerns so that policies and programs can be developed that will allow the project to move ahead with the support and understanding of the medical staff. This step is essential to the ultimate success and occupancy of the building.

ESTABLISHING THE ADVISORY COMMITTEE

After informally "testing the water," the hospital administration is now in a position to develop tangible programs for integrating the medical staff into the development process. The next step in accomplishing this objective is the establishment of a medical office building advisory committee to work with the administration and the governing board's building committee (see chapter 3) throughout the project.

The medical office building advisory committee is formed and appointed by the chief of staff and, ideally, consists of five to seven members, depending on the size of the hospital. In appointing the committee, the chief of staff should strive to have all of the major clinical departments of the medical staff represented. To ensure enthusiastic participation, most of the members should be interested in moving into the building. However, at least one member who definitely is not interested in locating in the building should be appointed to represent the interests of nontenant members of the medical staff and to alleviate any fear of discrimination that might arise. In addition to the physician members, the committee should also include at least one nonvoting member representing the administration of the hospital—someone intimately involved in the development of the project.

The committee membership will need to be approved by the governing board of the hospital. The committee itself will report to the chief of staff, the executive committee of the medical staff, and the hospital board, as needed.

RESPONSIBILITIES OF THE COMMITTEE

The advisory committee will serve a number of functions, but some of its more important duties are to:

- Represent the medical staff in all matters affecting the medical office building
- Communicate with and keep the medical staff informed of developments concerning the medical office building
- Help answer opposition to and criticism of the building
- Review and approve operational policies for the medical office building
- Review and advise on conditions of the lease, rental policy, or ownership agreement
- Determine the ratio of medical specialties to occupy the building
- Serve as a tenant selection committee
- Help recruit physicians for the building
- Reinforce, among the medical staff, decisions made concerning the building

Including the medical staff in the planning of the on-campus medical office building will take more time initially, but when the physicians help in the planning of the building, they identify with it, are more cooperative, and are more enthusiastic, thus saving time in the long run.

Provide Physician Input

Initially, the advisory committee will be very busy and will need to meet frequently. During the early planning stages the physicians will have many good ideas on services, that might be included in the building, such as central dictation, copying services, or delivery systems within the building. They may have valuable input in the consideration of sites, parking, connections to the hospital, and other similar areas. This type of input from the physicians needs to be obtained early, so that feasible ideas can be included in the building design.

This committee should have a close relationship with the consultants or architects working on the project and should be represented at any meeting at which physician input is needed. In addition, the committee should be kept informed at every step of the way in regard to plans for the building. The committee, in turn, will need to keep the entire medical staff informed of the project's progress.

Invariably, physicians will have questions, doubts, or outright opposition concerning the project. Doctors who will not move into the building will want to know how the building will affect their practices, whether their relationship with the hospital will change because of the building, and whether their relationships with other doctors will be changed by it. Through constant communication with the entire medical staff, the advisory committee will be able to answer these questions. Where specific opposition to the project is voiced, the committee will need to identify the opposition and take appropriate steps to answer the opposing view. Frequently, opposition and criticism are based on misunderstanding. When problems are handled factually and openly, trust and understanding usually result. This committee will also need to pass along legitimate criticism of and suggestions for the building to the hospital administration so that this important information can be acted upon.

As part of the communication process, many advisory committees publish periodic newsletters during the course of a project. A newsletter is one means of reaching all the physicians with exactly the same information and in written form so that it is less likely to be misunderstood.

Communicate Regularly

One of the most vital functions of the advisory committee is the development of operational policies for the on-campus medical office building. So important are these policies that an entire chapter follows to discuss the types of policies needed. Initially, many of them will be of a philosophical nature, such as whether rules apply to the physician in the practice of medicine within his own suite, how he will be treated by the hospital in the area of admissions and scheduling of surgery, any restrictions that are to be placed on the type of equipment he can operate in his own suite, and so forth.

These issues and others are paramount to those physicians who might be concerned about hospital control. For that reason, the policies need to be developed early in the project by the advisory committee in concert with the administration. Then, they must be approved by the governing board before they are presented to the medical staff as a whole. Thus, when the policies are presented to the medical staff, the physicians will know upon what basis the building will be operated, and they will have the pledge of the governing board that these policies, designed by the medical advisory committee and administration, will stand. Without clearcut policies, the hospital may have difficulty obtaining commitment from its medical staff members to locate in the building.

To protect the interest of the physicians, the advisory committee will also

Develop Operational Policies

review and approve the lease, rental policy, or ownership agreement to be signed later by the physicians. It can also offer suggestions to include items of particular interest to the physicians in the lease. The committee will openly discuss all aspects of allowances and costs, going over item by item the standard finishes that will be included in the custom suite designs and that will be included in the basic rental or purchase rate. (Contractual agreements are discussed in depth in chapter 12. Typical standard suite finishes are also discussed in chapter 15).

Establish Tenant Specialty Composition

Perhaps the most important responsibility of the medical office building advisory committee is to assist in determining the number of physicians by specialty and subspecialty to be located in the facility. The medical staff profile and master plan of the feasibility study will indicate how many physicians are interested in the on-campus medical office building, what specialties are needed to supplement the staff, and how many new physicians will be needed to provide replacement support for aging physicians. On the basis of that information, the consultants will have made a preliminary recommendation for a building to accommodate a certain number of doctors. The advisory committee will, in turn, take the information available and the number of doctors who can be accommodated in the proposed building and work with the consultants in developing a specific specialty composition.

The processes of developing the program and size of the building (see chapter 13) and working out the specific details of the specialty composition involve much give and take among the advisory committee, the hospital administration, and the consultants. It will be influenced not only by need, but also by local circumstances and practicality.

For example, a building might be recommended for 50 doctors. In order to have a well-balanced specialty composition, the advisory committee might determine that 30 percent of the physicians should represent the specialties of medicine; 30 percent, surgery; 20 percent, obstetrics and gynecology; 10 percent, pediatrics; and 10 percent, other specialties, including general and family practice. Having made this determination, the committee would then translate these percentages into specific numbers of subspecialties.

The subspecialties of medicine would represent 15 doctors under the percentage schedule above. When evaluating the feasibility study the committee might note, for example, that five internists, one neurologist, one oncologist, one allergist, and one psychiatrist are interested in locating in the building. In addition, four new internists are needed to replace older physicians who are reducing their practices, and three cardiologists are needed to fill vacancies on the staff and meet the needs of the community. Allowing for the fact that not every new physician recruited to the hospital is willing to locate in the office building, their specialty composition for medicine might look like this:

8   internists (assumes 3 of the 4 to be recruited will
        locate in the office building)
1   neurologist

1   oncologist

1   allergist

1   psychiatrist

2   cardiologists (assumes 2 of the 3 to be recruited will locate in the office building)

<u> 1 </u>   dermatologist (to be recruited)

15   total

Each of the major specialty areas would be treated in the same manner. Depending on actual circumstances, the percentages might be adjusted to blend with community medical practice patterns or specific goals of the hospital. For example, the hospital and the committee might have difficulty getting pediatricians to locate on campus, because they traditionally practice in residential areas, near their patients. In that case, the committee might adjust the initial percentages to include additional family practitioners, internists, or general surgeons. The committee will, however, want to strive for the ideal and make adjustments only when necessary for practicality and to meet changing needs.

Act as Tenant Selection Committee

The advisory committee will also act as a tenant selection committee, reviewing the results of the consultant's interviews with physicians and obtaining tenancy commitments from physicians on a first-come, first-served basis within the predetermined specialty composition guidelines. If a physician is not interested in locating in the building, but his specialty needs to be represented in order to complete the planned specialty composition, he could be asked to recommend a physician in his specialty who might be interested. In this manner, accusations of "bringing in competing doctors" can be moderated. Although this function as a tenant selection committee is largely completed during the building stages of the project, the committee should continue to function to some extent after the opening of the building. If changes in the specialty composition are needed because of changes in hospital services, availability of specialists, or new developments in medical treatment, the committee should handle those changes.

Assist in Physician Recruitment

By being in touch with the project from the very beginning, the physicians on the medical office building advisory committee will be well aware of the recruitment effort that will be needed in conjuction with the development of the medical office building. The presence of the building itself is a significant recruiting tool. Because of their intimate involvement in the project, the physicians on the advisory committee will also need to be involved in the recruitment of new physicians. Although much of the recruiting detail may be handled by hospital administration or a special committee of the medical staff, the availability of advisory committee members to talk with physicians being recruited can be invaluable. This critical area of recruitment and how the physicians can assist are discussed later in this chapter.

Reinforce Decisions

Finally, the advisory committee helps reinforce decisions. If a physician does not like a decision that has been made in the development of the project, he will at least know that it was reviewed and approved by the advisory committee. In many delicate areas, the advisory committee can make fair decisions that will be accepted by the medical staff; whereas, the hospital would reap significant criticism had it made the decision without the committee. For example, if a group of ophthalmologists wants to run the building's optical shop, the advisory committee would be the right group to help make a fair decision. Acting alone, the hospital would be subject to criticism whatever it decided. With the advisory committee and the hospital acting together to weigh all such matters as conflict of interest, community standards, the rights of the doctors, the consensus of the medical staff members, and the needs of the hospital, a decision could be reached that would be more readily accepted in such delicate circumstances.

COMMUNICATING WITH THE MEDICAL STAFF

Open, honest, and frequent communication with the medical staff is one of the most essential elements of developing good working relationships and positive attitudes about the project. Communication has already been mentioned as a function of the medical office building advisory committee. Because the committee is intimately involved in the development of the project, it is in the position to know what is going on and has, in turn, the responsibility for keeping the rest of the medical staff informed. How it goes about carrying out this responsibility can include any number of communication methods.

Communication with the medical staff should begin during the initial planning stages. Once the hospital has decided to proceed with a feasibility study and an advisory committee of physicians has been established, the first presentation to the whole medical staff should be planned. This initial briefing can take place during the regular medical staff meeting. It should include the announcement that an on-campus medical office building is under consideration and that a feasibility study has been initiated. It should include the introduction of the advisory committee and the explanation that this committee will be working closely with the project planners and will be representing the physicians throughout the decision making process. Further explanation should include a description of what will be done in the study and when it is likely to be completed.

Although the administrator of the hospital may instinctively want to make this first presentation, he should stay in the background. A better way is to have the chief of staff make opening remarks and give his endorsement as he introduces an independent party—the consultant or other person who is conducting the feasibility study—to make the presentation. Physicians are usually more receptive to a consultant than to the hospital administration, because they believe a consultant to be less prejudiced and have fewer ulterior motives.

Many medical staff members do not attend all staff meetings. Therefore, follow-up communication is necessary to make sure that all staff members know what is going on. The medical staff newsletter is a good vehicle for this additional communication. Where no medical staff newsletter exists, the advisory committee may want to create one to communicate with staff members for the duration of the project. In still other cases, the employee publication of the hospital might be a vehicle for written communication with both the medical staff and the employee staff.

A second major briefing of the medical staff needs to take place when the hospital has decided to go ahead with the project and has determined the ground rules for its development. The plans for the project and the policies that will govern its development should be explained to the staff. The hospital and advisory committee should point out the advantages of the particular building program as it is being designed, including such points as the anticipated improvement in patient care, the advantages of the type of ownership selected, the hospital's need to be financially efficient in order to provide new and better services for its patients and doctors, the optimum specialty composition that is to be maintained in the building, and the advantages of more convenience and less hassle for the physicians. These and other points were addressed in detail in previous chapters.

The important aspect of the second briefing is for hospital management and the advisory committee to present a complete picture of why the office building is being developed and what it is expected to accomplish for the physicians, the hospital, and the patients. The physicians should be given ample opportunity to ask questions, and all should be invited to have individual meetings with the consultants to learn more about the project, if they are interested in doing so. Again, all progress reports made at general staff meetings should be followed by written information appearing in the staff and/or employee newsletters.

Periodic letters from the administrator and/or the advisory committee can also be valuable communication tools. These letters can be especially effective for making major announcements and in issuing individual invitations to the physicians to practice in the building.

In short, all physicians, whether they come to staff meetings or not, whether they are interested in occupying the building or not, should receive all information concerning the building and have an open invitation to become tenants.

CHAPTER **10**

Marketing MOBs to the Medical Staff

The process of marketing the on-campus medical office building begins the day the hospital first considers the building. It is not a separate phase during which an articulate salesman tries to persuade doctors to sign on the dotted line. It is, rather, an effort integrated into the development process for the building.

The hospital has both a concept and a product to market. Much of the success of the office building depends on the hospital's success in gaining acceptance of the on-campus office concept from the medical staff as a whole, whether or not, as individuals, they elect to become tenants. The hospital wants its physicians to be supportive of its effort to improve patient care through the development of the office building and wants its physicians to look at the building as part of the hospital's long-range plan for quality, service, and stability. Second, the hospital needs to motivate individual physicians to choose to practice within the building. Unless the hospital is successful in selling its medical staff on both the concept of the building and the reality of practicing in it, progress toward achieving the objectives the building was designed to accomplish will be slow.

"A farmer wouldn't plant a seed without preparing the soil to accept it. Why should we ever try to sell an idea without creating the acceptance attitude," Cavett Robert has stated. "And as long as you live, you'll never find a method as effective in creating this acceptance attitude as learning how to make the other person feel important. And I don't mean that sickening, nauseating massage of a person's ego.... The best way to make people feel important: get the habit of considering the other person is important."[1]

Careful examination of the steps given in chapter 9 concerning working with the medical staff will indicate that they are, in fact, steps toward creating an acceptance attitude in the medical staff. They include involving the physician; asking for his opinions, needs, and desires; including him in the decision-making process; and communicating with him regularly—all steps that reflect the fact that the hospital considers the physician to be an indispensable member of the hospital team.

This, then, is the first step toward developing a successful marketing program for the office building: create an attitude of acceptance. Recognize initially that the physician is vital to the operation of the hospital and treat him accordingly.

"People don't care how much you know about your product or service until they first know how much you care about helping them solve their problem," Robert says.[2] This statement is the basis for the second step of marketing the office building. The discerning administrator will recognize immediately that any effort he expends toward solving the problems of his medical staff, toward helping his staff practice more effectively, is really effort toward accomplishing the goals of his hospital and providing better quality patient care.

Thus, the hospital's marketing program for the on-campus medical office building must hinge on two basic principles:

- The hospital must create an attitude of acceptance in the medical staff by considering and treating the physicians as important.
- The hospital must convince the physicians that it wants to help them solve their medical practice problems.

The hospital that assumes these two attitudes and develops its medical office building program around them stands a better chance of gaining the support of the medical staff and quickly filling the office building with dedicated and loyal physicians.

PHYSICIAN INPUT TO FEASIBILITY STUDY

Very early in the consideration of the project, hospital administration will have "tested the water" by informally discussing the idea of the office building with key medical staff members. As a result of those early discussions, some physicians undoubtedly indicated interest in and support for the office building. Those physicians should be invited to meet individually with the project planners or consultants during the feasibility stage to offer ideas and opinions on the project's development. In addition, any medical staff leaders who have not expressed interest and support should also be asked to meet with the consultants. Even though their feelings may be negative, their input is needed to see the total picture.

These individual meetings with the physicians are usually best conducted by the consultant or other independent party so that the physicians feel free to talk openly about how they feel about the building, and their working relationships with the hospital, and any apprehensions. An independent third party not only tends to give credibility to the hospital, but also encourages frankness on the part of the physicians (see chapter 3).

During these initial individual meetings, the physicians should be told about ideas being developed for the project. They should also be asked to express their ideas and opinions in a number of areas that affect the project. For example, they should be introduced to the idea of a balanced specialty composition for the building and asked what specialties they feel are underrepresented on the staff. They should be asked what type of ownership they would prefer, and about their present offices—rental rates, type of leases, and problems they have with their office situations that they would like to see solved in the new building. They should also be asked about specific facilities and services they would like to see incorporated into the new building. All of these questions can provide valuable input for the program design of the project.

In addition, if the physician expresses interest in becoming a tenant, he should be asked what his individual practice needs would be; for example, what type of suite he might want (solo, two-man, or group), including the type, size, and number of examining rooms and the type of waiting room and special rooms and facilities. Each physician should be reassured, however, that he is being asked for this information not as any kind of commitment to the building, but rather as a means for the planners to understand the type of facilities likely to be needed in the building in order to accommodate local practice patterns.

During this interview, the physician is likely to voice any reservations or fears he has concerning the development of the building. He may be worried about control by the hospital or whether the building tenants will be selected in a fair and equitable manner. These apprehensions and attitudes need to be known, so that appropriate programs can be developed in response to them.

DEVELOPING MARKETING STRATEGIES

These early interviews are essential not only to include the medical staff in the planning process, but also to develop marketing strategies that will respond to the physicians' needs beyond those for rentable space and bricks and mortar. To seek out the physicians' needs, desires, and opinions not only helps the hospital develop a better and more marketable program, but also helps create an acceptance attitude in the individual physician. It lays the groundwork for motivating him to move into the building later.

Once the feasibility stage of the project is past and the hospital has decided to proceed with the development of the project, a second briefing of the medical staff should take place, as mentioned in the discussion on communication in chapter 9. At that time, an invitation should be issued to all physicians to meet individually with the project planners or consultants to learn more about the building and explore any interest they may have in occupying the building. Those physicians who have already expressed some interest in the building should be issued a special, personal invitation, perhaps followed by a phone call from the administrator to set up an appointment for them.

At these personal interviews the actual process of motivating the physicians to move into the building begins, but experience has shown that only one type of approach is generally effective with medical staff members, and that is low key.

Discussion now becomes more specific regarding the project, the physician's desires and needs, his ideas on his own suite, and what he would want if he decided to move into the building. A preliminary suite design is drawn for the sake of discussion.

In addition, the planners will talk with the physician about key areas of interest. The number of referrals the physician can anticipate receiving from the hospital and other colleagues in the office building is not only interesting to the physician, but also one of the main motivating factors for his occupying the building. The physician will want to know which physicians are already interested in or committed to moving into the building. The planners will also want to reemphasize the advantages to the physician and his patients (see chapter 2) of the on-campus location.

HOW MUCH WILL IT COST?

The economics of occupying the building should be carefully discussed. Physicians are frequently unaware of the full rental costs of their current offices. Rents are set in numerous ways, and low sounding rents may, in fact, have hidden costs in fees for optional services, surcharges, and/or assessments. Consequently, the physician may need assistance in comparing his true rental rate with that being offered in the new building.

Project planners should quote the rental rates for the new building and what those rates include in the way of custom design, suite finishes, and services provided. They should also point out that the rates may sound high because they reflect new building costs and because they are being set for a building that will be completed a year or two in the future. The physician should be helped to project what his current office rental rate would be at that same time in the future. The planners will also want to compare point by point the quality, efficiency, and level of services of the physician's present practice suite with one in the projected building.

The physician needs to know every aspect of what he would be getting for his money in the new building in comparison to his current location. Sometimes his rent may actually be lower in the new location, but most times it will be more expensive in the on-campus medical office building. When that is the case, the physician needs to be made aware that typical office rental costs are normally about 5 percent of a physician's gross income. Even if the rental rate in the on-campus medical office building is 50 percent higher than his current rent, it would still normally amount to only 7 or 8 percent of his gross income. That figure should be compared to the minimum increase of 10 to 12 percent in his gross income that he can expect by moving into the building. On the basis of that information, many physicians consider the advantages of practicing in the on-campus office building to be worth an increase in rent.

In one community in Kentucky, the hospital helped a group of doctors who owned a building determine what it actually cost them in comparison to what the rent in the new hospital-owned, on-campus medical office building would cost. Here are the facts: Seventeen doctors were located in an old, dilapidated clinic building that did not conform to the fire codes. They had 90 employees. The doctors did not know how much they were spending on their own building, so the hospital helped them run a financial analysis. It showed that their space cost $5.72 per square foot per year. The cost of space in the new hospital-owned, on-campus medical office building was projected at no more than $7 per square foot. In addition, the clinic doctors employed a yard man, an elevator operator, four or five housekeeping employees, and two or three maintenance men—all of whom would not be needed in the new location. The bottom line was that these doctors were actually spending more for offices in a substandard building than they would be in a new, modern, and convenient on-campus medical office building. Further study also showed that the hospital-owned building would be less expensive for the doctors than constructing a new office building of their own.

Not every comparison of present offices with new on-campus offices will be that dramatic. However, that is the type of comparison the hospital and medical office building advisory committee can help a physician make as a part of marketing occupancy in the on-campus building to him. In addition, if the physician believes that physician ownership is the answer to all his financial investment problems, then the hospital will need to present information such as appears in chapters 5 and 7 about the actual costs in time and money of physician ownership.

Although the physician can actually come out ahead financially through either hospital ownership or physician ownership, depending on the details of the project and the local circumstances, the negative factors of management time, friction among doctors over management decisions, and other problems that appear to be inevitable under physician ownership can be real selling factors for the hospital-owned building and can be potential hurdles to overcome for a physician-owned building.

In all, the logical reasons for the physician to move into the office building need to make up a total package that is to the physician's advantage—the on-campus location, the economics, and the operating procedures and policies related to the form of ownership. Each factor that makes his decision to move into the building a good one should be reinforced. Keep in mind that although the hospital is looking toward patient care as its objective in developing the building, the individual physician has additional motives for moving into the building, including convenience and availability.

OVERCOMING DOUBTS AND APPREHENSIONS

The fact that physicians are likely to voice reservations or fears about the project as they are interviewed individually or as a group has already been mentioned. Essential to the success of the project will be overcoming these doubts. Consequently, wise leadership will anticipate them and plan to deal with them. Generally speaking, the most common reservations physicians have about locating in an on-campus medical office building are the following:

- Fear that the hospital will try to control the private practice of the tenant physician
- Fear that the hospital will discriminate for or against on-campus tenants in the matters of scheduling surgery, availability of beds, or providing certain services
- Fear that the hospital will play favorites in the selection of tenants for the building
- Fear that "in" and "out" groups will develop within the medical staff
- Fear of being looked on as an employee of the hospital
- Fear of being tied to only one hospital, particularly of losing referrals from physicians at other hospitals
- Fear of losing patients if he moves his office

Other problems that physicians may have with the on-campus location could undoubtedly be listed, but these seven are the most common.

The development process already described in this chapter and a marketing program that is concerned with building receptive attitudes, not just selling suites, are means of dealing with the apprehensions. Physician involvement, close individual working relationships, open communication—all contribute to better understanding and less suspicion and fear. In addition, three specific approaches can be taken in varying degrees to help alleviate these fears.

First, the policies of development and operation designed by the advisory committee and approved by the governing board of the hospital should specifically address many of these areas. These policies should remove all doubt as to how the hospital will operate in relation to the building and how it will deal with its medical staff—both tenants and nontenants.

Second, if the physicians are renting from the hospital, the lease agreement should be so designed that the physicians do not feel trapped by the hospital and they could terminate the lease under certain circumstances (discussed in depth in chapter 12). If the physicians are to be owners as well as tenants of the building, then the ability to move out is not so easily achieved (see chapter 4).

Third, the hospital should provide the physicians with the testimony of other physicians who have had the experience of locating in such a building. The doctors need a physician's point of view on the advantages and problems of being located on campus and/or renting from a hospital.

Fear of Control

For example, in response to the fear of control of private practice by the hospital, the advisory committee should have clearly stated in the operating policies whether or not any restrictions are placed on private practice. In most cases, the operating policies will state that the physician is free to practice as he chooses within the ethical procedures consonant with medical staff bylaws. The hospital gains no advantage by imposing restrictions on private practice within the on-campus medical office building. The hospital wants to encourage, rather than discourage, physicians to practice in the building. If, however, any restrictions are to be placed on the physicians in their practice suites (such as denominational restrictions against performing abortions on hospital property), then these restrictions must be clearly stated in the operating policies and understood by all doctors before they are asked to commit themselves to the on-campus location.

The former chairman of the medical office building advisory committee at Anaheim (California) Memorial Hospital, emphasized this point when he said, "I am unaware of any domination by the hospital over any individual or group of doctors. The hospital has not attempted any domination. The only requirement of being in the building is that the doctor be a member of the medical staff. If his privilege is revoked at the hospital, he must move out of the building. I have witnessed no attempt by the hospital to coerce any physician because he is a tenant. The fear of this is widespread, but a wise hospital will never attempt this type of coercion."[3]

If the hospital and advisory committee have adequately addressed the subject of control in the operating policies of the building and if the physicians understand that the hospital will live by these policies, then most problems of this nature will not arise. A lease that leaves the physician in a position of flexibility, as opposed to being tied to a multiyear and/or financial commitment, can also contribute substantially to alleviating fear. If the doctor knows that he has the flexibility of moving out of the building if the hospital should not live up to its part of the bargain, then he can usually be confident about both locating on campus and/or renting from the hospital.

Finally, the comments of other physicians located in on-campus medical office buildings can provide additional reinforcement of the hospital's position of noninterference. In the preparation of this book, a number of physicians in a variety of on-campus medical office buildings were asked about this particular issue. In every case, the physicians responded that they had experienced no interference. One physician's comments virtually summed up what they had each stated in different ways, "The hospital has in no way attempted to interfere with our manner of practice, and, as a matter of fact, has been most cooperative. There has been no discrimination to my knowledge in favor of tenant physicians in such areas as scheduling or admitting. Those of us who have been in a hospital-owned medical office building for some time have the same difficulty with scheduling and admitting patients as those who are not in such a building. We have difficulty when the hospital is filled, or when the operating room schedule is filled. Otherwise, we have no difficulty at all."[4]

Fear of Discrimination

His comments address both the fear of control and of discrimination concerning tenant physicians. Just as with fear of control, fear of discrimination must be removed by setting policies that state how all medical staff members will be treated—tenants and nontenants. The hospital must make clear its intention to treat all physicians the same, whether or not they decide to occupy the building. Typical of remarks made by physicians asked about discrimination was the one made by a Louisville doctor. When asked, "Does your hospital seem to discriminate in favor of tenant physicians in such areas as scheduling and admitting at the expense of physicians not located in the office building," he responded, "No. I wish they would, if in my favor of course."[5]

Tenant Selection

The most essential element of alleviating the fear that the hospital will play favorites in the selection of tenants for the building is the adoption of the policy of tenant selection presented in the previous chapter. If the policies of development and operation established by the advisory committee state that the committee will select tenants on a first-come, first-served basis within the guidelines of the designated specialty composition, then the most important step toward alleviating this fear has been taken. The second step is to communicate this policy to all members of the medical staff.

Cohesive Medical Staff

The fear that "in" and "out" groups will form within the medical staff is a legitimate concern. The hospital wants to keep a cohesive and congenial medical staff, and the physicians want to maintain their relationships with one another.

In this particular matter, how the hospital works with and deals with its medical staff will have greater impact than anything else, and equitable operating policies are an essential aspect of that relationship. Open communication in which every doctor, whether tenant or not, is kept informed of developments concerning the building as well as current activities at the hospital also helps. Generally, the problem of in and out groups is far more a reality in physician-owned buildings than in hospital-owned ones. The investment of the physician's money in the building is more likely to create a clique than in cases where the physicians are all still on an equal basis of renting.

Loss of Identity

The fear of being looked on as an employee of the hospital also can be alleviated through the operating policies. If a physician knows he will not be treated as an employee but will be treated the same as any other medical staff member, he can be more confident about occupying space on the hospital campus. The flexibility of his lease agreement and other physicians' experiences can also be helpful. One of the most important aspects of eliminating this apprehension concerns the architectural design of the office building. Although this point will be discussed later in this book, the hospital should make sure that its on-campus medical office building does not look exactly like the hospital. It should certainly blend architecturally with the hospital, but the office building must have a separate identity and, especially, a separate address so that the physician and his patients will associate his practice with the hospital, but not as an actual part of it.

Specialists' Concerns

The fear of being tied to only one hospital—perhaps not being able to get beds at other hospitals or losing referrals from physicians who practice at other hospitals—is expressed most often by "super specialists." Highly specialized physicians require a broad base of referrals to maintain their practice. In this situation, the operating policies and lease or ownership agreement have little effect. The physician needs the experience of other physicians to assure him that he is not jeopardizing his practice. He also needs to know that his "good referral manners" will have more to do with a continued healthy referral pattern than any office location he may choose. For example, if he is a specialist, a patient may be referred to him by an internist from another hospital. If, when the time comes for that patient to see an internist again, the specialist refers him to an internist in his own building, rather than sending him back to the original internist, little time will pass before referrals stop coming from the original internist. Courtesy is involved, and that depends on how the physician handles his practice—not upon where the practice is located.

A Honolulu urologist had been in practice for more than 20 years before he moved into the medical office building adjacent to the Queen's Medical Center.[6] Eight months later he commented, "I really can't believe it. During the past eight months, since I moved into the on-campus office building, my practice has doubled. Every advantage of the on-campus office that I was told about has come true."

This physician's experience testifies to the fact that a well-established specialist can move his office across town to an on-campus location and not only maintain his referrals, but actually increase them. Not every physician is likely to experience such a dramatic increase. However, this physician's experience also addresses the last of the apprehensions listed previously: fear of losing patients. Overwhelmingly the experience of physicians who have moved on campus will indicate that the referrals generated through the office building will more than compensate for any patients that may be lost—and, by and large, few will be lost.

A surgeon at the Baylor Medical Center, Dallas, summed up most adequately the experience of physicians in an on-campus medical office building that is properly developed and operated.[7] "To begin with," he said, "the hospital is not objectively interested in this as a real estate venture. It is a project involved in the overall development and future of the institution. There is, therefore, a certain professional understanding of each other's needs. When we have a particular need, therefore, then there is an understanding of this and it is met without any question. [The advantage of] the actual geographic proximity of the office and hospital are demonstrated so many times during the day that we could not begin to list them."

RECRUITING NEW PHYSICIANS

The physician from Baylor described a successful hospital-related medical office building as one "involved in the overall development and future" of the hospital. As such, the development of the building must be incorporated into the hospital's need to provide a balance of services under the supervision of a balanced tenant composition of qualified medical specialists.

Appropriate early planning, including the medical staff profile, shows areas of weakness on the staff. Some specialists are needed to fill in areas that are unrepresented or understaffed. Others are needed to begin picking up the load of doctors nearing retirement. On the basis of these needs, the medical advisory committee establishes a tenant specialty composition for the office building, including spaces to be filled by newly recruited physicians.

In turn, the building is designed with space in it for these physicians to be recruited (see chapters 13 to 15). Thus, a symbiotic relationship emerges between the development of the medical office building and a physicians' recruitment program. The building cannot fulfill its ultimate potential for the hospital without recruitment, and the success of a recruitment program is largely dependent upon the availability of suitable office facilities.

The recruitment process itself is highly competitive. "Recruitment of physicians is not only difficult, it is expensive," said one administrator.[8] "If one community is recruiting, there are advertising costs that will exceed $2,000 a month during the recruiting process. It takes many man-hours to answer letters, the phone, or to visit personally with physicians. Some physicians will come to the area on their own, but many will not, so the next expense is bringing in the doctors to look at the community. The new doctors coming out of school cannot afford this expense. Also there are many communities that do offer this service, so the doctors tend to go where the service is offered and omit the areas where it is not.

"If a doctor is recruited," he continued, "where does he set up his practice? If office space is not readily available he will not stay. Availability of office space is just as important as actual recruiting."

A high-quality hospital with good on-campus medical office facilities can mount a successful recruiting effort. Many young doctors are accustomed to teaching centers with offices on campus and with the newest equipment and are most easily recruited by hospitals with top-notch office facilities. New doctors understand how a referral system works, and they know they need to break into it. An office in a hospital-related medical office building with a guaranteed specialty composition is the best and quickest way for them to break into the referral system, and they know it.

Other Factors in Successful Recruitment

Whereas the medical office building itself is frequently the prerequisite to a successful recruitment program, two other factors will be the keys to success. They are the involvement of the medical staff and the hospital's willingness to work with new doctors in solving their practice problems.

Because of the availability of resources on recruiting, a lengthy discussion on recruitment techniques is not needed here. The hospital will need to lay plans for reaching physicians and recent medical graduates. A good marketing program, including advertising, marketing materials, and other tools, is important and should not be overlooked. However, the degree to which the hospital is successful in involving its medical staff will be a major factor in the success of the program. Especially the members of the office building's advisory committee should be closely involved in the recruitment program. They will be aware of what specialists are needed. They should be asked to recommend physicians they know who might be interested. They should go to other members of the medical staff and ask for their recommendations. They should be available to meet with physicians recruited from outside the community who come to look over the hospital, its facilities, and the community at large. The enthusiasm of supportive physicians can do more to recruit other physicians than any other single factor. They are a living endorsement of the advantages of practicing in that community and at that hospital.

The chairman of the advisory committee might take on the responsibility of discussing the office building and his experience with it when new doctors come from out of town. Often, these new physicians would be right out of training and inexperienced in relocating, and the availability of an experienced professional to answer their questions can give them confidence. A physician is also better able than other professionals to relate the opportunities for success to the doctor being recruited.

If the physicians are reluctant to get involved in the recruitment process, three factors might be pointed out to them. First, they have a certain amount of responsibility to the community that supports them—to provide high-quality medical care and to help recruit their own replacements. Second, by being involved in the recruitment process, the physicians are able to assure themselves that the new doctors will fit in with the present medical staff, creating and/or continuing congenial relationships. Third, the physicians themselves need to understand that a balanced group of specialists works to the advantage of all the physicians. It provides a good referral system and helps prevent overstaffing in one specialty area while leaving another vacant.

For physicians being recruited from outside the area, the final point in favor of the medical office building is the hospital's willingness to be flexible and work with them in solving their practice problems.[9] "How can a physician getting out of school equip his office?" asked one administrator.[10] "This is tremendously expensive. In most cases, the physician cannot do it, so it is up to the community to assist." Or the hospital can assist, by equipping the medical office for the physician and allowing him to pay off equipment costs through his rent.

"Who pays for the physician to relocate to the town?" he asked. "There are many communities that are now paying this expense, so the communities that do not get physicians may find this is the reason, even though they have gone through all the other processes of recruitment.

"Does the community offer a guarantee for the first year?" the administrator continued. "Many communities do, so it has become a way of life. If the community is unable to make this offer, most physicians will not consider a community."

In most areas, the offer of a guarantee is not as difficult as it may sound. A physician who is genuinely needed by a community usually will not lack business. For example, one hospital in rural Idaho desperately needed physicians. As a part of its recruitment program, the hospital guaranteed new doctors an annual salary for the first three years. The hospital has recruited 12 physicians and to date has not paid out the first dime in guaranteed salary. In every case the physician exceeded the income guaranteed for his first year in practice.

In other cases a guarantee may not be needed, but the hospital may want to give the new physician free or deferred rent for a period of time, while he is getting established. It may want to reduce the initial rent, with the difference being made up later, once the physician's practice has been established. In still other cases, the hospital may be able to provide equipment, services, personnel, and/or supplies to the new doctor with the cost being paid in increased monthly rental charges. All of these methods provide options for the new physician to be able to establish his practice, and any cost to the hospital will quickly be made up in increased revenues.

The hospital might even be able to work with an older physician who would like to have a younger associate. The hospital and the physician would become a recruitment team. In this case, the hospital might allow the physician to rent a two-man suite in the office building, but pay rent on only a one-man suite for a limited time until the new physician is recruited.

The hospital's flexibility in working with what the physicians need at a price they can afford is absolutely necessary for recruitment. The day may come when that is not the case, but today, the competition demands it.

MAINTAINING GOOD RELATIONSHIPS

All other considerations aside, a physician moves his office on campus because he wants to practice at that hospital. He either is already practicing there and intends to continue, or he wants to practice there. He would not move on campus unless he respected the reputation of the hospital and the level of care rendered there.

Consequently, the hospital has its reputation with the physicians at stake when the operation of the office building is concerned. To protect this reputation and to continue to build better working relationships, the hospital must first adhere to the operating policies developed by the advisory committee and approved by the board. Second, it should operate the building itself as if it were any other department of the hospital. This is most easily accomplished when the building is hospital owned. Third, it should continue to utilize the medical office building advisory committee to discern the needs of the building tenants and to help in making decisions in sensitive matters.

Fast Troubleshooting

The second step mentioned above is most in need of amplification. The importance of good housekeeping, maintenance, security, heating, cooling, and similar services is primary. Also, an effective method for handling all tenant problems and complaints quickly and efficiently is essential, Usually, this troubleshooting is handled by one person on the administrative staff.

Quick response in solving problems is what would be expected of any good landlord, but because the hospital has a unique relationship with the physician tenants and because of their mutual dependency on each other in the provision of high-quality patient care, the hospital can afford to be more sympathetic and cooperative with the doctors in times of crisis or need than a typical landlord would be.

When the hospital is landlord, it can anticipate problems and solve them before they arise or while they are small. The hospital can provide special assistance to the physicians that may help them solve their practice problems. For example, the individual physician may need assistance in obtaining the right kind of insurance. He may need to utilize hospital sterilization equipment to process instruments. He may have equipment such as an EKG or an EEG machine that is difficult to get serviced on an individual basis, but the hospital could provide a technician to recalibrate it for him. The hospital might be able to extend crisis service to the physician's offices—blue teams, for example. The hospital might even help facilitate a flow of patient records by extending the in-house delivery system into the office building. Inclusion of a paging system in the office building or of a physicians' directory in the hospital are other ways in which the hospital might further assist the physicians.

Promoting Understanding

If the hospital is running the office building itself with real concern for the tenants, then it promotes common action based on understanding between the hospital and the doctors sharing the facilities full time. In turn, working so closely with each other gives advantages to each not otherwise available.

One ophthalmologist said, "I feel that, because of hospital administration representation at our building tenant meetings and continuing communication through our building manager, those of us in the medical building have significantly greater input of our wants and needs in the hospital than do those physicians who admit to the hospital but have their offices elsewhere. I . . . have found my particular hospital to be a very agreeable landlord."[11]

The goal of the hospital-related medical office building is better hospital-physician relations, better understanding and support for the hospital, and improved patient care. When the hospital invests the small amount of time and service needed to continue good relationships with its physician tenants, the result is happy tenants. In turn, satisfied doctors pass on their satisfaction to their patients, preventing many problems with disgruntled patients and creating more understanding of the hospital staff.

From beginning to end, no single factor can be more important to the successful development and operation of a hospital-related medical office building than good relationships with the physicians.

NOTES

1. Robert, Cavett. Tape from Positive Thinking Rallies. Humaneering, Inc., Memphis, 1977.
2. Ibid.
3. Belt, M.D., J. A., chairman, physician's advisory committee. Anaheim (CA) Memorial Hospital. Recorded interview, Feb. 1976.
4. Letter to Drexel Toland & Associates from physician, Dec. 16, 1975.
5. Letter to Drexel Toland & Associates from physician, Dec. 9, 1975.
6. Morgan, M.D., A. Interview, Honolulu, HI, Jan. 1978.
7. Letter to Drexel Toland & Associates from physician, Jan. 13, 1976.
8. Reed, E. L. A summary of the physician recruiting process. Unpublished paper. Evanston, WY. Aug. 16, 1976.
9. For an outline of physician recruiting practices recognized for medical reimbursement process and, hence, consistent with the Medicare-Medicaid Anti-Fraud and Abuse Act, see Stiller, J. Legal Boundaries in Physician Recruitment Practices. *Hosp. Med. Staff.* 10:25, Sept. 1981.
10. Reed, E. L. Summary of the physician recruiting process.
11. Letter to Drexel Toland & Associates from physician, Jan. 31, 1976.

CHAPTER **11**

Policies for Development and Operation

Regardless of what form of ownership an on-campus medical office building takes, early establishment of policies for development and operation is essential to the building's ultimate success. Physicians who are going to associate themselves and their practices with an office building on a hospital campus need to know in advance exactly what kind of situation they are entering and what kinds of working relationships they will have with the hospital and with one another. Their support of the project will depend largely on the completeness of the information they have and the security they feel in the policies that have been established.

The development policies that follow are not optional, if a medical office building is to be successful. Consequently, the hospital should carefully examine itself and/or other potential owners of the building to ensure that these priorities are met. If these development policies cannot be accepted by the hospital and the owners of the project (if other than the hospital), the chances of developing a project that will ultimately benefit the hospital, its patients, and the physicians are substantially reduced. In fact, it would be safe to say that the project should be abandoned.

The actual operating policies contribute in varying degrees to the project's success. Many simply ensure a smoothly running project. Others protect the interests of the physicians, and still others protect the interests of the hospital.

DEVELOPMENT POLICIES

The six nonoptional policies for development of the building reviewed in this section are discussed in greater detail in other chapters. Because of their essential nature, however, they are reviewed here as the prerequisites to effective operating policies.

1. Establish the priority of improved health care as the single motivating factor for the development of the building.

As discussed in chapter 3, health care alone is the reason for the hospital's existence and, as such, can be its only motive for developing facilities on the hospital campus. Other benefits such as convenience for patients and physicians do result, but these are not the reasons for undertaking the project. The concepts of an on-campus medical office building as a real estate venture, a profit center, a tax write-off for physicians, a means of trapping or controlling physicians, or any number of other similar faulty concepts not only do not relate to the central purpose of the hospital, but may in fact interfere with or jeopardize that purpose.

2. Include the physicians in planning, programming, and setting policies for the building.

The previous two chapters have discussed this aspect of project development in great detail. Physician involvement is vital for two reasons. First, the physicians' input is needed to develop a project suited to the individual needs of the particular medical staff. Second, physician involvement is essential in cultivating attitudes of acceptance and physician support for the project.

3. Establish a standard of high-quality design and construction to be pursued throughout the project.

The office building reflects on the hospital. If it is poorly designed and cheaply constructed, then it will detract from the image of the hospital and breed discontent among the physicians. However, if it is a high-quality building throughout, then it will enhance the hospital's status with both physicians and patients. Chapters 15 and 16 detail the need for design and construction quality that is similar to, but different from, the hospital. Specifically, the need for sound control, superior heating, ventilating and air conditioning systems, parking, and elevators is discussed in detail. In addition, a policy that presumes custom designing of each suite for the specialist who is to occupy it is an important aspect of this high-quality design.

4. Establish a standard of high-quality management and maintenance to be pursued throughout the life of the building.

If the hospital owns the building, it should manage the building much the same as it would any other department of the hospital. That is, it should be assigned to one member of the administrative team, who should see that it receives superior housekeeping and maintenance services. In addition, when problems arise, he should handle them, just as he would any other departmental problems under his supervision. Most hospitals have better administrative management than other institutions or businesses in the community. Consequently, this expertise should be applied to the medical office building.

If the building is owned by someone other than the hospital, then the same high standards of management and maintenance must apply as a prerequisite for that ownership. When a building is located on the hospital campus, it reflects on the hospital, regardless of ownership, and for it to be poorly maintained or inadequately cleaned would be a detriment to the prestige of the hospital. In addition, poor management will quickly result in a disgruntled medical staff, thus creating new and greater problems for the hospital.

5. Develop and utilize the building as an integral part of the hospital's marketing program.

The office building may be a separate structure, but it cannot be separate from the goals and long-range plans of the hospital. The last two chapters touched on the fact that the medical office building is an important marketing tool of the hospital. It reaches the hospital's primary market: the physicians. For that reason, its development should be carefully coordinated with the broad marketing program for the hospital. As the hospital studies the community it serves and plans for the expansion, addition, elimination, or promotion of various hospital services, it must do so in concert with the medical staff. The planning of an extensive cardiac care department would, for example, be wasted without corresponding plans to see that sufficient cardiologists and other specialists were available to support and staff it. Thus, the program for the medical office building must dovetail with the hospital's master plan and marketing program. The medical office building is not an end in itself, but is, rather, just one of many aspects of the hospital's program to achieve its long-range goals. Failure to realize the building's integrated role in the total future of the hospital will result in a building that fails to reach its full potential.

6. Establish a balanced specialty composition for the building based on the hospital's and medical staff's needs, with tenant selection based on that composition.

Much has already been said about the specialty composition in the previous chapter. It is the critical issue upon which the effectiveness of the project hinges and relates to the needs of the hospital and the medical needs of the community in specific terms. If the hospital elects physician or investor ownership for the project, a prerequisite to leasing hospital land to the owner must be that the tenant composition by specialty will be developed and programmed in conjunction with the hospital and that the owner of the building will guarantee adherence to it over the life of the project.

OPERATING POLICIES

Operating policies prevent problems; they answer questions. They let the physician know where he will stand if he becomes a tenant of the medical office building. Most of all, they lay the groundwork for a smoothly running project.

Because they do provide information upon which a physician may partially base his decision to move into the building, many of the operating policies need to be adopted early in the project development, before the marketing of the building begins. The 23 policies presented here will serve as a checklist, touching on the critical issues of operation. A good list of operating policies will address each of these areas, although the specifics may vary from project to project. In addition, local situations may dictate the need for additional policies.

1. Base tenant selection on fair procedure established in advance.

The sixth development policy presented the need for the selection of tenants on the basis of specialty. That policy is not an option for a successful building. What may vary is how the tenants are selected within that guideline.

The most frequently used and best method is for tenants to be assigned space on a first-come, first-served basis within the established composition. For example, if the building has been programmed for three cardiologists, the first three cardiologists who commit to occupancy will be assigned space. If a fourth then decides he wants to move into the building, he will be put on the waiting list, regardless of whether other spaces still need to be filled. The cardiologist will not be given the space programmed for a dermatologist, for example, or other specialists.

In other situations, hospitals sometimes use the seniority system in assigning space. Physicians interested in the building would be asked in the order of their seniority and would be assigned space accordingly, still within the specialty composition guidelines. This system is used less frequently, probably because it tends to fill the building with somewhat older physicians, rather than with a broad spectrum of ages.

These or other methods for tenant selection may be adopted for the building according to the local situation. Whatever procedure is to be used should be decided upon early in the development process by the medical advisory committee and should be written into the operating policies. The committee should also make the procedure well known among the medical staff. Early development of this policy eliminates a number of concerns on the part of the physicians and prevents many potential problems as the building moves into the marketing and operational phases.

2. Do not require a financial contribution as a prerequisite for tenancy in the building.

This policy puts all physicians on an equal footing and makes space available in the building without regard to a physician's financial status. It is particularly important in recruiting young physicians just completing their training. The policy must state that no contribution to any hospital fund or service will be required as a prerequisite for tenancy of the building or even considered in the assignment of space.

In addition, if the hospital owns the building and plans to rent it, sufficient standard suite finishes or finishing allowances should be made so that a physician's suite can be completed for occupancy without the doctor having to invest in capital improvements (see chapter 15). Such a policy does not preclude a physician from spending money to customize his own suite decoration to whatever degree of elegance he may want. It does mean that a physician who does not want or cannot afford to spend anything extra on cabinetry, window coverings, floor coverings, elaborate decorating, and so forth, would not have to do so in order to have an operational and attractive office.

If an owner other than the hospital is to manage the building, the same principles must apply. If the form of ownership selected is, for example, a general partnership of all physician tenants or a condominium, then financial contribution as a prerequisite to occupying the building is likely. If this alternative is chosen, the hospital should be aware of the severe restriction it places on the building's usefulness as a recruiting tool.

3. Require medical staff membership as a prerequisite to occupancy (except for commercial establishments).

In a hospital-owned building, medical staff membership of the physician tenants is required to maintain federal income tax exempt status (see chapter

6). Regardless of ownership, however, the requirement for medical staff membership is vital to the building's effectiveness. If the building is to be owned by anyone other than the hospital, then a contractual guarantee should be established on this point. Physicians who are not staff members, but who occupy the building, would not necessarily detract from the hospital, but they would occupy space that could otherwise be filled by physicians who would support the goals and objectives of the institution.

4. Do not assess tenants of the building or allow any guild or auxiliary of the hospital to assess them.

Neither the hospital nor any of its related organizations should be allowed to take advantage of the on-campus location of physicians in this area. Because the physicians are most concerned about this type of activity, a prohibition on assessments should be made in the operating policies well in advance of the building's actual operational phase.

5. Continue the active involvement of the medical office building advisory committee in policy and disciplinary matters relating to the office building.

Although the advisory committee will not meet as frequently after the office building becomes operational, it should still be a functioning entity. In the event new policies need to be set or old ones amended, the advisory committee should be the body to do it. In addition, if problems arise with a tenant physician, the committee should be the body to determine action. For example, if a physician were seriously delinquent in paying his rent, the advisory committee should assist the hospital in dealing with the situation and talking with the physician. If the doctor failed to respond to the committee, then the committee would recommend appropriate action to be taken by the hospital.

The problem of a physician being seriously delinquent in paying his rent is usually symptomatic of other problems, and an alert administrator often will be able to work with the physician to help solve those problems, thus avoiding any need for action against him. The establishment of this policy of continuing advisory committee involvement does, however, assure tenant physicians that they will be continuously represented in the building's management.

6. Base changes in building tenancy on the established specialty composition.

This policy may seem somewhat redundant in relation to the first operating policy. However, the importance of maintaining a balanced referral group is such that a policy statement is needed. It should simply state that when a physician retires or moves out of the building for any reason, his space must be filled by a physician of the same specialty. That is, if a primary care physician moves out, he must be replaced by another primary care physician.

This policy is not inflexible, however. The advisory committee should review periodically the tenant specialty composition and adjust it to changing community needs and/or hospital programs. Thus, a controlled but flexible specialty composition can be maintained throughout the life of the building, assuring the physician tenants of good referral patterns and the hospital of a broad base of support.

7. Establish a policy of noninterference in the private practice of tenant physicians.

A good policy of noninterference will simply state that the physician is free to practice within his suite without any limitations, other than those spelled out in the code of ethics of the medical staff. That statement means the hospital cannot use the building to pressure the physician to practice at the hospital or to require him to admit patients to it. It also means that the hospital will not draw up rules or regulations that govern his practice within his suite.

Some physicians are fearful of hospital control of medicine and view the medical office building as a "foot in the door" leading to the hospital's dictating how the doctor is to practice. If no restrictions, other than those already required to be a medical staff member, are placed on the physician, then he can be more secure about moving into the building and will, in turn, be a better satisfied tenant.

8. Establish a policy of noncompetition between the private, on-campus physicians and the hospital.

This policy is actually the reverse side of policy 7, which says the hospital will not interfere with the physician's private practice. Conversely, this policy says the physician will not use his private practice on campus to go into competition with the hospital; that is, he will not take inpatients to his private office for such services as X ray and laboratory, for the purpose of collecting the revenue for these services himself.[1] Nor will he sell laboratory or x-ray services to other physicians or their patients at the expense of hospital provided outpatient services.

This policy can be extremely important when ownership other than by the hospital is being considered. Most other owners will want to establish competing laboratory, x-ray, and other ancillary services because of the anticipated income. A hospital would be foolish, however, to let its own campus be developed for the purpose of competition.

9. Allow the physician to have whatever equipment he wants in his office.

This policy is a continuation of policy 8. Although the physician agrees not to compete with the hospital in the sale of such services as laboratory and X ray, he certainly should be able to have whatever laboratory and x-ray equipment he wants for use of his nonhospitalized patients in his own private practice. Many hospitals want to prohibit the physician from having his own laboratory and x-ray equipment, but that would be classified as interference in his private practice. Most physicians will not want to duplicate the expensive equipment available to them through the hospital, but if they want to, it must be their prerogative.

10. Make available high-quality, convenient, fast, and reasonably priced ancillary outpatient services for the physicians on a strictly voluntary basis.

This policy is the conclusion of the previous three. If the hospital makes available laboratory, x-ray, and other services that are convenient, fast, high-quality, and reasonably priced, most physicians will opt to take advantage of them for their private patients. Such services should, however, be on a completely voluntary basis, with the option mentioned previously for the physician to have his own facilities for his own patients.

11. Establish a hospital policy of equal treatment for all physicians, whether tenants or not.

Doctors fear that the development of an on-campus medical office building will lead to the hospital's giving preference to on-campus physicians in such areas as admitting patients and scheduling surgery. For that reason a policy of equal treatment for all physicians needs to be set early in the project's development. After the building is completed and occupied, patients will be admitted and surgery will be scheduled on the same basis as before. When beds are short, the most seriously ill patient will get the bed. The hospital must set specific policies governing these procedures. If these policies are clearly stated and enforced, numerous problems and divisions in the medical staff can be avoided, and good working relationships, enhanced.

12. Give office building employees the same privileges as hospital employees in parking, training programs, use of the employee cafeteria, and so forth.

Just which hospital privileges can be extended to office building employees will vary from place to place. Basically, however, this policy accomplishes two objectives. It contributes to the attractiveness of the office building as a place for the physician to practice because it provides benefits to his employees that he would not otherwise be able to provide. It also promotes better relationships between the hospital and office building employees. Primarily, it encourages the two employee groups to come in contact with each other and to get to know each other better. The objectives are greater rapport and understanding of each other's problems and cooperation between the two groups.

13. Establish clearcut policies concerning parking.

Parking problems are a major irritation to physicians. They should be avoided through well thought-out policies. When they do occur, they should be solved promptly. A typical parking policy would be for all physicians to maintain their privilege to park in the hospital's doctors' parking area. If a parking garage is constructed in conjunction with the office building, the physician tenant would be given the option of continuing to park in the free physicians' parking area or of using the garage at the normal monthly fee charged. As previously stated, if the hospital provides employee parking, office building employees should be allowed to park there. They might also be given the option of paying for space in a new garage or an adjacent parking lot. Fairness of this policy is extremely important; however, the specifics will vary widely according to local circumstances.

14. Establish consistent office building hours and a system for doctors to enter when the building is closed.

One of the primary factors governing this policy is security. If the building is hospital owned, if it is near enough to the hospital, and if the hospital has sufficient security people available, the building might stay open 24 hours a day, just as the hospital does. More than likely, however, such a liberal policy will not be possible. Most buildings will be open to the public during specific hours every day—8 a.m. to 8 p.m., for example—and remain locked the rest of the time. During the hours the building is locked, security guards should make regular rounds. Because doctors may choose to work late or meet patients at their offices during off-hour emergencies, at least one door to the building should be keyed so that any key that opens an individual suite will also open that door. Thus, physicians can come and go as they please at any hour. In addition, that same key might be designed to operate one of the elevators in a multistory building.

Security is a major problem in medical office buildings for reasons such as drug-related thefts. The landlord has a responsibility to maintain the building in as secure a manner as possible, as well as make it accessible to its tenants.

15. Clean and maintain the building to the same high-quality standards of the hospital.

Because the on-campus medical office building reflects on the hospital, regardless of who owns it, the hospital must require that any owner clean and maintain the building to predetermined high standards. This policy will present little problem to the hospital, but other owners may balk at it, because of the additional expense it would require of them. If the hospital wishes to protect its reputation, however, this policy is not an option.

16. Determine which housekeeping services will be provided by the landlord, and state what will and will not be included in the tenant's rental or other agreement.

This policy avoids tenant/landlord conflict. Typically, housekeeping services might be provided Monday through Friday, possibly Saturday. Housekeeping would be done in the evening, and cleaning services might include the following:

- Cleaning floors—damp mopping or vacuuming
- Dusting—furniture, cleared surfaces, pictures, doorjambs, plastic plants
- Emptying ashtrays
- Emptying wastebaskets
- Cleaning bathroom fixtures
- Cleaning counter tops where no equipment or merchandise is sitting
- Vacuuming upholstered furniture
- Cleaning windows and sills (about once a month)
- Scrubbing tiles in bathroom (about once a month)
- Cleaning corridors and public areas

Cleaning services that would not be provided might include the following:

- Cleaning around microscopes or other breakable equipment
- Cleaning desk tops that have not been cleared away prior to the arrival of housekeeping personnel

An additional feature that the hospital can provide that ordinary landlords do not provide is special housekeeping assistance during the day. For example, housekeeping personnel could be called upon to clean up in cases of accidents, spills, or other similar situations.

17. Determine maintenance services to be provided by the landlord, and state what will and will not be included in the tenant's rental or other agreement.

Whereas the housekeeping policy addresses the daily care of the suite, this policy addresses the long-term care. Typical maintenance services that might be included in a tenant's rent are as follows:

- Lighting fixtures (other than the physician's own lamps)—maintaining bulbs and tubes, keeping fixtures in good working order
- Plumbing—leaking faucets, clogged toilets, keeping the system in good operating order
- Heating and air-conditioning—repairing broken thermostats, changing filters, keeping the system in good working order
- Periodic refurbishing of standard suite finishes— painting every five years, new vinyl floor covering as needed for wear
- Repair of general damage to the building and suites (other than that caused by the tenants themselves)

The type of maintenance services that would not be included might be the following:

- Additions or alterations to the suite done for the convenience of the tenant
- Maintenance of the tenant's own equipment
- Repair of damage caused by the tenant
- Replacement or refurbishing of optional suite finishes—wall coverings, carpets, and similar items

18. Establish a policy of uniformity in corridors, including doors and signs.

From the corridor all suites should look the same. Doctors should not be allowed to use fancy doors or other adornments in the corridor to make their suites distinguishable from the others. Instead, a policy that establishes standard doors and signs is best. Ideally, the owner should provide the uniform signs for each physician's door. He should also provide directory strips on each floor and in the main lobby or lobbies. This policy will maintain the aura of professionalism and quality throughout the building.

19. State clearly what the landlord's insurance policies cover and what must be covered by the physician's private policy.

Usually, the landlord will provide fire and extended-coverage insurance and public liability on the public areas of the building—elevators, corridors, parking lots, and such. The physician, himself, is responsible for public and professional liability in his own suite. He is also responsible for personal property insurance. Although specifics of policies may vary, this type of division of responsibility is common. For the protection of both landlord and tenant, a clear policy needs to be established before the building moves into the operational phase.

20. Establish a policy on sharing and/or subleasing space and on selling space.

If a physician is a rental tenant, the usual policy is for him to be able to share the space with another doctor on the staff, if he so chooses. A policy needs to state, however, that he alone can be the tenant, and if he vacates the space, it reverts back to the hospital. He cannot sublease the space without hospital approval. This policy is designed to protect the specialty composition in the building. It also prevents someone from circumventing the waiting list by subleasing.

If the physician is an owner-tenant, the building needs a policy that allows the hospital the first right of refusal in purchasing the physician's equity if he chooses to sell. A potentially unpopular policy, but one that the hospital needs to have in a physician-owned building, is that the physician must sell his equity if he moves out and must not be permitted to rent his suite (in the case of a condominium) to someone else, thus disrupting the planned specialty group. In a rental situation, these policies are a rather simple matter. Writing them into and enforcing them in an ownership agreement with individual physicians is considerably more difficult and complicated. The hospital should proceed with caution. It should be noted that if "the tenant" consists of a group of physicians, the same policies apply to the group as apply to the individual.

21. Set a date for paying rent.

Setting a date for payment of rent, with a possible grace period, is a simple policy matter. It prevents problems later and gives the physician a guideline for paying his rent. It also allows the advisory committee to speak to a physician about late payment if that becomes a problem. If late payment of rent is a problem, it is usually symptomatic of deeper problems, signaling the physician's need for assistance and counsel by the administrator or the medical staff members.

22. Allow physicians to move out of the building whenever they want to.

One of the most destructive moves a hospital can make is to try to keep a physician in the office building if he wants to leave. If the physicians are bound by a lease, it should be no more restrictive than the terms on which the doctor practices at the hospital. That is, if he wants to move out, his resignation from the medical staff should constitute breaking the lease and allow him to vacate the building. If he is removed from the medical staff for disciplinary reasons, he should be required to move out. If he becomes disabled, retires, or dies, he or his estate should be released from the lease. For a hospital to go against an estate of a doctor for the remainder of a lease would be incomprehensible. The hospital wants to have the space occupied by an active physician; it does not want a financial settlement.

23. Spell out all policies clearly, have them approved by the medical office building advisory committee and the governing board of the hospital, and distribute the policies to each prospective tenant.

The next chapter discusses the fact that some hospitals actually use an agreed upon set of operating policies in lieu of a lease. Some hospitals will not go that far. What is important is that the operating policies be established and approved by the medical office building advisory committee and the governing board of the hospital and/or owners and distributed to all prospective tenants. Some of the policies will be made a part of the lease or rental or purchase agreement. Others will simply be understandings of how business is to be conducted or how the hospital will act in relation to the office building. This mutual acceptance of the operating policies is vital, because it prevents many potential misunderstandings.

NOTES

1. A hospital rule on this point was upheld in *Cobb County-Kennestone Hospital v. Price 249 S.E. 2d 581 (GA., 1978)*.

CHAPTER 12

Leases and Contractual Agreements

To present detailed information on every type of lease or contractual agreement a hospital is likely to encounter in the medical office building development process would require a book in itself. For that reason, this chapter focuses primarily on the hospital-owned building, with special emphasis on the rental or lease agreement between the hospital and its physician tenants and the hospital and its commercial tenants. In addition, some basic guidelines are set forth concerning contractual agreements that are likely to arise when physician or investor ownership on hospital land is involved.

Because laws vary widely from state to state, the information that follows is somewhat general and is designed to be customized by the individual hospital. Each hospital is advised to engage the most qualified and experienced legal assistance it can obtain before entering into any type of legal agreement, particularly when ownership other than that by the hospital is being developed.

LEASES AND RENTAL AGREEMENTS WITH THE PHYSICIAN TENANT

Hospitals operating medical office buildings today practice a wide variety of options in the types of rental agreements and/or leases they use. Some hospitals have no lease at all. Others have multipage leases written in the most complicated legal wording. In between are a variety of other options. To categorize these options, however, four general types of agreements might be listed: the oral or gentlemen's agreement, the letter of understanding, the short-form lease, and the long-form lease.

Oral or Gentlemen's Agreement

Operating on the premise of the mutual goals and concerns of the hospital and its medical staff, a number of hospitals operate medical office buildings on the basis of an oral or gentlemen's agreement. The rationale for operating the office building without a lease is simply that the hospital operates all its services for use by the physician without a contractual agreement or guarantee signed by the physician. Many hospitals believe that the office building should be no exception and that it, like the hospital, does not need a contractual agreement if it is operated properly. The physician will admit patients and prescribe hospital treatment as long as the patient care and services provided are of high quality. Likewise, he will usually continue to occupy his office and practice on campus as long as the office building is run properly. In addition, many hospitals find the "no-lease" policy an effective marketing tool, especially when physicians are apprehensive about renting from the hospital.

Except for two factors, probably more on-campus medical office buildings would be operated without leases. First, many lenders today require leases. Second, in this day of increasing emphasis on legal matters and technicalities, many physicians want all agreements to be in written, legal form. Nonetheless, many hospitals still operate medical office buildings using only the gentlemen's agreement.

One of those hospitals is Baptist Memorial Hospital, Memphis. It operates four medical office buildings on the basis of oral agreements with the physicians. The hospital distributes a set of operating policies to the tenants, but those policies are signed by the hospital only. Perhaps a reflection of changing trends, however, is the fact that a new office building recently constructed adjacent to Baptist's new satellite hospital in the suburbs utilizes a lease. The existing office buildings around the main hospital will continue, for the most part, to operate on the basis of oral agreements.

Letter of Understanding

One step beyond the oral agreement is the letter of understanding. It is a simple statement in which the hospital agrees to rent space and the physician agrees to take the space and pay rent. Some provisions are outlined in the letter, but the concept is to keep the relationship between the hospital and the physician as simple as possible. Many hospitals use the letter of understanding successfully, usually in conjunction with a set of operating policies agreed upon by the board of the hospital and the medical office building advisory committee.

Appendix A is a typical example of a letter of understanding.

Short-Form Lease

Because of the requirements of some lenders, the preferences of the physicians, or other reasons, many hospitals prefer to use a formalized lease as the rental agreement between the hospital and the physician. Some leases are brief, mentioning only basic matters, whereas others are quite comprehensive. Some hospitals prefer the short-form lease because of the desire to avoid complicated legal entanglements with the medical staff and to let the physician know that the lease is not being designed to entrap him. Other hospitals prefer to spell out numerous covenants in order to avoid misunderstandings concerning the building and its operation. Either point of view can be valid, depending on local circumstances, the relationship between the hospital and its physicians, and legal precedents in the area.

An example of a short-form lease and some discussion of its covenants are presented in appendix B.

Long-Form Lease

A comparison of a short-form lease with a long-form lease will indicate the degree to which leases may vary. The long-form lease, shown and discussed in appendix C, is presented because it demonstrates almost every covenant that is normally included in a lease between a hospital and tenant physicians. For the most part, it is a lease stated in simple, understandable language. It is followed by a few additional covenants that sometimes appear in hospital-owned medical office building leases.

A subject that sometimes arises in relation to leases concerns restrictions by some church-related hospitals, primarily Roman Catholic, on medical practices that, although legal, are considered by the church to be morally unacceptable. Generally, the procedures found to be objectionable would be abortion, euthanasia, and direct surgical sterilization. The courts have upheld lease covenants prohibiting these and other procedures when the lease was clearly stated.

Moral Codes

Attorney Richard J. Ciecka has stated the matter clearly. He says:[1]

"The rules of judicial construction indicate that in drafting a restrictive covenant for inclusion in the doctor's lease Catholic health care institutions should:

1. Absolutely and in the clearest language prohibit those procedures to which they as Catholics are unalterably opposed;
2. Enumerate those procedures that are to be conditionally allowed and attach exhibits to the lease that carefully delineate the parameters within which these procedures may be performed;
3. Establish a procedure by which the existence of defaults and the propriety of questionable procedures can be determined."

Ciecka went on to provide some examples of covenants that might appear in Roman Catholic leases.

"In those dioceses which prohibit all direct surgical sterilization, the covenant might read:

Lessee will not allow the premises to be used for the performance of abortions, euthanasia, or direct surgical sterilizations whether or not they are medically indicated.

"In those dioceses where the *Ethical and Religious Directives for Catholic Health Facilities* are interpreted in such a way as to permit medically indicated sterilizations, the covenant might read:

Lessee will not allow the premises to be used for the performance of abortions, euthanasia, or direct surgical non-medically indicated sterilization. The lessee, in determining whether a sterilization is medically indicated, is to follow the criteria established by the medical-moral committee of _____Hospital, pertinent parts of which are attached to and made a part of this lease as Exhibit_____."[2]

Not every medical office building operated by a Roman Catholic hospital will include such lease covenants. Some hospitals depend on careful screening of physician tenants and upon a gentlemen's agreement between the tenants and the hospital. Other hospitals, rather than include such covenants within a lease, will simply require that the same code of ethics practiced in the hospital apply to practice within the office building.

Choosing the Right Agreement or Lease

Just what form of rental agreement or lease a hospital chooses depends much on the individual situation. Basically, the hospital should never wish to get into a litigation with a medical staff member, for such action has a detrimental effect on all hospital/physician relations. Consequently, some hospitals avoid long and complicated lease agreements. On the other hand, many hospitals believe that the best guarantee against misunderstanding is a lease that spells out all details of the agreement. Some physicians may feel more comfortable with such an arrangement, and many lenders may require it.

However, the one thing that should be avoided in all agreements is any attempt on the part of the hospital to trap or control the physicians or in any way secure their loyalty through an entangling legal agreement. It will not work, and it is bad business.

In the final analysis, a lease does not guarantee that a physician will practice medicine at a particular hospital or that he will support its services. Only a hospital that provides high-quality patient care and an office building that is run with the best interests of the physicians at heart can capture the loyalty of the physicians and maintain it. Consequently, whatever the type of rental agreement or lease, it should be designed with only one end in mind: the development of understanding, good working relationships, and a smoothly operating building.

LEASES WITH COMMERCIAL TENANTS

Whereas the hospital may choose to have oral agreements or letters of understanding with tenant physicians, a lease agreement is mandatory for commercial tenants.

Commercial leases vary and are usually negotiated with each tenant, depending upon the enterprise. As a rule of thumb, rental rates for commercial space are 50 percent higher than rental rates for physician office space. In addition, they also may carry a percentage of gross sales so that the tenant pays whichever amount is greater—the base rental or the percentage of gross sales. However, the rental rate and percentage are both negotiable items, and high volume, high profit enterprises such as pharmacies usually pay higher rates than lower-profit businesses such as food service operations.

A typical commercial lease (in this case, a pharmacy) is shown in appendix D. The example was selected because it covers the most important covenants of a commercial lease and it is written in clearly understandable language. Additional discussion of the commercial lease appears in the appendix.

It should go without saying that any hospital developing any lease, whether with tenant physicians or with commercial establishments, should do so only with the help of qualified, experienced counsel. All general lease provisions presented in the preceding discussions and appendix D are just that. Every lease must be customized to meet the requirements of state and local laws as well as the needs of the individual situation.

LAND LEASES

Land is becoming more precious every day, and the hospital that is fortunate enough to own sufficient land for growth and development is wise to keep control of it. Consequently, when ownership other than by the hospital is considered for the on-campus medical office building, a land lease is usually involved. When a hospital leases rather than sells land, it not only maintains flexibility for future development, but it also is able to retain some control over the building's development and operation.

Land leases, however, tend to be quite lengthy and complicated—too lengthy, in fact, for an example to be presented here. However, three essential guidelines can be given, to help protect the hospital developing a land lease.

1. Do not subordinate ownership of the land to the mortgage holder.

In the event the building should get into financial difficulty, the hospital does not want to be in the position of losing its land to the mortgage holder. It does not want to have to buy back both the building and the land in order to have the project survive and the hospital campus remain intact. Consequently, if possible, the hospital should not subordinate its interest in the land.

However, most lenders will either require subordination of the land or a more substantial capital outlay on the front end by the owners of the building. If front-end cash is a problem, as it might be with a physician partnership, then the hospital's desire not to risk its land could affect the financial feasibility of the project. The decision is a complex one, and the risk must be weighed against the potential return and against other ownership alternatives that would not require subordination. Only the hospital can make that decision, but it would be wise to consider long and hard before subordinating its land.

2. Utilize clauses and covenants to the fullest.

Clauses and covenants in the land lease are one of the few ways that the hospital can maintain some control over an office building it does not own. Consequently, they should be utilized to the fullest to protect the needs and interests of the hospital. Chapter 5 touched on some areas that could and could not be included in a land lease. Some of the more important aspects that need to be addressed in the lease include:

- An all-medical, or health-care related, building
- Medical staff membership as a requirement of tenancy
- Means for controlling the physician specialty composition
- Commercial services related to the medical needs of the building tenants and not in competition with the hospital
- Provision for holding space vacant for recruitment
- Provision for hospital utilization of space that it might need
- Initial quality of architectural design, including esthetics, design efficiency, and functional efficiency

- Standards for high-quality construction and materials
- Standards for maintenance

In addition to these covenants, the hospital also needs to make sure that the land lease includes an adjustment for taxes, a periodic adjustment of the rental rate in relation to inflation (every 5 to 10 years), an option to buy back the building on reasonable terms, and a clause that states the landlord's failure to exercise his rights does not constitute waiver of these rights (this clause is easily overlooked). These covenants and clauses are particular ones that the hospital should not omit. In addition, the lease will need to include all the standard clauses and covenants of a commercial land lease.

3. Retain a qualified, experienced attorney and listen to his advice.

The importance of a well drafted document with the hospital's interests protected cannot be overstressed, nor can the means for obtaining that document: the counsel of both a well qualified and an *experienced* attorney. Experience is emphasized because even some of the most qualified attorneys do not have the specialized knowledge necessary to draft a good land lease between a hospital and owners of the medical office building on hospital property.

One hospital that made the mistake of signing a land lease without careful scrutiny by experienced attorneys now lives with a nightmare: an owner who has offended the medical staff, causing many of the doctors not only to refuse tenancy in the building, but also to leave the community; a building that is occupied by tenants whose businesses are totally unrelated to the hospital and its objectives; the alternative of buying back the building, but at a cost roughly $5 million higher than if the hospital had developed and owned the building itself; and a clause in the land lease that prohibits anyone else, including the hospital, from developing an office building on hospital property as long as the lease is in effect. The importance of good legal counsel cannot be overemphasized.

PARTNERSHIP AGREEMENTS AND CONDOMINIUM RULES AND REGULATIONS

The last major contractual area in which a hospital may find itself involved with regard to a medical office building includes partnership agreements and/or condominium rules and regulations.

"There is no such thing as a simple set of condominium rules and regulations," said attorney Lewis Donelson.[3] "In fact, condominium rules and regulations are one of the most complicated legal documents around.

"Partnership agreements may not be quite as complicated," he continued, "but they are certainly a potential source of problems and misunderstandings. Problems arise when there is a difference between an individual's equity ownership and the space leased. The agreement needs to be clear on what happens when a doctor leaves or dies: how will the sale of the partnership be handled. Provisions must be made for making decisions. Unless otherwise stated, each general partner has an equal vote, and decisions are made by majority rule. A simple agreement will not suffice."

Because of the complicated nature of these agreements, no attempt will be made here to delve into a detailed discussion of them. If the hospital wants to protect its interest and see that good agreements result, it should, first of all, involve itself in the drafting of these agreements. If the hospital is the initiator of the project, it can have considerable input into the condominium rules or the type of partnership agreement. This input can both improve the quality of the documents from the hospital's point of view and cover potential trouble spots.

Second, the hospital should, once again, seek the counsel of qualified, experienced attorneys. No single statement is more important nor sums up this chapter more completely.

NOTES

1. Ciecka, Richard J. Moral-legal considerations of medical office building sponsorship. *Hospital Progress.* November 1974.
2. Ibid.
3. Donelson, Lewis, attorney. Interview. Memphis, August 1978.

CHAPTER 13

Programming the Project

The development of a program for the hospital-related medical office building is prerequisite to the development of a properly structured and architecturally successful building. Program development is that aspect of the project that translates planned hospital programs, community and medical staff needs, and the needs analysis data of the feasibility study into an objective-oriented building. The programming process takes into account the hospital master plan, the marketing plan of the hospital, as well as the individual input of the medical staff members, with the end result being a program that defines occupancy for the building, the size of the structure, and a time frame in which it is to be developed.

The importance of the program is that the office building is not developed as an end in itself, with size based on the number of doctors signed up and occupancy based on who happens to be available. It is that vital aspect of the project development that links every major design decision to the needs and goals of the hospital, the medical staff, and the community.

PROGRAMMING OCCUPANCY

Occupants of an on-campus medical office building can usually be grouped into three major categories—physician tenants, hospital departments and/or diagnostic and treatment services, and commercial establishments. In order for a building to be designed to the appropriate size for long-rage effectiveness, the space requirements of each of these three tenant groups must first be projected.

As the hospital begins thinking of physician tenants in real terms, it will want to consider the number of physicians usually needed to support the number of beds in operation. In an urban area a good rule of thumb is one physician to every five beds. That would mean that a hospital of 200 beds would need the equivalent of 40 full-time physicians actively admitting patients. That figure should then be weighed against the consideration that about 25 percent of the hospital's active admitters are never likely to move into the building. They either already own offices, are permanently settled as part of a group, or are not interested in an on-campus location. Although this particular rule of thumb is not scientifically defined, it addresses the issue of whether or not the

Physician Occupancy

hospital wants to plan its on-campus office facilities in relation to the number of beds in operation and planned for the future.

In a similar manner, the hospital master plan and marketing plan must play an important role in programming, for not only does the hospital need to relate the occupancy of the building to the number of beds, but also to the types of services offered and/or planned by the hopital. For example, if the hospital is planning the addition of a particular service, it will want to program space into the office building for the physicians needed to staff that new service.

In the discussion of the feasibility study in chapter 3, mention was made of the need for the coordination of master planning of the hospital and programming of the office building. In addition, a brief description of the types of information to be gathered in the analysis-of-need section of the feasibility study was included. At this point, project planners must take the needs analysis data, the master plans for the hospital, and the knowledge of the number of physicians needed to support the hospital and begin to translate them into real numbers.

Community factors

The first consideration is the demographic and health facilities information developed in the needs analysis. Is the community growing, changing, or dwindling? Is it economically depressed or thriving? What services are being adequately provided to the community by one or a combination of several hospitals? What services are needed? In addition, the hospital should consider the general market for office space in the area, such as prevailing rental rates and the availability of suitable space, as well as the existing relationships between hospital administration and the medical staff. These factors, when linked to the current size and services of the hospital, tend to indicate the hospital's need to be conservative or aggressive in projecting the needed occupancy of the medical office building.

Physician interest

The next step will be to consider the information collected in the study of medical staff interest. In that study physicians were interviewed in depth, without a member of the administration being present (see chapter 10). During those interviews, each physician had the opportunity to express the degree of interest he might have in the project, to discuss what factors he would consider essential for his participation in the project, and to determine what his space needs would be if he were to move into the building. At that time some physicians stated a definite interest in the project, some were definitely not interested, and others stated interest but will make up their minds more completely as time passes. On the basis of these interviews, the number of physicians who are definitely interested in the project can be determined.

The hospital should realize that in these interviews the physicians expressed interest, not commitment. It would be unfair to the physician to have asked him for commitment at that early stage, before specific plans, time schedules, and rental rates or ownership options had been determined. In addition, if the number of physicians who expressed interest was fairly low, the hospital should not be disturbed. Because of sensitive referral relationships and because some physicians may be planning to leave a group or a partnership, a number of physicians will indicate their interest only after the project has become a certainty, that is, after construction is under way or even substantially completed. Experience has shown that on the average only about one-third of a building's total occupants will definitely express interest at the early interview stage. Another third will usually make the decision during the construction phase of the project, and the final third are usually physicians recruited to fill medical staff needs or who decide to move in after the building has been completed.

Specialty composition

To the number of physicians who have expressed interest should now be added the number of physicians who need to be recruited in order to balance the specialty composition of the medical staff. The medical staff master plan, developed in conjunction with the medical staff profile in the feasibility study, will indicate the numbers of physicians needed and their specialties.

In specific, a good medical staff profile will have examined the medical staff by specialty and subspecialty in relation to the general rule of thumb for a balanced medical staff:

Internal medicine and specialties of medicine	30%
General surgeons and specialties of surgery, including a few dentists and oral surgeons	30%
Obstetrics and gynecology	20%
Pediatrics	10%
Other, including general and family practice	10%

This comparison will have shown gross imbalances, if any, in the specialty composition and pinpointed major areas where improvement is needed.

In more detail, a well analyzed profile will have compared the current medical staff to physician-to-population ratios for the service area. In a community with only one hospital, such a study will have indicated what specialists can be supported by the population base and the number of generalists who are needed to care for the people in the service area. In more highly urban areas, the physician-to-population ratios will have been related to the entire community, with consideration given to the number of physicians practicing primarily at other hospitals. This information will not only give the hospital considerable insight into the numbers and types of physicians needed and who can be supported by the community, but also a realistic picture of specialists for whom to program space in the building, based on physicians already practicing within the community and those who can or should be recruited.

In this manner, the hospital may discover, for example, that although no oncologist is practicing in the service area, the population is sufficient to support one, and, in fact, cancer patients are having to be referred to distant cities for treatment because of the lack of an oncologist. In such a case, the hospital would want to program space in the office building so that an oncologist could be recruited.

Once the research aspects of the medical staff profile are completed, much of the work in translating those statistics into specific numbers of physician specialists to be included in the building is worked out jointly by the project planners and the medical office building advisory committee (see chapter 9). Frequently, in fact, if a particular specialty is needed or if additional physicians in a specialty are needed, the physicians themselves will mention these needs during their personal interviews. Consequently, the physicians should be a primary source for pinpointing voids or weak spots in the composition of the medical staff.

Replacing aging doctors

Finally, the hospital must now consider the age of its medical staff, and program space in the building for physicians to be recruited to replace aging doctors. If the hospital is to maintain a balanced and viable medical staff, it must be aware of physicians' practice trends as they relate to age. The medical staff profile will have correlated age and admissions and may well have indicated specialty areas in which the hospital is vulnerable to potential retirements. In addition, hospitals should be aware that American Medical Association studies indicate that the average physician peaks around age 50, with his practice gradually tapering off until he retires completely.[1]

For these reasons, a hospital developing an on-campus medical office building should develop a five-year program to recruit new physicians to replace physicians 55 years of age and older. This replacement does not mean that the new recruits will push the older doctors out; on the contrary, the older physicians are usually the hospital's most enthusiastic supporters. The intent of this recruitment program is to attract young physicians to begin building their practices during the time that the aging doctors are decreasing their practices and considering retirement. Often, older physicians encourage this process by allowing new physicians to join their established practices. The replacement is planned and gradual and prevents the hospital from finding itself in the position of having, for example, five or six of its heaviest admitters retire over a short period of time, with a resultant sharp drop in admissions.

In addition, this five-year recruitment program is usually set up so that the first two years of the program would take place during the time the office building is being developed and constructed. The remaining recruitment would be carried out during the first three years of operation of the building.

The preliminary program for physician occupancy would then include (1) the total number of current medical staff members who have expressed interest in locating in the building and those who experience has shown identify themselves after construction starts, (2) the number of physicians to be recruited to balance the medical staff composition and provide needed new specialists (the total needed would be reduced by approximately 25 percent to allow for those new doctors who would not want to locate in the building), and (3) the number of physicians to be recruited to replace aging physicians (again, this number is reduced by approximately 25 percent). The total obtained from adding these three groups together will be a good preliminary indication of the number of physicians for whom space should be programmed.

Hospital Occupancy

In addition to programming space for physician tenants, the hospital must consider its own needs and how the medical office building will relate to the hospital. For example, prior to the development of an on-campus medical office building, ambulatory care in the hospital is usually centered around the emergency department and outpatient clinics. With the development of the medical office building, however, ambulatory care will now be centered in the office building, by virtue of the physicians located there and the patients who will visit them. For that reason, the hospital may want to examine its whole concept of ambulatory care and make full utilization of the office building as an ambulatory care center. It will need to consider whether to include such services as day surgery, laboratory, X ray, patient education, physical therapy and rehabilitation, chronic hemodialysis, occupational therapy, mental health programs, multiphasic screening, and similar outpatient services within the building. A medical staff auditorium, conference room, and teaching rooms are other facilities that should be considered for inclusion in the medical office building.

Particularly if a hospital is crowded for space, is heavily utilized, and wants to expand in the most economical manner, it will want to evaluate carefully its own needs as it develops the occupancy program for the medical office building. Office building construction is considerably less expensive than hospital construction because of less stringent code requirements. Consequently, the shifting of some nontreatment functions, as well as outpatient services, to the medical office building can provide an attractive means for creating more in-hospital space. Medical records, central supply, public relations, and some administrative functions are of the kind that might be relocated. By and large, as long as the hospital does not include patient beds (overnight confinement) and general anesthesia or certain medical gases within the office building, the code requirements for the office building will remain unaffected, and construction can be considerably less expensive than for hospital expansion. For special hospital services such as day surgery, it may be possible to isolate the service from a code standpoint so that the remainder of the medical office building is not adversely affected.

The hospital must also consider in advance the increase in utilization of the hospital's laboratory and x-ray facilities that the medical office building will generate, provided those services are conveniently located, reasonably priced, and sufficiently fast. The hospital must have the capacity to handle this increased utilization. Many hospitals already have that capacity, and the increase will, in effect, improve efficiency. Others, however, must plan for expansion of these facilities. The hospital needs to decide if it will expand these facilities in their current location, establish branch facilities in the office building, or move some of these facilities to the office building altogether. These planning decisions must be made in the early stages of the project's development so that appropriate space can be programmed into the office building.

Some other areas will need to be coordinated between the office building and the hospital. For example, consideration must be given to whether or not the office building will utilize the hospital's central power plant. Many hospital power plants are large enough to handle the office building requirements, or the expansion of the hospital plant may provide for a more efficient operation, both from a standpoint of energy use and its attendant costs and from a standpoint of ease of maintenance. A remote location for the noisier equipment is often desirable, as well. The hospital must, however, be willing to spend the money necessary to get proper architectural and engineering advice early in order to evaluate properly such areas as energy coordination and conservation. Failure to plan carefully in these areas can be costly as well as detrimental.

Thus, through careful coordination of the hospital's master plan and marketing plan, the hospital must decide specifically what hospital functions, if any, are to be included in the medical office building. These functions should then be itemized individually and added to the preliminary list of occupants for the building.

Commercial Occupancy

Finally, the hospital must consider what commercial occupants are going to be included in the building. Generally, the primary reasons for including commercial services in the office building are to provide convenient services for the physicians, patients, and employees within the building and to provide an additional source of income for the building so that the cost to the physician of practicing there can be kept as low as possible. In short, the commercial services should enhance the marketability of the office building and should contribute to its overall objectives.

The most important commercial services to the physicians, patients, and hospital are laboratory, x-ray services, and pharmacy. Laboratory and X ray have already been touched on in the discussion of possible diagnostic and treatment services to be included in the building, but they should also be considered "commercial" in nature because they may well be leased to independent firms or individuals for operation.

In addition to these three most important services, any number of other related establishments might also be considered for inclusion in the building. Some of the more typical businesses are an optical shop, limb and brace shop, uniform shop, orthopedic shoe shop, restaurant or coffee shop, hospital supply company, and barber shop or beauty shop. A number of hospitals also include some hotel rooms in the medical office building. These rooms are usually occupied by families of out-of-town patients in the hospital or out-of-town patients themselves who need only outpatient treatment. Such hotel rooms provide convenient and economical accommodations for those who need to be near the hospital. In addition, the hospital might also consider physician oriented services such as central medical transcription, copying service, general typing, and computer billing.

In deciding which of the many commercial services to program for occupancy in the building, the hospital must consider several factors. First is the fact that the IRS limits commercial establishments in office buildings owned by not-for-profit hospitals. The IRS states that for a building to remain income tax exempt, commercial establishments included in it must be able to show a "causal relationship" to the purpose of the building (see chapter 6). How that causal relationship is interpreted varies somewhat from IRS region to region, but the types of businesses listed above are generally considered acceptable.

A second factor the hospital must consider is the need for the service. For example, a building with no ophthalmologists is not likely to need an optical shop. On the other hand, if several orthopedists are practicing in the building, a good limb and brace shop conveniently located might be both a great asset to the patients and a successful business enterprise. If the hospital currently houses a gift and/or flower shop, it may want to move that shop to the office building, and if it has not previously had room for a gift shop, it might want to operate or lease one for the convenience of hospital visitors.

The two last factors to consider in deciding on commercial services are physician interest in the service and hospital willingness to provide it. For example, the physicians might be highly interested in a medical transcription service and a branch operation of medical records so that they could complete their work more conveniently, but the hospital might be unwilling to go to the effort and expense of setting up such a service. Or, the hospital might be willing to provide computer billing services for the physicians through the hospital computer system, but the doctors might be suspicious of the hospital's having access to their financial records.

The relationship to the purpose of the building, sufficient need, physician interest, and hospital willingness are all factors to be considered as the hospital decides on which commercial services to program into the office building. Development of the commercial enterprises in the building can be tricky business because of these and other factors. Consequently, the hospital is wise to investigate thoroughly before making its decision. For example, one hospital in a large urban area included a uniform shop in its office building. Because the shop was a small operation, however, it could not compete pricewise with other uniform shops in the city, and employees did not use it. The shop had a difficult time paying its rent and generally was a drain on the building, rather than a business asset. In the same building, the hospital rented space to a nationally known fast food operation. Because of stiff competition around the hospital, however, this operation did not do well. As with the uniform shop, the hospital had difficulty collecting rent. In both cases the hospital did not investigate thoroughly enough the real need for these businesses, particularly with regard to the competition already established nearby.

Own, or lease?

After investigating thoroughly and deciding which commercial enterprises to program for inclusion in the building, the hospital has yet another decision to make before the programming of occupancy is complete. That decision is whether the hospital will own and operate the commercial enterprises or whether the space will be leased to private operators. Although this decision does not *have* to be made at this early stage, the next step—programming space—can be far more effective if it is developed in conjunction with the actual shop owners or tenants.

In the areas of greatest concern—pharmacy, laboratory, and X ray—the hospital will usually want to maintain control and will probably want to own these operations outright. The reasons for hospital ownership of these services are two-fold. First, they can be areas of substantial profit, and the hospital will want to protect these sources of outpatient income. Second, the hospital already has capabilities in these areas and will want to prevent competition from diluting the efficiency of the hospital departments.

In the case of laboratory and X ray, the hospital will normally want to handle referrals from the medical office building through its existing facilities, particularly if the hospital's facilities have the capability of handling greater capacity without physical expansion. If the hospital's facilities are already operating at maximum capacity, branch operations may be established in the medical office building to handle the increased work load, or the existing department might be expanded.

The method by which referrals from the office building to the hospital's lab and x-ray departments are handled can be a ticklish proposition. Some doctors will invariably want to work in totally different ways from other doctors. For example, some may want to draw specimens themselves and use the laboratory only for processing them. Other doctors may want the lab to handle everything. In the area of X rays, some physicians may want to read the X rays themselves, without the hospital's radiologist. Others will want the consultation of the radiologist. Billing and third-party reimbursement are other areas that physicians may want to handle in different ways. Consequently, the hospital should be prepared to be flexible and to work with the physicians in developing systems that will be agreeable. Through hospital ownership, usually the most flexible and attractive system for the doctors can be worked out, while protecting the hospital's sources of outpatient income.

Ownership of the pharmacy is a somewhat different matter. Although the hospital will usually want to own this potentially profitable business, it can do so only under certain restrictions. For example, the hospital cannot sell medications and drugs in the retail pharmacy that have been purchased under the not-for-profit hospital's quantity discount. In some cases, the hospital will operate the pharmacy as a separate corporation, with purchasing and storage of pharmaceuticals completely separate from the hospital. In other cases, because of various legal requirements, it is simpler and more practical to lease out the medical office building pharmacy altogether. A thorough study of tax laws, state and local restrictions, if any, and community standards should be made before the hospital decides how to handle pharmacy ownership.

Where other businesses are concerned, the decision on hospital ownership will be primarily a matter of how much expertise the hospital may have and how much it wants to maintain total control over the business versus the expertise of private operators and the hospital's desire not to be involved with the management of the businesses. Whatever the hospital decides, it must be fair in allocating commercial space, especially if it is a community and/or county hospital. It has a responsibility to the community that supports it to be fair to local businessmen in the selection of owners for the various businesses.

Competitive proposals

Usually, the hospital will want to work with the medical office building advisory committee in taking competitive proposals for the various businesses to be included in the building. All bidders would be asked to submit detailed proposals of what they intend to provide and what they expect from the landlord in regard to their space. The following questions and information should be included as part of the standard proposal form:

- What type of commercial business/service will you operate?
- What products or services will you provide or render?
- What days and hours will your shop be open?
- What type organization is yours: individual, partnership, or corporation?
- What would be your inventory value?
- What size shop will you require in square feet? Describe your physical requirements for: store space, work area, storage, toilets, exhaust system.
- What is your rental offer: base plus percentage of gross (based on finished space—walls, floor, ceiling, lighting, roughed-in plumbing, and all utilities)?
- What length of lease will you require (lease term with what options at how many years each)?
- Please submit the following:

References: Number of Years

  Supplier _____   _____
           _____   _____
  Bank   _____   _____
           _____   _____
  Other   _____   _____
           _____   _____

Other store locations:
Current financial statement:
List of financial partners, if any:

On the basis of the information provided in the proposals, the hospital and advisory committee should be able to select stable organizations that have submitted the best financial offers for operation of the businesses.

At this point the preliminary program of occupancy is complete. It consists of a list of physician tenants (both currently interested and to be recruited), a list of hospital services and/or departments to occupy space in the building, and a list of commercial businesses and/or services to be included in the building. On the basis of this preliminary list, the space program or size of the building can now be developed.

PROGRAMMING SPACE

Programming space means combining the academic data of research with the subjective data of perceived needs and blending them into a practical solution—one that will work architecturally and financially. The process begins by assigning space requirements to all tenants listed on the preliminary occupancy program by determining what kind of space and type of suites the physician occupants will need and by assessing the number of square feet that will be needed by each of the hospital and commercial occupants.

From these data a preliminary total of net square feet needed in the building can be derived. In turn, the architects, planners, or consultants use that preliminary total to initiate the design of the building. Because certain building sizes and configurations are more efficient than others, adjustments to the space program may be needed in order to provide an architecturally efficient building. For example, 10,000 square feet of net rentable space per floor is a good and commonly used standard for multistory buildings, because it combines both architectural efficiency with flexible layout potential. On the other hand, if a building is designed with more than 14,000 square feet of net rentable space per floor, spaces are generally too large for good, functional layouts. Thus, the preliminary total square footage may need to be adjusted upward or downward in order to accommodate efficient, functional design.

If adjustments are needed in the space program, the hospital and the planners will need to reevaluate the proposed occupancy for the building, including reexamination of the number and specialties of physicians, hospital functions, commercial establishments, and the number of spaces being held vacant for recruitment. On the basis of this second look, the hospital and the planners can determine whether to make needed adjustments toward a larger or smaller building. Much discretion must be used in this evaluation. However, the tendency of many hospitals is to be too cautious in sizing the building, resulting in a building that will not fully support the hospital, uses up valuable land without providing maximum benefit, does not provide the recruitment facilities necessary to maintain a viable staff, and will force considerably higher construction costs for a second building, if needed.

As the reevaluation of spaces being held for recruitment takes place, the hospital and the planners will want to consider several points. Are the recruitment goals realistic, based on the availability of physicians? Is too large a percentage of space in the building programmed for recruitment? Usually about 30 percent is practical. Can the hospital afford to hold the space vacant in the building while the new doctors are being recruited?

In considering the financial aspects of holding space for recruitment, the hospital must keep in mind the "investment potential" of doing so. For example, if construction of the building costs approximately $70 per square foot, then the cost of a typical suite of 1,000 square feet would be $70,000. The real cost to the hospital of that space is amortization, which is about a 10 percent constant, or $7,000 per year. That is a $7,000 per year investment for a one-to-five year period, depending on how long the space is held open prior to renting. When the physician is recruited, he will generate approximately $300,000 of gross income per year for the hospital.[2] Assuming he settles in the community and practices for 20 years, that investment of between $7,000 and $35,000 would generate about $6 million of income to the hospital, without considering inflation. Conversely, without the office space available, the hospital's ability to recruit that same doctor would be severely hampered.

Finally, the preliminary building as sized will need to be evaluated. The building must be considered according to how much it will cost, how much the hospital can afford, and whether the building as sized will be financially feasible based on its projected operating budget. Again, adjustments in size and structure may be necessary to produce a viable project.

Sizing the building is a subjective undertaking. No "one-two-three" set rules can be laid down to make it clear-cut. The expertise of the building planners and designers and the discretion of the hospital will ultimately determine whether the building is sized appropriately or not. If, however, the preliminary occupancy program, architectural efficiency, and financial feasibility are all considered concurrently, then a viable building size can result.

PROGRAMMING THE TIME FRAME

The third aspect of programming the project is outlining a time frame for its development. It involves understanding how the many separate aspects of the project dovetail into a coordinated effort.

Although projects are going to vary widely according to size, location, and problems that must be taken into account, the same basic phases of development must be programmed for most projects. For example, most undertakings will include preliminary planning, design, construction, startup, and operational phases. The length of time to be programmed for each phase, however, will vary considerably according to the specifics of the project.

For the sake of discussion, a typical project of 60,000 square feet might be developed according to the following time frame (see figure 1, page 146).

Preliminary planning: The entire process of programming the project, including programming the time frame, usually falls within the initial planning stage of the project, that is, within the feasibility study itself. From the time the hospital decides to pursue the question of an on-campus medical office building until the time the feasibility study is completed, requires about three months. That means that at the end of three months the medical staff profile, the evaluation of hospital needs, services and service area, the preliminary interviews with the medical staff to determine interest, the medical staff specialty composition, the preliminary sizing of the building with schematic drawings and site plans, the selection of the best ownership vehicle, and a proposed operating budget to indicate the financial feasibility of the project should all be completed. During this initial time of study, the medical office building advisory committee should be set up and functioning, and the hospital should also start investigating possible alternatives for financing the project.

By the end of this preliminary planning phase, the time frame should be programmed for completion of the project. Not only should the time frame include the project itself, but also it should include any other projects that must be completed in relation to the development of the office building, such as expansion of laboratory facilities or the construction of a parking facility.

Failure to dovetail the related projects with the time frame of the office building can have costly results. For example, one hospital developed a 60-doctor office building and a 400-car parking garage independently of each other, instead of programming a coordinated time frame for the two. As a result, the parking garage was scheduled to begin operation one-and-a-half years before the office building was completed, meaning that it would lose substantial amounts of money during that time. The hospital was unable to get the long-range financing it wanted for the garage. An already expensive project became an even greater financial burden on the hospital, all because of failure to plan early in coordinating related projects with the development of the office building.

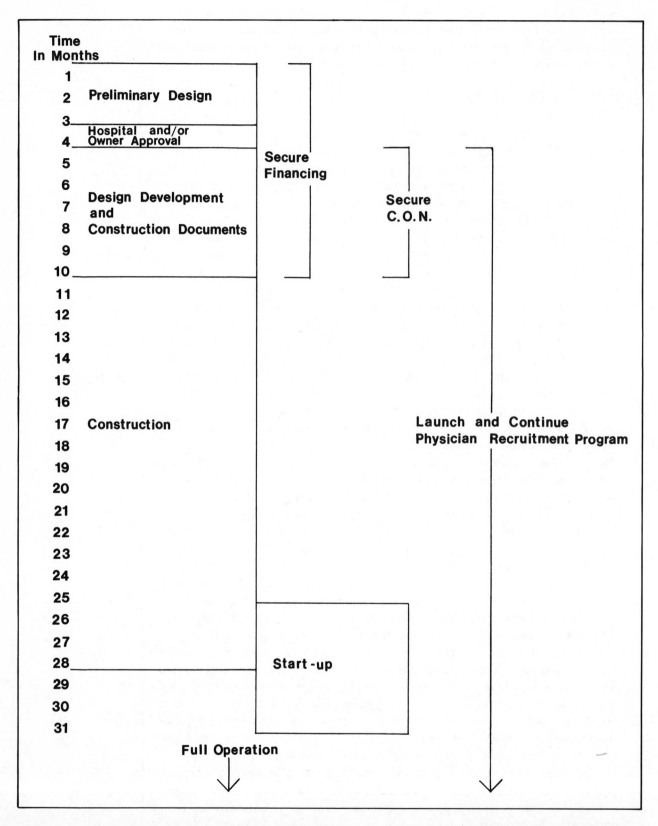

Figure 1. Programming time frame for a typical 60,000-square-foot project is shown in diagrammatic form.

Hospital and/or owner approval: The board of the hospital should be prepared to make a decision on whether or not to proceed with development of the office building as soon as the preliminary planning is completed. Thirty days should be sufficient time to make this decision. Failure to make a prompt decision can ultimately jeopardize the project itself, since the hospital tends to lose credibility with its medical staff. Time delays curb the enthusiasm of the physicians, and since construction costs continue to escalate, any delay adds to the cost of the project.

Design development and construction documents: Up to six more months are usually necessary for the architects and planners to take the schematic drawings that were prepared as a part of the feasibility study and proceed with the design development and construction documents for the building's shell. Because the best time to market the office building is during construction, the hospital should be emphatic in not waiting for interior designs to be completed before the building is put out for bids and construction is begun. Facsimile floor plans and density studies will be completed during this phase in order to facilitate bidding and construction while custom suite designs are being completed (see chapter 16). Although designers will be meeting with building tenants throughout this period in order to begin marketing the building and custom designing the interior spaces, this process will continue throughout much of the construction phase of the building. During this six-month period, the hospital should also complete the certificate of need process and pursue the completion of financial arrangements so that by the time the design and construction bids have been completed, the hospital has financing in hand and can proceed with hiring the contractors. Many projects have been delayed for months because the hospital failed to begin early enough to secure financing, and money was not available when it was needed. Finally, the physician recruitment program needs to begin and gradually intensify throughout the remainder of the project.

Construction: For the actual construction phase of the medical office building, the hospital can program about 18 months. During this time interior suite designs will continue to be planned so that by the time the shell is completed, interior finishing can begin. Near the time all construction is to be completed, suites that are not committed to specific doctors can be designed by prototype, constructed, and held for the specialists to be recruited.

Start-up: No office building is going to be completed one day and filled with tenants the next. Time must be allowed for the physicians to move in as the suites are completed floor by floor. This period is called the start-up phase. In a 60,000-square-foot building, this period would last about six months and would overlap with the construction phase. Doctors would begin moving in as the first suites are finished and while interior finishing continues on other suites. The ideal time to program the beginning of the start-up phase is in July. Presumably the hospital will have been recruiting new physicians during the periods of planning and construction. Because most residents complete their training in June, July is an optimum time to have office space available for them to move in. It is more effective as a recruiting tool, and it means the hospital will not have to hold suites vacant for several months until the new recruits have completed their training. Throughout this start-up phase of the project, the hospital needs to remain flexible in working with the physicians. Some will not be able to move in just as soon as their suites are completed because of existing leases and other problems. Others may need extra effort put in on completing their suites early because of their need to vacate the offices in which they are currently located.

Operation: Usually, by the end of six months the hospital can anticipate that all rented suites will be occupied and most of the major bugs worked out of the building. Although minor problems may need to be handled throughout the first year of operation, the hospital can anticipate business as usual by the end of the six-month start-up period.

A properly programmed time frame can add immeasurably to the success of the project, whereas improper planning can create devastating delays that can cripple the project's effectiveness. A time frame that is presented to the physicians early in the planning stages and is subsequently adhered to throughout the development of the project builds the hospital's credibility with the medical staff. Conversely, a project filled with false starts and delays will dampen the physicians' interest as well as their respect for the hospital. The hospital must also remember that physicians who eventually move into the building must have sufficient lead time and accurate target dates to plan their changes of office location, so that leases can expire or be handled in some manner. Partnerships may be formed, expanded, dissolved, and otherwise changed at the time of the move. The physician's livelihood is involved, and if he is to believe in the hospital and plan adequately for the future, he must have a time frame to work within. Careful and appropriate programming of any project's occupancy, size, and time frame is a prerequisite to its ultimate success.

NOTES

1. Cantwell, James R., editor. *Reference Data on Profile of Medical Practice.* 1975-76 ed. Chicago: American Medical Association, 1976, p. 161.
2. Figure based on analysis of fiscal data supplied by clients of Drexel Toland & Associates, Inc., 1980.

CHAPTER **14**

Planning in Relation to the Medical Complex

Despite the difficulty of looking ahead 5, 10, or 20 years, foresight is an essential aspect of developing an on-campus medical office building. The hospital needs a clear picture of where it is headed and where it will be down the health care road. It needs to develop its long-range goals and objectives, based on a realistic description of the area and the people it will serve, on the kinds of services and programs it plans to incorporate and market, on projected rates of utilization, and on reasonable estimates of beds and facilities it will need in the future. The long-range development and marketing plans of the hospital will dictate to a large degree the type of medical staff needed, and the hospital will want to program its medical office building around the needs, demands, and requirements of the medical staff who will occupy it.

Already the trend for the future is not so much the addition of beds, but the expansion of ancillary services, especially outpatient treatment. Emphasis is being placed on preventive medicine and ambulatory care. These ancillary areas, most likely to be expanded in the future, are also the areas with which the medical office building needs to be coordinated. Consequently, careful planning must take place that will incorporate optimum convenience and efficiency with the maximum options for expansion in the future.

The governing board of the hospital may have difficulty visualizing the need for a second office building before the first is even under construction. The board may have difficulty looking at the hospital's potential needs for expansion 10 or 15 years down the road. Consideration of these needs, as difficult as they are to visualize, is essential if the hospital is not to work itself into a corner. No hospital wants to find itself in the position of needing to expand a wing, only to have an office building standing in the way—particularly if that office building could have been located elsewhere.

NEW VERSUS REMODELED SPACE

As the hospital and its planners look at the total medical complex, a number of structural alternatives may come to mind in the consideration of providing physicians' offices. In some situations the decision may need to be made whether to build a new office building or to utilize an existing building by renovating it. A number of considerations will influence the hospital's ultimate decision. Some of the more important are cost, land use, flexibility, efficiency, and prestige.

Cost is undoubtedly one of the most important considerations, and, by and large, remodeling is very expensive. In fact, in most situations the renovation of an old building will cost as much as or more than the construction of an entirely new building of the same size. A number of problems, such as mechanical and electrical systems that must be replaced and structural obstacles that must be circumvented, contribute to the high cost of renovation. In addition, the hospital will have difficulty getting firm bids from contractors, who normally work on a cost-plus basis on remodeling jobs.

A second factor that will influence the decision whether to build or remodel is the hospital's land use situation. In actuality, this factor may be a deciding one. If a hospital has sufficient land to program a new medical office building, cost alone will usually dictate the use of new construction over remodeling. However, some hospitals are so cramped and face such severe land use problems that renovation may be the only possibility for providing on-campus offices. In the latter case, careful examination of renovation possibilities is in order.

In general, however, the result of remodeling is less flexibility and more compromise. A new building can be custom designed for the physicians' needs, but remodeled space not always can be. Invariably the building to be remodeled will have inappropriate types and locations of elevators, inadequate lighting, inappropriate types and locations of windows, and inefficient rentable depths. Support columns and load-bearing walls may limit interior design flexibility, and mechanical systems, such as plumbing and air-conditioning, if not replaced, will certainly provide design obstacles.

Probably one of the most typical remodeling projects considered by hospitals is the conversion of an old nurses' dormitory into a doctors' office building (see figure 2, page 158). It serves as a good example of the types of problems that arise in remodeling existing space. Usually, an old dormitory is designed for a one- or two-bedroom suite with a toilet. The depth of the suite will normally be from 18 feet to 22 feet. In contrast, the optimum depth of a physician's practice suite is 28 feet. The shallow depth of the nurses' dorm means that the physician's suite will have to be long and narrow, with an interior corridor that serves examination rooms on one side only. With an optimum rentable depth, on the other hand, the suite can be designed to be more compact, with less square footage, and with an interior corridor that serves rooms on both sides (see figure 3, page 158). In addition, the location of windows in the old building may also inhibit the placement of walls, causing rooms to be either larger or smaller than needed. The designer of the physician's suite loses almost all flexibility in the remodeling situation, for he will have to design the suite around what will fit in the building, rather than what the physician actually wants and needs.

Not only is flexibility lost, but efficiency is also lowered. A corridor that is 10 feet long and serves one examining room on each side is more efficient than a corridor that is 20 feet long and still serves only two examining rooms, which are side by side. In addition, under these circumstances, the design of a suite for a group of physicians would be so long that the office personnel might need roller skates to get from one end to the other. The result of this loss of efficiency is that fewer physicians can be accommodated in the older building than in a new building of the same square footage, and the physician himself will have to rent more space than he might otherwise need.

Prestige is the final factor to be considered in a new building versus a remodeled building, and either type of building could be prestigious, depending on circumstances. A new, well designed building will usually reflect an aura of professionalism and prestige. However, if it were built at the expense of tearing down a particularly fine or historic building, it might never overcome the stigma of historical destruction in the public's eye. Conversely, a particularly fine old building, if renovated, could be quite prestigious, but a poor quality, unpleasing old building, even if renovated, might never overcome the stigma of its past.

Although the shell is usually all that is redeemable of an old building when it is converted to a medical office building, a few other factors might influence the hospital to consider renovation. An old building may be designed and constructed with materials and detailing no longer economically feasible today, and the hospital may want to preserve the building shell because of its quality and esthetics. Also, some old buildings on the hospital campus may have been constructed through fund-raising drives, and family members of large contributors may still be active on the hospital board or as contributors. The hospital might consider renovating, rather than tearing down, an older building in deference to them. Finally, existing landscaping, which takes many years to replace, may be a consideration.

Generally, the factors to be considered indicate that new construction is usually preferable to a renovated building. Cost, flexibility, and efficiency are all on the side of the new building. If, however, new construction is totally impossible because of the land use situation or because a historic building is involved, then renovation can still be a viable alternative. Although careful planning is needed before renovation is undertaken, in cases where competition demands an on-campus medical office building for maintaining a viable medical staff, the decision to renovate can be a good one for the hospital's long-range future.

IN-HOSPITAL SPACE VERSUS SEPARATE BUILDING

Another planning decision the hospital may need to make in regard to the total medical complex is whether to locate the physicians' offices within the hospital or in a separate building. Although this decision would largely be made in relation to new construction, it might also be made in regard to renovating existing in-hospital space.

A hospital that is considerably overbuilt might consider converting existing space into physicians' offices. As mentioned earlier, however, remodeling costs are expensive, and existing in-hospital space usually has the same problem of inefficiency as an old nurses' dormitory. If a hospital does have unused space (and does not foresee the need for that space for a number of years down the road), if it is in great need of recruiting physicians, and if it does not have the capital to begin new construction, then the remodeling of in-hospital space is a possible alternative and one that has been used successfully under these circumstances.

Where new construction is concerned—an office wing or floor of the hospital versus a separate building—three factors will usually indicate the separate building to be the best alternative.

The first factor is physician attitudes. Many doctors do not like the idea of having offices directly within the hospital. They consider in-hospital offices as a threat to their independence and as a loss of individual identity. Physicians in general are very sensitive to the possibility of being looked upon as "employees of the hospital." They frequently prefer the separate building because they believe it provides them with autonomy, and it does, in fact, provide them with a limited form of "advertising."

Cost is another important factor, and hospital construction is considerably more costly than office building construction because of the restrictive codes concerning the hospital. Although these codes can be circumvented to a large degree by providing proper separation between the office wing and the hospital, separate building construction is usually the more economical method for providing physicians' offices on campus.

Convenience and security are two balancing factors that must also be considered as the hospital decides between in-hospital offices and a separate building. On the one hand, in most cases in-hospital space would be even more convenient for the physician and his patients than a separate building. The physician would have a minimum distance to travel between his office and his hospitalized patients, and outpatients would have a short distance to travel to ancillary hospital services. On the other hand, the same factors that create this extra convenience also produce related problems. Inpatient and outpatient traffic flow can be more difficult to control and coordinate. In addition, security is more difficult to maintain. An office wing that is open to every floor of the hospital will be far more difficult to monitor than a separate building with a single connection to the hospital. The same is true for a single floor of the hospital being utilized for offices.

In general, the separate building is the preferred choice as a method for providing on-campus physicians' offices. It combines maximum independence for the physicians, the most economical construction costs, and the minimum of security problems while still maintaining convenience. This alternative is, however, just that, an alternative. Physicians' attitudes vary from location to location, and individual hospitals find themselves in differing circumstances that may affect their decision. Careful evaluation of the individual situation is the only sure way of determining the best alternative.

INTERIM FACILITIES

Some situations demand physicians' offices on campus immediately, regardless of the fact that it may take some time to develop a building program. Under these circumstances the use of interim facilities may be a valuable part of developing the long-range plans of the hospital.

If circumstances dictate that a hospital needs to get physicians on campus immediately, if a hospital wants a doctors' office building but cannot afford it right away, or if a hospital needs to recruit physicians now, not later, then the use of interim physicians' office facilities may provide the immediate answer while long-range planning and/or permanent facilities are being developed and implemented (see figure 4, page 159).

One form of interim facilities is the use of a prefabricated building or portable building such as a trailer until permanent arrangements can be made for physicians' offices. For example, one hospital faced a number of problems—it was located in an old building, the census was low, new doctors were needed desperately, but before new doctors could be recruited, the hospital had to upgrade its laboratory, x-ray, and other facilities. The problem was made even more difficult because the hospital did not have the money for both upgrading its facilities and building a physicians' office building. Its long-range plan was to construct a building for 12 doctors, but its interim solution was the purchase of a temporary office building. In this case the hospital selected a portable building that was customized on the inside and large enough to house four physicians' offices. It was an attractive building and one that could be converted for other purposes later, or even sold. It cost the hospital (in 1975) $120,000 installed, or $24 per square foot.

With on-campus office space available, the hospital was able to recruit four new doctors whose presence helped increase the census and utilization of ancillary services. With greater income, the hospital was able to begin improvement and expansion of the laboratory and the x-ray and emergency departments. Once all these steps were completed, the hospital was then in a position to seek the needed financing to begin construction of its 12-man building.

In another situation, a hospital used in-hospital space for interim facilities. This hospital was suffering from a lack of physicians, low census, and substantial financial losses annually. It needed an office building to use as a recruitment tool, but it simply could not afford a greater debt service. In this case a shelled-in floor of the hospital that was not needed for beds in the foreseeable future was converted to physicians' offices. Since that time a number of physicians have been recruited, the hospital census has increased, and the facility has gone from deficit to profitable operation. Now the hospital is in the position to build an office building for additional recuitment and to accommodate physicians who already have expressed an interest in locating on that hospital's campus.

By and large, the use of in-hospital space as interim offices is most suitable for medium to small size communities with only one hospital. Doctors who are new to a community will usually accept this type of arrangement if the rent is attractive enough. In larger communities, the greater competition among hospitals for the recruitment of physicians makes this type of temporary arrangement less viable.

One of the real assets of utilizing interim facilities during the development of a long-range office building program is that physicians begin to come on campus immediately, rather than a year or two down the road. They not only provide a good foundation for hospital operations, but also they usually become enthusiastic supporters of and salesmen for the medical office building when it is constructed. A hospital can have no better salesmen for an office building than a group of physicians who can speak well of the arrangement and can influence their colleagues.

PLANNING THE SITE

Site planning in relation to the total medical complex and its long-range needs is another essential aspect of developing an effective on-campus medical office building. In reality, it is a simultaneous process with consideration of structural alternatives because examination of the available land may, in fact, dictate the type of structure that is to be built or indicate that renovation of an existing building is the only practical alternative.

No one factor alone will determine the ideal site of an on-campus medical office building, but rather a series of at least 10 factors must be considered in the evaluation of every potential site. If each potential site is measured against these criteria and evaluated on the basis of how well it fulfills each criterion, the site with the greatest assets and fewest liabilities will usually prove to be a wise selection.

Identity. A good site for a medical office building should provide the building with an identity of its own and one that is easily recognized by the patient. The building should be visible from the major thoroughfares, not hidden behind the hospital building. It should be recognizable as "the medical office building" so that it will not be confused with the hospital. Although architectural design provides some of the recognition, site also contributes to this quality. For example, a site separated from the hospital structure by 40 to 60 feet helps establish identity. In addition, the building site should be such that it can have its own patient access from the major thoroughfares, separate from the hospital access, and the building should be so located that its street address will be both one that residents of the community will know and that can be readily found by persons unfamiliar with the area.

Physical connection. A building site that provides an optimum connection with the hospital proper is also important. Although not every medical office building will be physically connected to the hospital, a protected connection is not only desirable, but also essential in many climates. It allows the physician to conduct a "shirt-sleeve" practice as he goes between his office and hospitalized patients. Consequently, a good site should be located so that the medical office building can be connected to the hospital, preferably into a corridor leading to the outpatient laboratory and the x-ray department in the hospital. Consideration of patient, physician, and staff pedestrian traffic patterns is important here. In addition, the ideal site will enable this connection, such as an enclosed walkway, to be on grade, because an on-grade connection is far more economical to construct than a tunnel or a skywalk.

Accessibility. Accessibility to the hospital's outpatient services is an important aspect of the site of the medical office building. As mentioned earlier, the outpatient departments are those most likely to be expanded in the future. Their ability to be expanded must not be blocked by the medical office building, but if the patients of the physicians located in the medical office building are to be referred to the hospital's outpatient departments, then the departments must be accessible. A physician does not want to have to send an ill or injured patient all over the hospital campus to receive an X ray and have laboratory work done, nor does the hospital want to encourage extra traffic throughout the hospital. Trying to locate an on-campus medical office building near the outpatient departments without blocking their expansion may seem to be somewhat of a paradox, but it is possible and is one of the more important requirements for a good site.

Parking. A good site for an on-campus medical office building must also include space for sufficient parking. Providing for adequate parking now, as well as planning for adequate parking a number of years in the future, is an essential aspect of developing the entire medical complex as well as the development of a medical office building. On the average, in a large medical office building the hospital must allow a minimum of six spaces per physician; in smaller buildings, more spaces per physician should be allowed. This minimum assumes that in most buildings of 30 doctors or more only 60 to 65 percent of the physicians will be in their offices at any one time. If enough land is not available for the needed parking spaces, then the development of a parking garage and its appropriate site must also be included in the planning for a medical office building. Ideally, the parking should be located conveniently near the office building, preferably adjacent to, rather than under, the building.

Traffic flow. Planning traffic flow around the hospital can be a complicated aspect of site consideration. Both vehicular traffic and pedestrian traffic must be considered. A hospital is already a heavy traffic area even before the medical office building and its physicians, personnel, patients, families, and suppliers are added to the problem. A good site will be one that allows the medical office building, the hospital, and the hospital emergency room all to have separate access. In addition, the separate automobile access to the medical office building needs to include a loading and unloading area where patients in wheelchairs or on crutches can go and come from the building with ease. It should be covered and should be free from steps. A good site for the medical office building will be such that a person can drive right up to the patient access area, unload patients, continue to the parking area, and then be able to return easily at departure time. Because many people will be parking and walking to the medical office building, a preferable site will not have its parking area located across a heavily traveled thoroughfare. For safety's sake, intersections on the hospital campus should be kept to a minimum. One other factor in site consideration in relation to the traffic flow is how other construction in the area will affect traffic. The hospital should be aware of other buildings being constructed in the area, should be in contact with their planners, and be aware of what those buildings will do in influencing the traffic flow in and around the hospital and its medical office buildings.

Compatibility. Compatibility with the long-range plans of the hospital is another aspect of site selection that is important. As the hospital develops its long-range goals and development plans, consideration should be given to what areas of the hospital may need expansion in the future. Any possible needed expansion should be detailed into the land use program for the hospital campus. In turn, sites under consideration for the medical office building should be evaluated on the basis of how compatible they will be with the various alternatives included in the hospital's long-range plans.

Expansion. In addition to being compatible with the hospital's possible expansion needs, the sites being considered must be evaluated on the basis of their own expansion possibilities. Although consideration of expanding a medical office building may seem premature during the site selection process for the building, additional space is so often needed a few years hence that this consideration is quite important. In particular, a good site should allow for economical, functional, and horizontal expansion of the medical office building, whether in the form of an addition to the building or construction of a second building. The ability to expand horizontally is particularly important because it allows expansion to proceed with a minimum of disruption to existing physicians' offices. Vertical expansion is not a good alternative because it is rarely economical and can be quite disruptive to the building's tenants.

Availability. The availability of the land being considered for construction of the medical office building can be a critical factor. Does the hospital already own the land? If not, is the land available for purchase? At a reasonable price? Is the land zoned so that an office building can be constructed on it? If not, how difficult will it be to obtain a variance in the zoning code? Will the inclusion of commercial services in the building require a zoning variance? Is the land encumbered by a mortgage? If so, how difficult will it be to clear that mortgage so that financing of the new construction can be obtained? Are there any restrictive covenants on the land? Utility easements? Consideration must also be given to any code requirements, including setbacks or necessary distances between buildings. All of these questions must be answered, and how they are answered may greatly influence the selection of a site. A site that is readily available and totally unencumbered would always be preferable, if availability alone were the only deciding factor, but when other factors are considered, a less readily available site might be a first choice. In such a case, a careful investigation should be made before the development of a building proceeds too far. Buildings have been blocked because neighbors rallied to prohibit the hospital from obtaining a zoning variance or from converting previously residential property into an office building site.

Site improvements. The greater number of improvements needed in a site, the more costly and less desirable it is in relation to this consideration. Possible site improvements that need to be considered are grading, filling, demolition of existing buildings, correction of drainage problems, and any surface or subsurface conditions that might require special treatment. The load-bearing capacity of the soil and what will be required to establish an adequate foundation can be very important, as well as consideration of any possible caverns, fissures, or subsoil conditions that could create problems.

Esthetics. Consideration should also be given to the general esthetics of a proposed site. Although this may not be a deciding factor, it might well be an influencing one. A good site will provide an attractive view from the windows of the building, but even more important, a good site will not block the view from the patient rooms of the hospital. A good site will also be one that will lend itself to an overall attractive appearance of the hospital campus. It should provide a blending of buildings with the ability to be landscaped and lighted in a similar, although not identical, manner as the hospital.

One other consideration that might be added to this list, particularly in areas of extreme heat or cold, would be site selection based on energy factors. Although the majority of energy conservation techniques relate to design rather than location, some site factors can be important. For example, in areas of extreme cold, the building site that provides maximum exposure to the sun and minimum exposure to northerly winds would be desirable. The opposite might be true in a very hot climate.

A site that fulfills all the "ideals" for an on-campus medical office building will be rare. For that reason, the selection process needs to include an evaluation of all potential sites according to the maximum number of preferred characteristics and the importance of those characteristics. Although an individual situation may involve factors other than those listed here, these basic guidelines will provide a strong foundation for evaluation and selection of an optimum site.

With the type of structure and the site carefully selected in relation to the present and future needs of the hospital, the hospital can be reasonably confident of the quality of its planning and the long-range effectiveness of the on-campus medical office building.

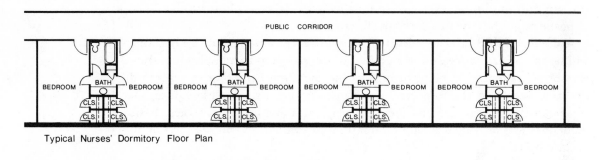

Typical Nurses' Dormitory Floor Plan

Conversion of Dormitory to Two-Physician Office

Figure 2. These floor plans illustrate a typical nurses' dormitory and how that space would be converted into a two-physician practice suite. In order to fit into the dormitory structure, the converted suite has to be designed in a long, narrow configuration. Although the remodeled suite includes the same number and size of rooms as the suite in figure 3, it requires 2,266 square feet of area, because of the inefficient use of the long interior corridor.

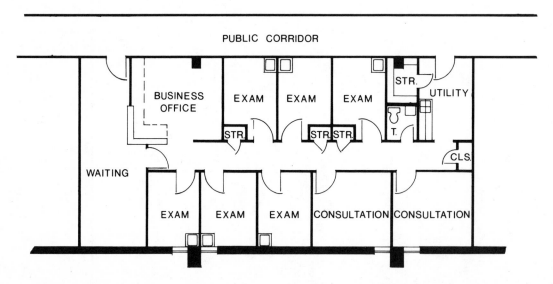

Figure 3. This floor plan illustrates a typical two-physician suite in a well designed medical office building. It encompasses 1,689 square feet. Compare this layout with floor plans in figure 2.

Figure 4. This small building was constructed for interim physicians' offices across the street from the Cullman (AL) Medical Center. It provided a place for physicians to practice while the on-campus medical office building was being constructed adjacent to the hospital.

CHAPTER **15**

Designing the Building

Developing the appropriate design for the on-campus medical office building plays a significant role in the success and effectiveness of the building. In some ways, the medical office building is not unlike other office buildings, but in the aspects in which it is different, the differences are all-important to the physicians and their patients.

In recent years, medical technology and the practice of medicine have been changing rapidly. The natural conclusion one might draw from the changes is that physicians' architectural needs in their offices would be changing with the technology. But that conclusion is true to a surprisingly limited extent. For example, the primary reasons physicians move from old offices into new are not because of architectural obsolescence. "The forces of relocation include changing referral patterns, newer buildings, prestige, real estate speculation, new partnerships and a need for additional adjacent space which may not be available," reported one architect.[1]

Changing medical practice has affected physicians' offices primarily in two areas. Individual office suites tend to be larger now, to accommodate group practices and some enlarged work areas. Also, because of the greater emphasis on preventive medicine and greater use of hospital ancillary services on an outpatient basis, more high-rise office buildings are being constructed.

Even though more and faster changes can be expected in health care delivery, little seems to indicate that a major change will take place in the basic requirements for examining rooms, treatment rooms, nurses' work areas, and storage spaces. As more and larger group practices and health maintenance organizations come into being, business offices and waiting rooms may be concentrated together in one area of each floor, but other major changes in physicians' architectural needs do not seem to be imminent.

Primarily, then, as a hospital begins the design process for an on-campus medical office building, it needs to concentrate on quality, efficiency, flexibility, and meeting the particular needs of its physician tenant members. Although the hospital will want a building designed for adaptability as some needs change, it need not be preoccupied with the building's architectural obsolescence, unless the building is poorly designed initially.

QUALITY AND ESTHETICS

Overall quality of the on-campus medical office building should be high, but the building must also be reasonably economical so that it is marketable. The design goal is quality without extravagance.

When completed, the medical office building should be superior to other commercial office structures in the community, especially in materials, sound control, and mechanical systems. It should complement the hospital and project a professional image equal to that of the hospital. A well designed office building of high-quality construction will satisfy and attract the physicians who are accustomed to working within the surroundings of the hospital itself.

Esthetically, the on-campus medical office building should be designed to be as attractive as possible within the economic limitations of the project. Although the functional qualities of the office building will dictate much of the form of the building, these qualities should in no way hamper the end result of an attractive building.

An important aspect of esthetics is blending the new structure with the existing hospital building and campus. Although the two buildings should relate architecturally, they should look more like first cousins than identical twins (see figure 5, page 177). Because the hospital is frequently an older structure built of outdated materials, duplication of design is usually esthetically undesirable as well as impossible or impractical. Conversely, an updated design that blends with the old can actually improve and modernize the appearance of the whole hospital campus.

The same attention to and the quality of the exterior esthetics of the office building need to carry through into the lobby, elevators, and public areas of the building. Because the lobby presents the first impression to the patient of the interior of his doctor's office, it needs to be tastefully furnished with colors coordinated attractively. Signs in commercial areas should be controlled so that they conform to the esthetics of the building. Elevators need to be nicely appointed with carpets and decorative wall finishes. Finally, interior signs and graphics, which begin with the lobby directory and directional signs and end at the door to the physicians' suites, need to be carefully designed for uniformity, functional clarity, and visual attractiveness.[2]

EFFICIENT BUILDING TYPES

Because of economic ramifications, the efficiency of the building design is very important. Primarily, efficiency refers to the percentage of rentable space in relation to the total space of the building. Rentable space is defined as that space occupied by the tenant within the walls surrounding his suite, thus, the greater the percentage of rentable space, the greater the income to be derived from the building.[3]

In an on-campus medical office building, a minimum of 75 percent of the total square footage should be rentable space, preferably 80 percent or more, up to 85 percent. (More than 85 percent usually results in inefficient interior suite design.) With 80 percent of the space rentable, only 20 percent remains as core space—elevator shafts, stairwells, public corridors, public toilets, janitors' closets, electrical and telephone equipment rooms, duct shafts, and other mechanical spaces.

To arrive at the optimum ratio of net rentable space to core space, the designers of the building will need to take into account any number of factors.

For example, many of the details of the core elements in the building are dictated by local building codes—number, size, and types of toilets; number and location of exits; corridor widths and requirements for the handicapped, to name a few. Consequently, the designers can improve efficiency by carefully planning core areas, but they cannot improve efficiency by decreasing the size of areas specifically stated in the codes. One method of increasing the efficiency of stairs, elevators, and lobbies is to design at least 10,000 square feet of rentable space on each floor of the building. Not only does that create a desirable rentable space to core ratio, but it will also allow sufficient flexibility in combining a variety of types and sizes of practice suites on each floor of the building.

Still another method of increasing efficiency of building design is the use of appropriate rentable depths between the public corridor and exterior wall of the building. Depths of 28 feet have been found to be preferable in most buildings, with a deeper space (up to 40 feet) used only at one or both ends of the building to accommodate large group practices. The 35-foot to 40-foot depth is not efficient for the majority of one-physician and two-physician suites that will be needed in the building. Common practice in the design of most commercial office space is the use of 40-foot rentable depths throughout the building. Unfortunately, however, in a medical office building, any increased efficiency achieved by providing deep space in all areas of the building is greatly outweighed by corresponding inflexibility of internal suite design that results. As will be pointed out later, optimum flexibility in suite design is obtained in the building by aligning all interior corridors within the suites in a continuous loop around the building so that expansion of suites can be carried out by simply removing the portion of interior partition separating the aligned corridors within two or more suites. In order to maintain both aligned interior corridors and optimum-sized rooms on either side, a rentable space depth of 28 feet in most of the building is necessary.

When all of these factors are considered, along with any number of specifics of a given situation, three major building configurations usually emerge that provide optimum efficiency, while still maintaining the interior design flexibility. These building configurations are the rectangular building with a center core, the modified center-core building, and the double-loaded single-corridor building.

In the rectangular center-core building, all the core elements are located in the center of the building with the public corridor surrounding the core in a race track fashion (see figures 6a and 6b, page 178). Rentable space is continuous and unencumbered around the center core to the exterior of the building. This type of building design is most desirable from a functional standpoint. It is compact, convenient, and provides the greatest flexibility in suite design, expansion, and remodeling. When well designed, this floor plan can be 80 percent to 82 percent efficient as defined on page 162. It is still a little less efficient than the double-loaded single-corridor building, but it has an additional advantage. When large suites are to be designed, they may be located across the short side of the building, incorporating part of the other-

Rectangular Center-Core Building

wise public corridor into the suite (see figure 7, page 179). This procedure can increase building efficiency to about 82 percent or 84 percent, but it requires careful planning. Core elements must be arranged appropriately so that if part of the corridor is used for tenant space, the building will still meet fire and safety code requirements. The length of dead end corridors, for example, is limited by code requirements.

Modified Center-Core Building

The modified center-core building can take on several different shapes. For example, it can be a long and narrow center-core building, with the core elements arranged in a line down the center rather than in a cluster configuration (see figures 8a and 8b, page 180). This variation is used primarily where the site dictates a building narrower than the average center core. Any number of other shapes can also be included in the modified center-core design—an L-shaped building, a cross-shaped building (see figures 9a and 9b, page 181), a building with offset modules (see figures 10a and 10b, page 182), or other variations with protrusions outside the rectangular shape. In these various instances, the public corridor still runs primarily around the core elements in a race track fashion, and the building maintains approximately the same efficiency as the standard center core. However, some flexibility is lost. If the core is elongated, the ability to include some of the public corridor in large end suites is usually impractical because of the creation of dead-end corridors that are too long to meet building egress codes. In other shapes, stairs or other elements of the core may project into what would otherwise be rentable space, creating less flexibility in suite design.

Double-Loaded Single-Corridor Building

The double-loaded single-corridor building is long and narrow with a single corridor down the center (see figures 11a and 11b, page 183). Core elements can be located in a variety of places, but are commonly placed on one side of the corridor somewhere near the middle of the building. This type of design works well for T-shaped buildings and is also easier to expand than other types of buildings (see figure 12, page 184). It is also the most efficient of the building configurations, usually 82 percent to 84 percent or more. The functional efficiency of this type of building is also good, but it is not as flexible and easy to work with in designing large suites for group practices. One problem of the double-loaded single-corridor building is that space is not continuous around the building; it is divided by the core elements at some point, limiting expansion and rearrangement options for the individual suites near the core. In addition, some core elements such as stairs almost always project into rentable areas, creating odd-shaped spaces that are workable but much less flexible and convenient in meeting physicians' needs and in coordinating suites throughout the floor.

Although many factors influence what type of building is designed in any given situation, site requirements and the number of doctors to be accommodated usually exert the greatest influence. By and large, the double-loaded single-corridor building works best for smaller buildings, and the center-core configurations work best when many physicians with a wide variety of needs must be accommodated in the building. Site restrictions or limitations may, of course, establish the parameters of the size and type of building that can be integrated into the medical complex.

CRITICAL DESIGN ELEMENTS

Four design elements need special attention in the planning and development of a medical office building if it is to function properly, and more especially, if the physicians are to be satisfied with their offices. These four elements, always mentioned by physicians as sources of irritation and dissatisfaction, are sound control; heating, air-conditioning, and ventilation; elevators; and parking. Each of these design elements is of paramount importance in the construction of a successful medical office building.

Because of the confidential and very personal nature of what is discussed in a physician's examining and consultation rooms, sound control is vital. Design and construction of proper sound-attenuating elements in a medical office building costs money, but it is money well spent.

Metal tracks in continuous floating ceilings act as conduits for sounds from one room to another, and therefore floating ceilings covering an entire suite should be avoided. Instead, demising partitions between suites should extend all the way up to the structural slab above, and partitions dividing rooms within a suite should extend a minimum of six inches above the ceiling. All partitions between suites and around treatment and consultation rooms should have sound-attenuation batts within them. Because they are thinner and provide less sound control, movable partitions should be avoided. Although some remodeling will be needed over the years, it will not be frequent enough to warrant the use of that particular type of partition. If properly designed, the building will be flexible in its ability to have suites redesigned with a minimum of partition modifications or construction. Consequently, the loss of sound control through the use of movable partitions is far worse than any slight advantage gained.

Another common practice in design that should be avoided is the use of a double junction box for placing electrical outlets back to back in a wall that separates rooms. Although this method is cheaper than installing completely separate outlets, it creates a direct passage in the wall through which sound can be transmitted. Electrical outlets in such instances should be at least four inches apart.

The return air system also requires special attention, because it can transmit sound from room to room through ceiling return air openings. Where strict control of acoustics is required, a sound-attenuating duct boot behind the ceiling grill helps resolve this particular problem. In addition, ceiling blanket insulation can be used for more critical areas.

Still other design elements that contribute to good sound control are the use of solid core doors, carpeting wherever practical, and quiet-flushing tank type toilets. Some of the design elements mentioned in regard to sound will contribute somewhat to the cost of the building, but these additional costs make the difference in an ordinary commercial office building and one designed especially for the high quality, professional practice of medicine.

Sound Control

Heating, Ventilating, and Air Conditioning

The heating, ventilating, and air conditioning system (HVAC) should be a good, economical system that will provide a medial temperature of 72 °F. to 75 °F. in an energy-efficient manner. The designer of the building must remember that the system is being designed for the comfort of the sick, elderly, and very young, as well as for the office personnel. For that reason, the system must not be designed with only one control per floor. Instead, each 1,000 square feet of space (the size of a typical one-man suite) should have at least two zones that can be controlled thermostatically within the suite. Usually the preferable arrangement is for the waiting room, business office, and work areas to be grouped into one HVAC zone (usually a building interior zone) and for the examining rooms to be grouped into another (usually a building exterior zone) so that they can be kept warmer for disrobed patients. Zoning exterior office spaces separately from interior office spaces is important, because one will often require cooling while the other requires heating. The installation of radiant heat lamps in examination rooms where patients are likely to be disrobed can provide additional comfort for them.

The ventilation system should be 100 percent ventilating; that is, air should be completely changed in all spaces over a specified period of time. The air must also be distributed properly to provide for unnoticeable air flow and quiet operation. Local code requirements will often dictate standards for air change, recirulation, humidity, and filtration performance.

Elevators

Good elevator service in a medical office building is very important. Slow elevators are a source of irritation to both physicians and patients, and complaints about elevator service are among the most frequently mentioned by physicians. Doctors dislike waiting on elevators, especially if they are late in getting to their offices or if they have been called out on an emergency.

In designing the building, the architect should plan on a minimum of one elevator for every 25,000 square feet of net rentable space or portion thereof. Although buildings of three floors or less can usually justify the use of less expensive and slower hydraulic elevators, a larger building will need the more expensive and faster electric traction type. The minimum speed for medical office building elevators should be 250 feet per minute. Hospital type elevators are not necessary in the medical office building. A standard passenger type elevator cab with 5 feet by 7 feet of clear interior space and 42-inch-wide center opening doors will accommodate an ambulance type stretcher. The elevators should have controls on both sides of the door, and they should be carpeted so that most of the dirt on shoes is taken off at that point and not later in the hallways and suites. Replacement of elevator carpeting is considerably cheaper than additional cleaning and replacement of corridor and suite carpets.

Parking

Adequate parking is the lifeline of any medical office building. It needs to be convenient to the building and sufficient to handle the patient load. For the sake of equality as well as possible tax purposes, physicians' parking should be in the same location for all doctors, whether tenants or not. Patient parking needs to be adjacent to the medical office building if at all possible. Employee parking can be somewhat less convenient, probably in the same area as hospital employee parking. For sufficient parking to handle the patient load, an average of six spaces per doctor should be provided. Although this number will vary somewhat according to location, it will usually be adequate. It is based on the premise that at any given time only about two-thirds of the physicians will actually be seeing patients in their offices.

The importance of high quality design and construction in the areas of sound control, HVAC, elevators, and parking cannot be overstressed. These four areas are of great concern to the physicians, so they must be important to the hospital if it hopes to provide a building that will be marketable to the prospective physician tenants and that will keep them satisfied.

DESIGNING FOR FLEXIBILITY

Flexibility is significant because a building's ability to respond to changing needs will lengthen its economic life. Minor changes, such as minor partition changes within a suite, minor electrical and lighting changes, additional power for new equipment, and changes in the telephone system, will be necessary throughout the life of the building and should be assumed when the building is designed. More extensive changes will be needed less frequently, but the building's ability to accommodate these needs will be the real test of its flexibility. Some of the more extensive needs for change may include the following:

- Combining several small suites into one larger suite or modifying a large suite to make several small ones
- Converting an entire floor to serve one specialty or group practice or even converting an entire building for a group practice
- Eliminating private clerical and waiting space
- Sharing common rooms and equipment
- Providing centralized services for records, supplies, and billing
- Incorporating space for ambulatory patient treatment and recovery without admission to the hospital
- Requiring private work areas for paramedical personnel and doctors' assistants.

A number of steps can be taken in designing a building for maximum practical flexibility. The structural frame of the building, for instance, needs to support the weight of the structure so that few, if any, interior walls are load-bearing. Thus, the movement of walls to accommodate changing needs is not inhibited. Second, outboard (exterior) perimeter columns are preferable to inboard (interior) ones because they leave inside walls unencumbered, increasing the flexibility of individual suite design by eliminating offset or jogged partitions and the creation of small wasted alcoves by protruding columns. Concrete or steel structures that span from exterior walls across the rentable space to interior columns also contribute to flexibility by eliminating structural support columns within physicians' office spaces.

Modular fenestration design in small increments is important. For example, the use of narrow, vertical windows (24 inches to 30 inches wide) also contributes to flexibility along the periphery, because these windows are less likely to inhibit the location of interior partitions. Also, windows with a 42-inch to 48-inch sill height not only allow greater privacy within examining rooms, but they also make it possible for cabinets and work areas to be placed under the windows on the outside walls.

Because of the large number of toilets and sinks within a medical office building, flexibility in the plumbing system is important. The use of drop ceilings with mechanical, electrical, and plumbing systems run in the space between the ceiling and slab makes relocation of plumbing and electrical service relatively easy.

Perhaps of greatest concern in designing for flexibility is the need to be able to enlarge or redesign suites (see figures 13, 14, and 15, pages 185 and 186). The insistence on certain plan relationships between adjacent suites can assure this type of flexibility. If interior corridors within suites align in a continuous fashion around the building, then two suites can be connected by removing the partition between the two continuous corridors (see figure 16, page 187). Care should be taken not to block this corridor with plumbing or extensive cabinetry or special equipment. The placement of a storage closet at the end of this corridor is often a good use of the space without impairing the suite's ability to be remodeled.

Design and construction of a flexible building can add to the cost of the project. The qualities that contribute to flexibility are frequently not the most economical way to construct the building, but, as with the essential design elements, the additional cost of designing and constructing a flexible building will lengthen the life and usefulness of the structure.

CONNECTION TO THE HOSPITAL

The greatest convenience for doctors and patients is achieved in an on-campus medical office building that is physically connected to the hospital. Ideally, the connection should be at the first floor commercial level so that pedestrian traffic passes by the various establishments. As far as the hospital is concerned, the connection should attach to an area where outpatient registration and outpatient services are convenient. Having the admitting office nearby would be another plus. For the sake of the doctors, the connection to the hospital should be located near the medical records department, preferably so that they will pass by it when going and coming from the hospital.

Several types of connections work well between the hospital and office building. Climatic conditions, site restrictions, and cost usually dictate which type is most feasible. The least expensive type of connection would be a simple sidewalk or covered walkway at ground level. This connection is minimal and would rarely be recommended, since it provides little or no protection from the weather and does not allow the physicians and patients to go and come without a coat or other protective garments during inclement weather.

In many respects, the ideal connection would be an enclosed walkway on grade (see figure 17, page 188). It is less expensive than a tunnel or skywalk (bridge), and yet it provides convenience and protection from the weather.

The greatest drawback to this type of connection would be possible traffic flow problems on campus. The site may not be able to accommodate an on-grade connection.

Usually, the second most desirable connection is an enclosed skywalk (see figure 18, page 189). It is particularly desirable when a well traveled driveway separates the office building from the hospital. A skywalk is less expensive than a tunnel, but more costly than an on-grade connection. The problems associated with skywalks are that they can be visually unattractive if not designed properly. Also, the city's minimum height requirement for the skywalk may not be compatible with the floors of the building, or the city may have an ordinance that does not allow pedestrian walkways over thorough-fares. Another problem is that a skywalk frequently has to connect to a patient floor of the hospital.

Although a tunnel is an excellent means for connecting the office building to the hospital, it is also the most expensive (see figure 19, page 190). It provides excellent all weather protection, but because it is not visible from the outside, it usually requires some form of security protection, electronic or otherwise. In addition, angles, corners, deep ramps, and steps should be avoided in the design of a tunnel.

One other means of connecting two buildings is by designing them to touch at some point. This method is not recommended because it tends to eliminate window space, to create inefficient office arrangements, and to block the view from hospital windows. On-grade, skywalk, and tunnel connections are all preferable to placing two buildings together.

INDIVIDUAL SUITE DESIGN

The design of the individual physician's suite is the heart of the medical office building. For the building to do its job of providing the physicians with a high-quality, efficient, professional atmosphere for practicing medicine, the suites must be custom designed to meet the specific requirements of each physician. The design problem, then, is to provide custom layout within the standard format of the building.

Although most physician's suites have certain elements in common, they tend to vary according to the physician's specialty, age, background, and training. Some physicians, for instance, want separate examining and consulting rooms. Others want to consult in the examining room, so they have larger examining rooms with a desk in them. Ophthalmologists vary between those wanting to use a long alley for refraction (see figure 20, page 191) or those who want to conserve space and use mirrors (see figure 21, page 192). Each variation is a matter of training, habit, and personal preference.

"Generally each physician will rent about 800 square feet of space so that with circulation, partitions and shafts, 1,000 gross square feet per physician is a useful planning tool," explained one architect.[4] "Excluding psychiatrists, surgeons request the least space, as little as 600 square feet. Gynecologists and orthopedic surgeons are near the top at approximately 1,000 square feet [see figure 22, page 193]. Physicians with practices that employ technicians—in radiology, EEG and EMG, for example—tend to require the most space."

Influential Factors

The physician's specialty affects both the size and arrangement of the suite needed. Primary care physicians usually have large practices and require larger waiting rooms and business offices as well as more examining rooms. As already mentioned, surgeons require less space because they have a hospital-based practice, with the office used only for preoperative and postoperative visits. Because of their limited office practice, they have smaller waiting rooms and business offices, fewer examining rooms, but possibly larger consultation offices. In addition, a surgeon may require a wider examining room because he may need access to both sides of the examining table.

In contrast to the needs of primary care physicians and surgeons, internists usually work from the right side of the patient on the examining table and can use a narrower examining room, with the table against the wall. Pediatricians, also, have other special needs such as a waiting area for sick babies and children. They would also have high utilization of a utility room where babies are weighed and measured and where injections are prepared. Examining rooms, on the other hand, can be small because examining tables are usually against a wall so that babies cannot roll off the back side of the table. Ear, nose, and throat specialists are different still, for they will usually not use an examining table at all, but rather an ENT chair with a treatment stand. They can use a very small examining room, as small as 5 feet by 7 feet (see figure 23, page 194). Although the examples of varying needs could continue through all the specialties, the significant point is that each physician has specialized needs according to his practice, and a well designed medical office building will be able to accommodate these needs.

Age Factors

Age is another factor that influences a physician's individual suite design. Young doctors are usually afraid of renting too much space. They tend to underestimate their space needs. An experienced designer will know what the physician will need according to his specialty and will be able to encourage the young doctor to rent the appropriate amount of space. If he takes too little space, he will regret it in a year or two because of the expense and inconvenience of having to move or to expand. In other cases, a young doctor may want to provide space for an associate who might be coming along in a year or two, but he really cannot afford to do this. If the hospital has a policy of holding space open for physicians being recruited, it will want to help the young doctor in this situation.

In contrast to the new practitioner, older physicians may want to rent very small suites because they are cutting back on their practices, or they could want extra space to accommodate a new physican to take over their practice. The age of a physician may also influence how much space he needs for the storage of medical records (particularly if he has accumulated records over the years without culling them periodically). An older physician may also have special needs for incorporating equipment into his suite. Older doctors in certain specialities, such as orthopedics or internal medicine, may already own x-ray or laboratory equipment and want it included in their suites; whereas a younger physician will usually make greater use of hospital equipment rather than purchase his own.

Individual practice patterns also influence how a suite should be designed. The physician's path through the suite as he practices, the patient's path as he is examined and treated, and the flow of paperwork (paper path) are all traffic patterns that need to be taken into consideration so that suites can be designed for optimum efficiency. The designer needs to know if the doctor talks with each patient in his consultation office or if he moves from exam room to exam room, consulting in the examining rooms. The patient traffic flow will influence the location of the laboratory, utility areas, and toilets. The business office must also be carefully located so that it is convenient to the waiting room and so that patients pass by it on their way out of the suite. How paperwork is handled also influences the layout of the suite. The designer needs to know if all patient charts are pulled in the morning, whether the doctor examines the charts at the examining room door before seeing patients, and whether he returns the charts to the office or leaves them on the examining room door for the nurse to handle. How and where billing and insurance forms are handled are also important.

For optimum design of a suite all of these factors must be considered. A good and experienced designer who is well aware of specialty needs, practice variations, potential internal traffic patterns, age, and training variations can contribute significantly to the success of an office building. Needless to say, poor suite design can be a tragedy for the physician and his staff who must work within the suite and for the hospital, which is interested in keeping the physician tenants satisfied and productive.

Although the previously mentioned factors all contribute tc variations within suites and the need for competent, custom design of the doctors' suites, certain factors are still common to all practice suites. Virtually every suite will need a reception/business office, a waiting room, examining and treatment rooms, a private office, utility and laboratory area, toilet, storage, and a second entrance.

Reception/business offices are rarely too large, and are more commonly too small. A good rule of thumb is to allow a minimum of 50 square feet for every employee who works in the reception/business office, plus space for files and record storage. Unfortunately, the business office is the area in which the physician frequently tries to cut corners, and he usually regrets it, because of the cramped working conditions that result. A reception window or counter should be open between the office and the waiting room, but the door into the office should be located off the interior corridor, rather than between the waiting room and office (see figure 24a, page 195). Another good feature is to have a counter or alcove at which bills are paid between the office and interior corridor (see figure 24b, page 195). It provides a place for patients to discuss and pay their bills in privacy. In some larger practices, the business office may be separate from the reception office. In those cases the reception office is usually small, 8 feet by 11 feet for example; the business office is larger and contains the records and files.

Practice Patterns

Reception/Business Office Needs

Waiting Room

The waiting room of a physician's suite is very important to the patient. It needs to be large enough, usually four seats for every examining room, and it needs to be attractive and comfortable. Lamps might be used instead of fluorescent ceiling lights to give a warmer, homelike atmosphere. Large spaces might be divided by partial walls or room dividers to provide more wall space and more privacy for the patient than is available in one large open room crowded with people (see figures 25a and 25b, pages 196 and 197).

According to one newspaper science writer's report, a professional practice consultant, Robert P. Levoy, has sat in more than 5,000 physician's waiting rooms from New York to San Francisco and concludes that many a doctor would not want to be a patient in his own office.[5]

The consultant reports that he had seen waiting rooms furnished with worn plastic chairs patched with strips of masking tape, walls painted a depressing institutional green, worn linoleum, and in general resembling a railroad station. He urges that physicians furnish their office with varied seating that accommodates people of different ages, sizes and shapes, because men, as a rule, like to cross their legs and prefer a chair with arms, whereas women like a straight-backed chair.

The consultant observes that older people or patients with arthritis and other crippling diseases have difficulty in getting up, so an armed high chair firmly anchored to the floor suits them best. Heavy patients need extra-large chairs, and children enjoy small chairs.

He adds that few people settle by choice on a sofa or a love seat already occupied by a stranger; they serve a decorative rather than functional purpose. Finally, he urges warmth in furnishings, not chrome and leather.

Examining Rooms

For the physician, the examining rooms are of paramount importance because they are his work area. The examining rooms will vary considerably according to specialty. As already mentioned, an ENT specialist should require the smallest examining rooms, as small as 5 feet by 7 feet. Internists and pediatricians, for the most part, require rooms on the small side, usually 7 feet by 11 feet. As a rule, surgeons require more space, usually a minimum of 8 feet by 11 feet, because they need access to both sides of the examining table. Orthopedists need large rooms because they deal with patients in casts, on crutches, and in wheelchairs.

Although examining rooms vary considerably, a few basic principles of layout remain fairly constant. Ideally, the door into the room will be on the right side of the room (see figure 26, page 198), and it will open into the center of the room rather than against the adjacent wall. Such an arrangement allows the examining table to be located on the left side of the room so that when a patient is on the table, his head toward the corridor wall, he can be examined from his right side, the preferred method by most primary care physicians. In addition, the table can be placed away from the wall or diagonally, allowing access to both sides. Examining rooms with doors on the left and the layout reversed are also acceptable to physicians who do not examine the patient exclusively from the right side. The peculiar opening of the door transforms the door into a visual shield when opened, rather than allowing anyone in the corridor to see the patient on the examining table.

The sink is usually best located on the same side of the room as the door (see figure 26, page 198), thus allowing more freedom of space on the examination side of the room. In those situations where a dressing alcove is needed, the best location is usually in the corner behind the door, at the end of the examining table. A curtain on a track can easily be installed, which will allow privacy and make good use of this sometimes wasted space. Finally, if a physician is to have several examining rooms to be used for the same purpose, they should be similar in size and arrangement. The physician will find extra convenience in having all equipment and supplies in the same locations as he moves from room to room.

Other Areas

Virtually every physician will have a private office, but the size and furnishing of it will vary according to how it is used. If he uses it exclusively, then the room can be small. If he consults with individual patients in the office, it will need to be somewhat larger. If he consults with entire families, it will need to be larger still. An average private office would be about 11 feet by 12 feet, and an office used for family consultation would measure approximately 11 feet by 15 feet. A psychiatrist will usually have the largest private office, because he will usually see most of his patients there, rather than in an examining room.

The utility room/laboratory area is primarily the work station for the nurses. In this area many supplies are stored, syringes are prepared, instruments are sterilized, babies are weighed, and laboratory tests are run. In addition, it may serve as a coffee room and general clean-up room. Although a few specialists who do no laboratory work in their offices may not need a utility/laboratory area, most physicians will. Because it is a high traffic area, a door that closes is not usually needed between it and the interior corridor of the suite. A cased opening is usually sufficient.

Every suite needs a second entrance so that the physicians and employees can come and go without having to walk through the waiting room, as well as to meet some fire code requirements. This second entrance is also usually a part of the utility area in order to facilitate the delivery of supplies directly to the area where they are used.

Every suite needs a toilet, and in some suites one toilet for the staff is enough, but if specimens are taken, another toilet may be desired. The patient toilet is preferably located adjacent to the utility/laboratory area so that a specimen pass box can be installed between the toilet and the lab. Such an arrangement is convenient for the laboratory and also saves the patient from having to carry his specimen down the corridor to the laboratory.

Adequate storage areas are the last feature that should be standard to every suite. Although storage of records will normally be accommodated in the business office, and many supplies will be stored in the cabinets of the utility/laboratory area, most suites will need at least an additional 4-foot by 5-foot storage room with shelves from floor to ceiling on three sides. A small coat closet is also recommended, preferably near the second entrance.

Custom designing of high quality physicians' practice suites is an intricate process that requires competent, experienced designers. Although the hospital will want to do all it can to accommodate the needs and desires of each individual physician in his suite design, some consideration should also be given to future use of the suite. To the extent that unusual sizes or configurations of examining rooms and other features can be avoided, the suite will be more easily adaptable to the next tenant who may occupy it.

STANDARD SUITE FINISHES

Before actual custom suite designing begins, a decision must be made concerning what will be provided in the standard finished suite at the customary rental rate and what will be charged to the physician as an extra cost. A wide range of finish products are available for suites, and the architect and/or interior designer will want to give special consideration to the attractiveness, appropriateness, durability, and maintenance requirements of the various products available. Although projects vary from allowances for finishing to charging physicians for virtually all finishing work, the most equitable and satisfactory approach is to provide all the basics needed for a suite to be operable, with the amenities to be added at the physician's direction and at extra cost to him. Such an approach makes it possible for a young physician with little capital to move into a standard finished suite without an investment in improving the suite itself. An established physician who wants a more lavishly appointed suite can also have it, but at an additional charge.

Typically, the standard finished suite would include the following:
- A completely finished suite ready for occupancy
- Painted plasterboard partitions with metal studs
- Vinyl asbestos tile flooring with molded rubber base throughout
- Acoustical tile ceiling with adequate recessed fluorescent light fixtures
- One electrical outlet for every 12 lineal feet of wall
- Optimum sound control
- Solid core wood doors
- Sink and/or cabinet unit in each examining/treatment room
- Sink and cabinet unit in utility/laboratory area
- At least one public and one private entrance
- At least one toilet per initial 1,000 square feet and one more for each additional 800 square feet
- At least two thermostats to control corresponding heating, ventilating, and air-conditioning zones
- Ample telephone outlets with dual conduit for intercom
- Receptionist's opening, with plastic laminated counter, between waiting room and business office
- Utilities, except telephone
- Housekeeping services
- Maintenance
- Fire insurance on hospital-provided portions of the building
- Liability insurance for the building as a whole and for public areas only.

Other finishes that some physicians might want would be charged directly to the physician at the contractor's cost. These finishes might include the following:

- Carpeting (with credit given for omitted tile)
- Additional wall treatments such as wallpaper and paneling (with credit given for omitted paint)
- Extra casework, laboratory equipment, and millwork
- Additional electrical service and lead protection for tenant's x-ray or similar equipment
- Alterations and redesigning of suite
- Compressed air, vacuum, natural gas, or oxygen
- Insurance coverage for damage to tenant's personal property
- Personal and public liability insurance coverage.

With a clear understanding of what finishing materials or special construction will or will not be charged to him, the physician is better able to work with designers on a suite that not only meets his needs, but also his financial expectations.

OTHER DESIGN DETAILS

In a chapter of this length, touching upon major points of design is all that is possible. Many other areas must also be carefully planned in a well designed building.

Signs and graphics are vital. From the directory in the main lobby to the individual name plates on each physician's door, the graphics must be easy to read and understand, consistent, attractive to the eye, and coordinated with other building graphics. Directional signs must be carefully planned and appropriately placed if they are to function adequately.

The type of mail service the building will receive must be considered even as the building is designed. Will the postal service deliver mail to each suite, to a central mail room, or to mail boxes in a central location? Each type of service would require special design features in the building—mail slots in suite doors, a mail room, or a postal box area.

Types of public toilets must also be considered. Does the building code require wheelchair toilets on every floor or just in the lobby? If ever a building were designed with consideration for the incapacitated or handicapped, it should be a medical office building. All facilities should be readily accessible to such patients. Ramps, wide doorways, and toilets that will readily accommodate a wheelchair are just a few of the special features that should be considered.

The importance of good design is summed up succinctly by George F. Lull, M.D., former secretary-general manager, American Medical Association: "The many diagnostic tools of modern medicine call for a well designed and functional medical office or unit. Mistakes in planning are costly, not only in terms of misspent money, but in terms of lost time and resulting inefficiency. A physician who conducts his practice from a physical setup designed to meet his own and the community's needs can provide better medical service to his patients, since he can make the best use of his own time and facilities."[6]

NOTES

1. Diaz, James R. The hospital-affiliated medical office building. *Architectural Record,* 157:57, Feb. 1975.

2. For more in-depth information, see the American Hospital Association's book *Signs and Graphics for Health Care Facilities,* no. 1262, 1978.

3. For a more detailed definition, see the current *Downtown and Suburban Office Building Experience Exchange Report,* published annually by the Building Owners and Managers Association International.

4. Diaz, James R. The medical office building. AIA Journal. 60:28, Aug. 1973.

5. Snider, Arthur J. Scourge of doctor's waiting room is more than old magazines. Chicago Daily News Service. *Commercial Appeal.* Section 1, p. 23, Sept. 22, 1974.

6. American Medical Association, editor. *A Planning Guide for Establishing Medical Practice Units.* Sears, Roebuck Foundation Grant, n.d., p. 2.

Figure 5. The medical office building adjacent to Methodist Hospital-South, Memphis, was designed and built at the same time as the hospital. Consequently, the architectural blending of it with the hospital was simpler than with older hospitals. Although the office building blends architecturally with the hospital, it also maintains a separate identity, because of such factors as the distance between the two buildings and the similar, yet not identical, window patterns.

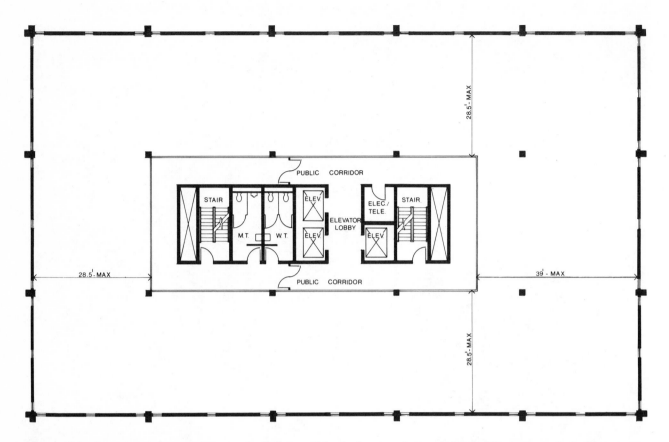

Figure 6A. A rectangular center-core building will include elevators, stairs, lobby areas, and other core elements in the center of the building with the public corridor encircling them in racetrack fashion. This building configuration provides continuous rentable space around the core, and is basically 80 to 82 percent efficient.

Figure 6B. The twin towers of the Baylor Medical Plaza, Dallas, are typical examples of rectangular center-core buildings. A similar floor plan is shown in figure 6A. These office towers are adjacent to the Baylor Medical Center.

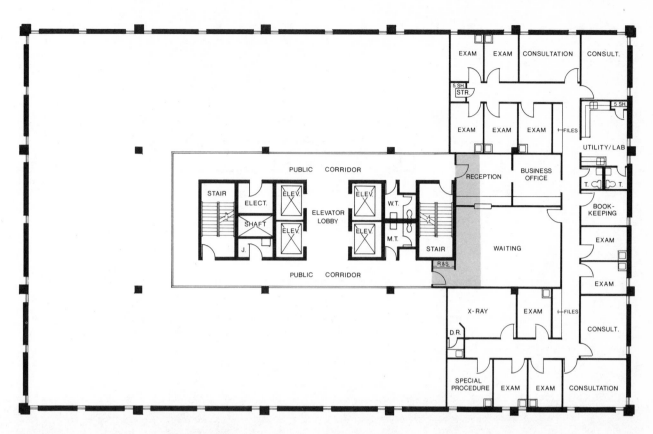

Figure 7. A center-core building can be made even more efficient when a large practice suite is fitted across the short side of the building, utilizing that portion of the public corridor in the suite. Such an arrangement can increase the building's efficiency to 82 or 84 percent.

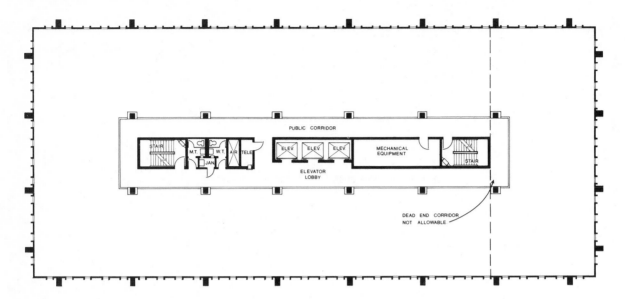

Figure 8A. The modified center-core building can take a long, narrow form. The elongated center-core is efficient, but the corridor at the ends of the building cannot be utilized as rentable space for large suites because of the creation of long, dead-end corridors.

Figure 8B. Located on the campus of Baptist Hospital, Jacksonville, the Laurette J. Howard Doctors' Building is a typical example of a modified center-core building that is elongated. A typical floor plan is shown in figure 8A.

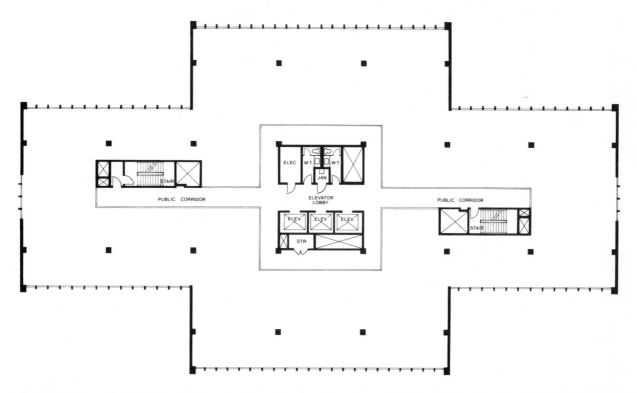

Figure 9A. The modified center-core design can also be cross-shaped. However, stairwells project into the rentable areas making the flow of space less continuous and the building somewhat less flexible for suite design.

Figure 9B. The Bauer Professional Building adjacent to St. Mary's Hospital, Long Beach, CA, is an example of a modified center-core building in the shape of a cross. The three-level parking garage seen in the foreground was designed as a part of the medical office building.

Figure 10A. A modified center-core design can have offset modules. As in the cross-shaped design, stairwells project into the rentable areas.

Figure 10B. This medical office building, located on the campus of the Queen's Medical Center, Honolulu, HI, is an example of a modified center-core building plan with offset modules, as seen in figure 10A. The offset seen here is repeated on the other side of the building, in reverse.

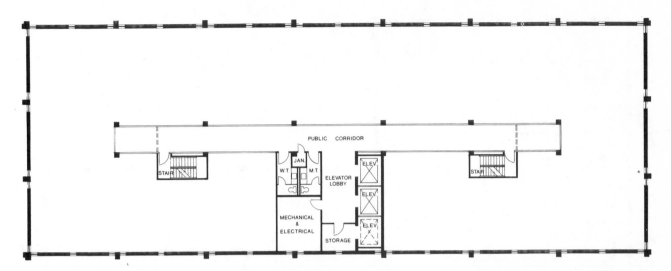

Figure 11A. The double-loaded single-corridor building is usually long and narrow. Although very efficient, the core elements interrupt the flow of interior space.

Figure 11B. The Cullman (AL) Medical Center used the double-loaded single-corridor configuration similar to that in figure 11A for its on-campus medical office building (foreground). Although hidden by the "fins" that project from the office building, vertical windows extend from top to bottom of this building.

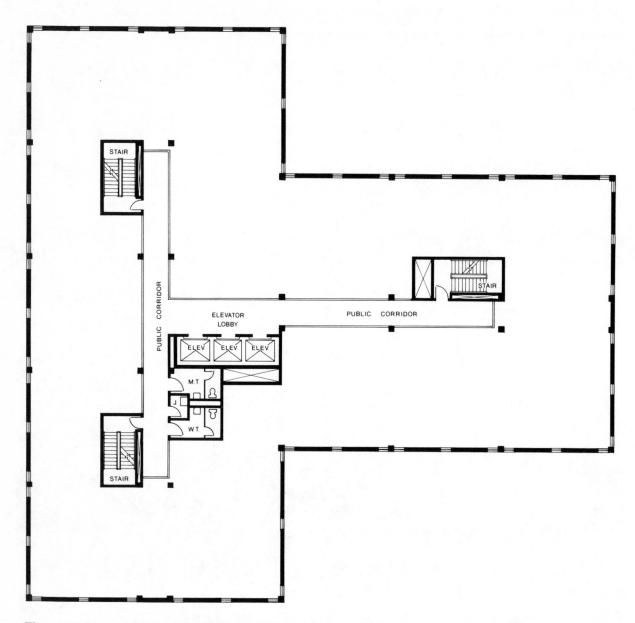

Figure 12. The double-loaded single-corridor design also works well in a T-shaped building.

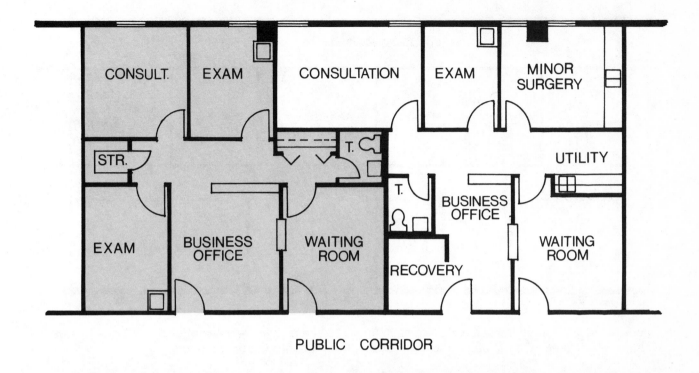

Figure 13. The two adjacent suites illustrated are designed poorly. Interior corridors in the two suites do not align completely, and the location of the toilets is such that extensive partition and plumbing changes would be required for the two suites to be joined, if expansion were required. In addition, the location and arrangement of other areas, such as business offices and waiting rooms, is such that the two suites could not be readily combined into a larger one if required.

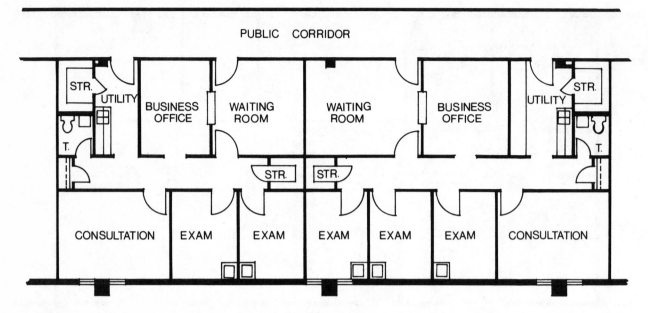

Figure 14. In contrast to the suites illustrated in figure 13, these two adjacent suites are designed conveniently and efficiently. Only storage closets separate the continuous interior corridors.

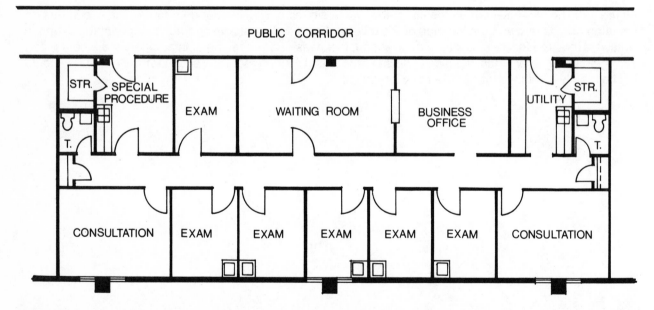

Figure 15. By removing the common storage room partitions, plus making a few other wall changes on one side of the interior corridor only, the two individual suites illustrated in figure 14 could readily be remodeled into one large efficient suite.

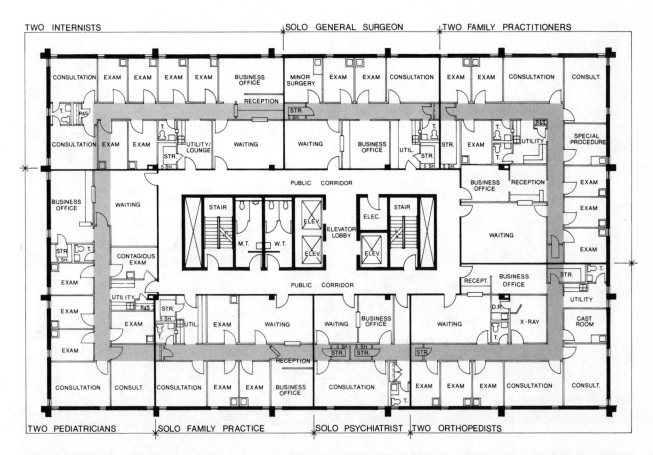

Figure 16. Interior corridors within the individual suites that align in a loop-type arrangement around the building add considerably to the architectural flexibility of the building.

Figure 17. An on-grade connection between a hospital and its adjacent medical office building can be designed to be an attractive part of the campus. In addition, it is usually more economical to construct than a tunnel or bridge. This enclosed walkway connects St. Francis Hospital, Memphis, with its office building.

Figure 18. An attractive sky walk or bridge connects St. Joseph Hospital (left), Fort Worth, with its medical office building across the street. A bridge can be an effective connection when a thoroughfare must be crossed. It is usually less expensive than a tunnel.

Figure 19. This tunnel under a major thoroughfare connects two medical office buildings with Baptist Memorial Hospital, Memphis. The natural light and attractive view provided by the sunken garden at right add considerably to the esthetics of the tunnel.

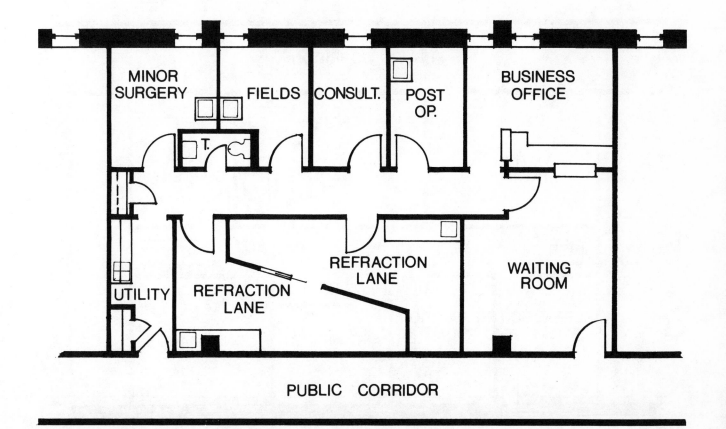

Figure 20. Because of different training, some ophthalmologists prefer 22-foot refraction lanes, whereas others prefer to use mirrors. Customized suite design can meet either need. This plan accommodates refraction lanes.

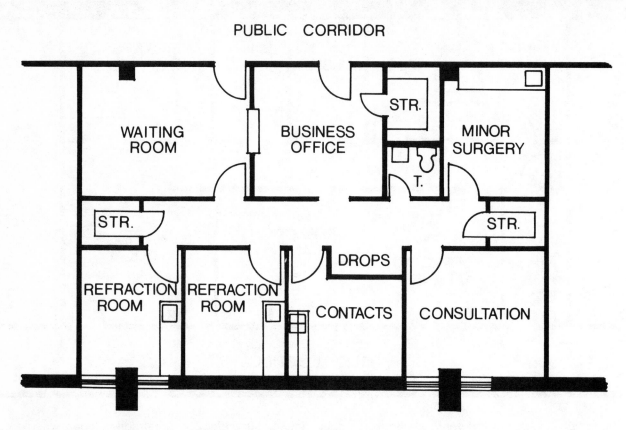

Figure 21. This suite is designed for ophthalmologists who prefer to use mirrors.

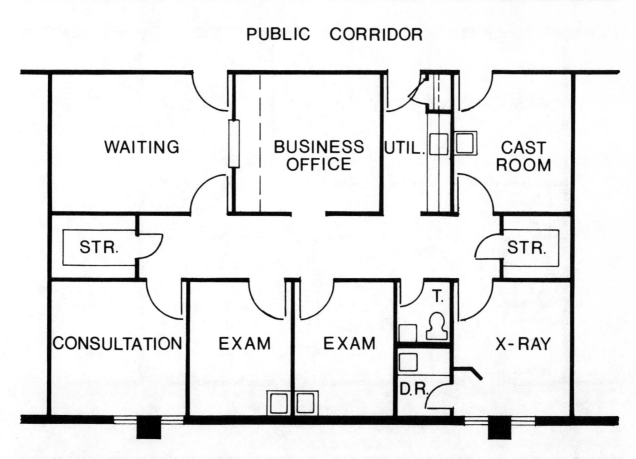

PUBLIC CORRIDOR

WAITING

BUSINESS OFFICE

UTIL.

CAST ROOM

STR.

STR.

CONSULTATION

EXAM

EXAM

T.

D.R.

X-RAY

Figure 22. Although the suites designed for different specialists have many points in common, they also require custom features. For example, an orthopedic surgeon will usually need a larger suite than an otolaryngologist because the orthopedist needs larger examining rooms and wider corridors to accommodate patients on crutches and in wheelchairs. For the same reason, the orthopedist will have standard hung or conventional swing doors (as opposed to reversed swing doors), making access to the examining rooms easier.

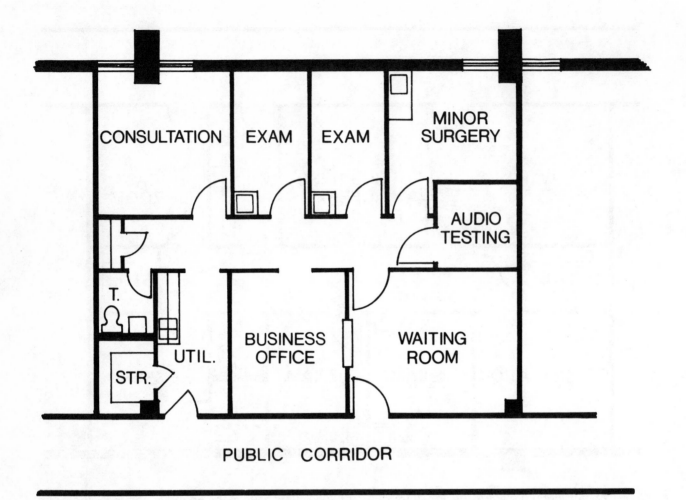

Figure 23. The typical otolaryngologist's suite shown here is 1,045 square feet, as compared to the orthopedic surgeon's suite, which is 1,282 square feet.

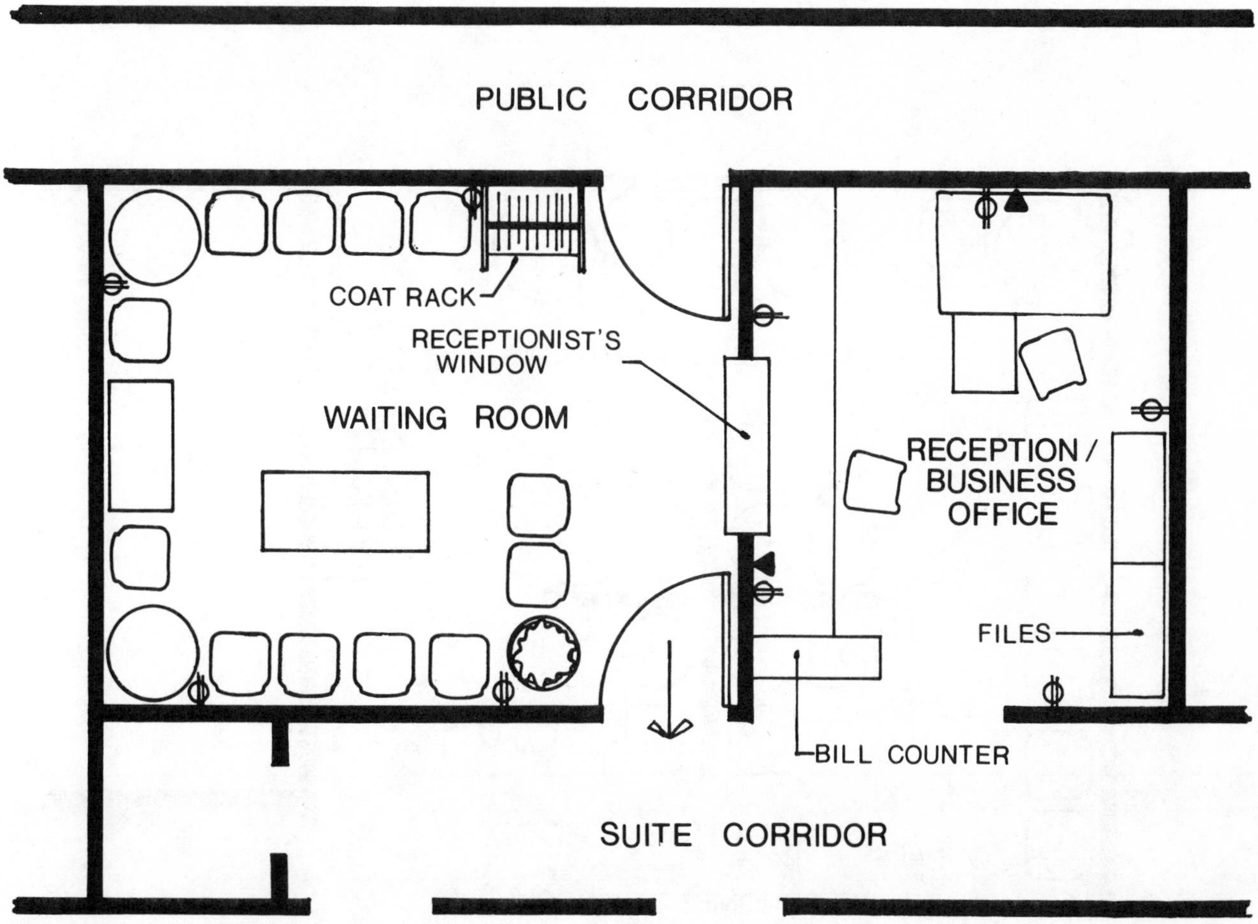

PUBLIC CORRIDOR

COAT RACK

RECEPTIONIST'S
WINDOW

WAITING ROOM

RECEPTION /
BUSINESS
OFFICE

FILES

BILL COUNTER

SUITE CORRIDOR

Figure 24A. A reception window or counter should be open between the reception/business office and the waiting room. In addition, a counter for paying bills between the office and an interior corridor allows the patient to handle business transactions in private. This counter is also used for rescheduling appointments.

Figure 24B. The typical plan of the receptionist's window and counter for paying bills, shown in figure 24A, is seen in this office. The receptionist's window is simply an opening with a counter between the waiting room and the business office, and the bill-paying area is a smaller opening and counter between the interior corridor of the suite and the business office. During business hours, the door between the waiting room and the interior corridor would be closed.

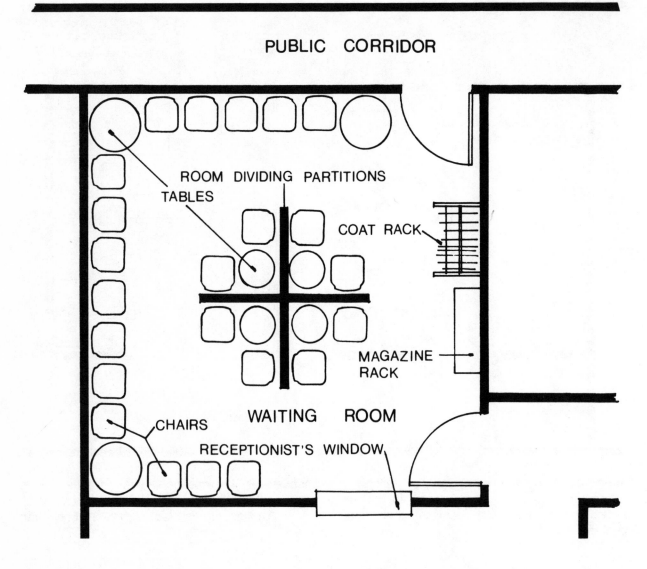

PUBLIC CORRIDOR

ROOM DIVIDING PARTITIONS

TABLES

COAT RACK

MAGAZINE RACK

WAITING ROOM

CHAIRS

RECEPTIONIST'S WINDOW

Figure 25A. Partial partitions added to a large waiting room reduce the coldness of the room and help patients feel more comfortable by providing grouped seating and more privacy.

Figure 25B. This large waiting room in a family practice suite is made to appear smaller and cozier through the creation of small seating alcoves. At left, partial partitions with decorative turned posts extending to the ceiling create areas for two to four persons to be seated. At the rear of the room, additional seating alcoves are created by full partitions, but with large, homelike picture windows in them. The windows and the partial partitions allow the receptionist to see waiting patients, whereas the wall arrangements provide some privacy for waiting patients. In addition the use of wood and leather chairs, table lamps (rather than overhead lighting), flower arrangements, and pictures add warmth to this waiting area. No sofas are used, and for patients who have difficulty sitting and rising from a chair, all chairs are sturdy and have arms.

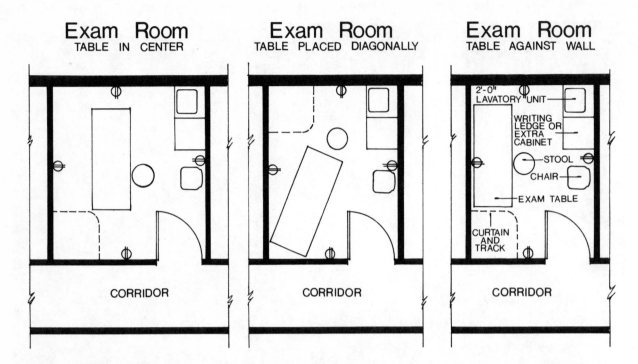

Exam Room
TABLE IN CENTER

Exam Room
TABLE PLACED DIAGONALLY

Exam Room
TABLE AGAINST WALL

2'-0"
LAVATORY UNIT

WRITING
LEDGE OR
EXTRA
CABINET

STOOL

CHAIR

EXAM TABLE

CURTAIN
AND
TRACK

CORRIDOR

CORRIDOR

CORRIDOR

Figure 26. A well designed examining room has a door that opens on the right side of the room and into the center of the room rather than against the adjacent wall. This location allows the door to act as a visual shield for the patient on the table when the door is open. The sink is usually located on the same side of the room as the door, providing more freedom of movement on the examination side of the room. A curtained dressing alcove can usually be placed behind the door, depending on where the physician likes his examining table located. This arrangement adapts well to the physician who likes to work from the right side of the patient, who likes a table diagonally located, or who likes to be able to move entirely around the table. Examining rooms with doors on the left and the layout reversed are also acceptable to physicians who do not examine the patient exclusively from the right side.

CHAPTER **16**

Construction Logistics

The process that begins with developing a medical office building program and ends with a completed structure is often complex and includes many sub-procedures.

A hospital may choose to use a conventional method of construction with competitive bidding of the entire construction package. It may choose to negotiate a construction contract while developing a building through various fast-track or phased construction methods. It may turn the entire project over to a turnkey developer who will handle the entire process. It may choose to employ or not to employ a construction manager. Or, it may choose any number of combinations of these and other alternatives.

An in-depth discussion of every alternative of construction development would be overwhelming. Consequently, this chapter will briefly present the pros and cons of the most frequently used alternatives. In addition, the author will present what he believes to be the most flexible and effective process for getting an on-campus medical office building built and occupied. The reader must, in turn, select for himself the alternatives that best fit his particular situation.

DESIGN/CONSTRUCTION METHODS

One familiar design/construction method might be called the conventional method, since it is one of the oldest and most familiar processes. The conventional method involves completing construction drawings and specifications before the job is put out for bids or negotiated with contractors. Both exterior and interior design details are set before a construction contract is sought. The primary advantage of this method is that it is considered the safest. All loose ends are tied, and total costs can be accurately determined before work begins. Its major drawbacks are that it requires more time from beginning to end than other construction procedures and that it does not allow for the flexibility of individual suite design throughout the construction of the project. It requires that physicians make decisions on interior suite design before construction documents go out for bids, and most physicians are reluctant or unable to commit themselves to so many details so far in advance.

The fast-track or phased construction method is another means for designing and constructing an office building. In this process design and construction go on simultaneously, with the design aspect staying one jump ahead of construction. For example, site preparation may begin before the building design is complete; footings may be poured while the structural steel is being bid; the structural steel may be going up while exterior design details are finished; elevators and mechanical systems may be bid and installed while interior design details of public areas are completed, and so forth. The job is broken down into segments, sometimes as many as 20, and each segment is bid or negotiated separately as the project moves along. The advantage of this method is that a building can be constructed very quickly. For example, a 60,000-square-foot office building in Florida was completed in seven months from the first day design began until tenants were moved in. The disadvantages include the fact that no final cost is determined before work begins, although reasonably accurate estimates of cost can usually be made. Also, errors in design are more likely to occur under the accelerated program, and, by and large, most medical office buildings are neither large enough, complicated enough, nor in need of such speedy completion to justify the fast-track method.

An additional construction method that has appeared on the scene for on-campus medical office buildings is the turnkey approach. This method's primary advantage is convenience, because it allows a package dealer to develop, design, and build the project, turning the keys of the finished building over to the hospital or owner. However, this approach has two major disadvantages: cost and loss of control. Although the cost of the package deal is likely to sound very good because it is usually a guaranteed price, that guaranteed price can be one of the most expensive methods for constructing a building (see "Common Construction Contracts," page 201). In addition, the hospital or owner has considerably less to say about how the design/build team is put together (that is usually predetermined by the packager) and is generally less involved in the whole development process than with other construction methods. Because the development of an on-campus medical office building is a part of the total hospital program and complex, this lack of involvement, though convenient, can produce serious consequences, both in loss of authority and in the hospital's having to live with someone else's errors. If a hospital chooses to use the turnkey approach for on-campus medical office building design and construction, it should be sure that it has a staff representative or consultant or both intimately involved throughout the development, design, and construction of the project.

EMPLOYING A CONSTRUCTION MANAGER

The employment of a construction manager is one other alternative for expediting the design and construction of an on-campus medical office building. It is an approach that can be used in conjunction with varying construction methods. Usually, when a construction manager is hired for a project, he supervises the construction process and keeps a running account of what everything costs. He may put together the bid packages and negotiate the major subcontracts, in which case he functions almost as a general contractor. In other situations, he may act more strictly in a supervisory capacity, functioning more as the hospital's watchdog and project coordinator. The hospital needs to decide before it hires a construction manager exactly what he is expected to do and whether the hospital is looking for the "general contractor" or the "owner's representative" type of manager.

Whether or not a hospital really needs a construction manager for an on-campus medical office building depends largely on the size of the project. Most construction managers charge a percentage fee and are more interested in large projects. Generally, a project would have to be at least 60,000 to 80,000 square feet before a manager would be interested in it. Smaller projects, with a good general contractor and a good architect on site, would usually not require a construction manager.

If, however, a project is very complicated or if time is critical, a construction manager can be valuable and worth his fee. For instance, if construction of the medical office building were to be near the emergency department or were to block the emergency department entrance temporarily, or if other hospital functions were to be disrupted, a construction manager could be very useful in expediting work and in getting fast action through difficult times. He could be extremely valuable in planning and enforcing time schedules that coordinate construction on the medical office building and any concomitant hospital construction. He can play a vital role in seeing that each step gets done exactly when it should so that disruptions are both planned and brief. Many top-quality general contractors can do the same, however. Clearly, the need for a construction manager is dependent upon circumstances, and only through examination of the total hospital program can the hospital board and administration determine whether or not this type of assistance is needed.

COMMON CONSTRUCTION CONTRACTS

Construction contracts can be let through a number of different methods, but the most common are competitive bidding and negotiation.

Competitive Bidding

Competitive bidding in its purest form involves distributing a complete set of construction documents for bid to interested and qualified contractors. The bid package includes a complete set of construction drawings and a complete set of specifications. The interested bidders, in turn, submit their sealed bids for the total cost of the project. The low bidder is usually selected and a contract signed for him to do the job.

Used in conjunction with the conventional method of construction, competitive bidding of a complete job is most frequently utilized in medical office buildings that are government-owned, primarily because the law usually requires competitive bidding on facilities owned by a city, a county, a state or the federal government. Although it is considered a safe method for determining costs and does give the bidders the incentive of competition for producing their best price, it also has drawbacks.

The sequence of completely designing, bidding, and constructing the building is, as mentioned earlier, a slow process that allows little flexibility for the physician. As a matter of fact, the completion of all interior office designs (if they are appropriately custom designed) before a medical office building is bid is quite difficult. Fortunately, however, most hospitals, including government-owned ones, are able to seek bids on a facsimile plan of office designs, with unit prices quoted on the units of work required to finish the interior. Such a procedure considerably lessens the lack of flexibility of the conventional competitive bid process.

Another drawback of competitive bidding of a completely designed job is that this process does not take advantage of early purchase of materials. Other types of construction contracts often bring the contractor into the picture much earlier than at the point when all drawings and specifications are completed. Consequently, other methods allow the contractor to purchase many of the standard building materials much earlier. When materials are not purchased until the total design is complete and the job is bid, as much as 18 months may have passed, with resulting increases in building material costs (as much as 15 percent). Any advantage thus gained through the competitive bid process may be lost by the slowness of this method. Where construction is concerned, time truly is money.

The slowness of the competitive bid process has one other drawback that is primarily psychological in nature. Once an announcement is made concerning the development of an on-campus medical office building, time becomes critical. Physicians want to see action to confirm in their minds that the building is actually going to be constructed. Although breakneck speed is not required, a design/build method that expedites the building's early development and construction contributes considerably to a kind of marketing momentum that begins to build as the physicians first hear about the building, contribute to its planning, see construction begin, commit to their own occupancy of the building, and assist in recruiting new physicians. Because this marketing momentum can be vital to the building's success, delaying factors should be avoided when possible, including construction methods that require substantially more time.

Although the process of designing, bidding, and building is not usually the recommended method of on-campus medical office building construction (unless required by law), competitive bidding can be very helpful and can be applied successfully in combination with other types of construction contracts to produce effective cost control without delaying the project. To some extent, competitive bidding may be used in the selection of a general contractor with whom a construction contract will be negotiated. For example, a number of contractors might be asked to submit proposals on the basis of one of the forms of negotiated contracts. Because several were being considered, the contractors would be encouraged by the competition to put the best possible terms into their proposed contracts. In addition, once a general contractor is selected, competitive bids may be solicited for some aspects of the project, such as in the selection of subcontractors or in the purchase of certain materials.

Negotiated Contracts

Negotiated contracts, which are frequently used for construction of on-campus medical office buildings, are usually negotiated on a cost-plus-percentage basis or on a guaranteed maximum price basis.

A cost-plus contract means that the contractor will charge an agreed-upon percentage over the actual cost of the project. The percentage the contractor will add to the base cost is a negotiable item that must be determined before the contract is signed. Generally, it will range between 10 and 15 percent. This type of contract is most frequently used for projects that involve renovation because most contractors will not commit to a firm price on a job that may involve many hidden problems. A cost-plus contract can also work for new construction, if the hospital is convinced of the absolute integrity and honesty of the contractor and his employees. It is also necessary for the hospital to have someone on its staff who is familiar with construction methods and costs and who can bird-dog the project. Although, in theory, a cost-plus contract can be an economical means for constructing a building, it is very vulnerable to contractors who might be inclined to pad costs, and it includes no incentive for the contractor to keep costs down. In addition, because no maximum is determined before the project gets under way, this method is very difficult to sell to the board. A cost-plus contract should be utilized with great caution.

A guaranteed maximum price contract provides the advantage of a ceiling on project costs. The hospital should realize, however, that when a builder guarantees a maximum, he is going to set a price high enough to make sure he does not lose money on the job. Thus, the initial price quoted will be higher than the ultimate cost. This point is of particular importance as a hospital examines the financial feasibility of a project.

Because a guaranteed price is always likely to be high, a hospital considering a guaranteed maximum contract should always include in the contract a provision for the hospital and contractor to share all cost savings below the guaranteed price. This procedure provides an incentive for the contractor to save money and guarantees that part of these savings is passed on to the hospital. Typically, the cost savings might be split 50/50 or 75 percent hospital/25 percent contractor. Usually, one of the best contracts is a combination competitive bid/guaranteed maximum in which several contractors submit proposals for the negotiated contract, the best is selected, and a savings split percentage is agreed upon.

One more variation on the negotiated contract might also be considered for medical office building construction. It is a hybrid that is basically a cost-plus contract with a guaranteed maximum price. In reality, this contract is not that much different from a guaranteed maximum price with shared cost savings, but it does allow the hospital to put a ceiling on the cost-plus method if, for some reason, a cost-plus contract is required.

EFFECTIVE COMBINATION

When all of the constuction methods and types of contracts are considered, one of the most flexible, economical, and effective means for designing and building an on-campus medical office building is the combination of a design/build team using a modified fast-track (phased) method of construction. This combination works especially well with a guaranteed maximum price contract with shared savings.

The first step in this procedure is the development of the program for the building. This step is carried out by the owner, consultant, and/or architect through the various methods outlined in chapter 13. Schematic drawings of the building are developed, as well as facsimile floor plans, density studies, and outline specifications. The bid package (to be discussed in depth in the next section) is submitted to interested and qualified contractors for their proposals for the job. A contract is negotiated with the contractor who submits the best proposal for the job, and work can begin. Although the contractor will be selected for the entire job, the project will actually be broken down into three separate segments for construction: basic site preparation, foundation and building shell, and interior finishes.

Once the contractor has been selected, the remainder of the design/build team needs to be put together as quickly as possible. The team includes the design engineers (mechanical, electrical, and structural) and the major subcontractors (plumbing, mechanical, electrical, and dry wall). At this point construction can begin on the first phase—basic site work—based on the schematic drawings and site plan. Included in this phase would be the preparation of the parking area, excavation, grading, filling, and any other ground preparation. Getting started quickly on this phase stirs up interest among medical staff members, starting the ball rolling on the marketing program.

At the same time that site work is being done, final construction drawings are being prepared for the shell of the building and some final drawings are being developed for interior spaces as physicians decide whether they want to move into the building. The great advantage of having a complete design/build team assembled before construction drawings are completed is that team members can each contribute in their areas of expertise. The team should meet periodically as the construction drawings are done so that each can learn from the other. Usually, numerous problems can be avoided and considerable amounts of money can be saved as a result of the team approach to working drawings.

After working drawings of the shell are completed, then construction can begin on this, the second, phase of the building. Shell construction includes the foundation, structural frame, exterior, core, mechanical and electrical systems, and such. During this phase of construction, the design/build team will want to meet periodically to present and discuss problems arising in specific areas. This procedure achieves a greater coordination of the project and contributes to more expeditious completion of the work.

During the second phase of construction, work continues on the completion of the drawings for interior spaces. As doctors decide to opt for occupancy in the building, their customized suites are designed. Working drawings for all the public areas are also completed. Consequently, as phase two of construction is completed, phase three can be starting up and individual suites can be finished for occupancy.

This dovetailing system allows great flexibility and a fast construction start for the building. Experience has proven that it works well and can be readily adjusted for varying local needs. Presented here in outline form only, more details of this modified fast-track or phased construction system with the design/build team will follow.

PREPARING THE BID PACKAGE

In order to receive maximum effectiveness from the design/build team using the modified fast-track method of construction, the hospital or owner must prepare the right kind of bid package for the selection of a contractor. The following bid package, which should be developed only after the program for the building has been developed, is based on the assumption that to select a contractor the owner will use the recommended method of competitive proposals in combination with a negotiated contract:

1. Schematic drawings. The first item to be included in the bid package is a set of schematic drawings of the shell or, in some cases, final drawings of the shell. (Usually final drawings are available only if the bidding or negotiations have been delayed). The schematic drawings should show the basic configuration of the floor plan; the basic structural system; the mechanical, electrical, and master plumbing systems; the elevations illustrating exterior materials; a few necessary sections; and a site plan showing necessary drives, parking, utilities, landscaping, and such.

2. Facsimile floor plans. Because completed interior drawings are usually not possible at this point, facsimile floor plans are a necessary part of the bid package. The facsimile floor plan should show an entire floor laid out in suites of various sizes and configurations. It should attempt to illustrate all of the materials in the proper quantities that would be needed to finish the floor at such time as custom designed suites can be developed. The facsimile should reflect proper density of materials, proper number of sinks, toilets, doors, electrical outlets, telephone outlets, standard cabinets, overhead light fixtures, and linear feet of partitions. In short, all of the units of work needed to finish the interior space should be shown in maximum density on the facsimile plan. An architect and his consulting engineers who have considerable medical office building experience or a qualified consultant can produce facsimile floor plans that are 95 percent accurate upon which to base bids. In essence, the facsimile floor plan might be compared to the pieces of an erector set. When the building is complete, the actual floor plans will look nothing like the facsimile, but all the pieces will be there in varying configurations.

In addition to providing the facsimile floor plans, the owner should instruct the bidders that they will be able to order 80 percent of all the materials required to finish the interior spaces according to the facsimile plan at such time as they are awarded the contract. The remainder will be ordered, if needed, at the time the final custom layouts are issued to the contractor.

3. Design criteria. The inclusion of a construction check list or design criteria in the bid package is an important part of establishing construction quality. The design criteria should specify the types, quality, and construction or installation of all materials to be used in the building, from electrical outlets to mechanical systems. For the purpose of bidding, the design criteria may include either specific brand and model numbers for items listed or they can be preliminary outline specifications, describing only the types and quality of materials to be used.

4. Unit price list. An itemized list of all the units of work required to finish the interior spaces should be included in the bid package. In addition, each bidder should be instructed to quote the number of units he is bidding. That is, if he were quoting a price on the electrical outlets, he would, first of all, state the number of total outlets projected for the entire building, based on the number shown on the facsimile floor plans. The price for electrical outlets should then be based on the total outlets counted, and the price should include the unit price or the price per outlet. He should also quote add or deduct prices for use in computing the cost if more or fewer outlets are required. This procedure forces the contractor to expose his unit prices and protects the owner from being charged inflated prices for change orders or for adding, for example, extra electrical outlets or more doors than originally bid. It also establishes the price for allowing credit to the owner if units are not used in the final design. Consequently, at the end of the project a relatively simple accounting of units used in the building can be compared to those bid on the basis of the facsimile plan, and total credits or charges can be computed.

The unit price list should also include some optional items that may be desired by the tenants, such as wood paneling, carpeting, vinyl wall covering, and extra cabinetry. By establishing the unit prices on the optional items in the bidding stage, the hospital protects the physician from being charged inflated prices for optional interior suite finishes and, thus, prevents a situation that could create ill will between the physician and the hospital. By having available both deduct prices for standard items and add-on prices for optional items the physician knows exactly where he stands. He can determine the cost of optional carpet, for example, by taking that total cost and subtracting the credit he will receive from not using the standard vinyl flooring. If he wants his own contractor or decorator to do interior finishing for him, he will know exactly how much credit he will receive for each unit not completed by the general contractor, and he can compare that credit with the cost of contracting for his own work.

One other inclusion should be made in the bid package in relation to unit prices. It is a statement such as the following, "The prices quoted herein are valid for the duration of the construction contract." Having unit prices valid for all segments of work for a specified period of time protects the owner from cost escalation of labor, materials, fixtures, and other aspects of the work. Any and all revisions, credits, deletions, and/or alterations, therefore, are valid and cost protected for the duration of the job. Unit prices should include profit, overhead, and taxes.

RECORD KEEPING AND CHANGE ORDERS

After the contractor has been selected, but before construction begins, procedures should be set up for both record keeping and processing change orders.

If, during the construction process, the contractor keeps careful records of the number of standard items per floor that he uses and the number of standard items he has left of the total he bid, impending cost and material overruns can be spotted before it is too late. He can go to the design/build team members for reevaluation and adjustments to be made, so that the costs can be controlled. For these reasons, the contractor should be instructed to keep running records and to report periodically how the utilization of items is progressing.

The first rule in dealing with change orders is to expect them and be prepared for them. Particularly in interior finishing, change orders can always be expected. Doctors change their minds, and their requirements change. A smart owner will make arrangements with the architect, engineers, and contractors for handling the change orders before construction ever begins. Fees should be set for redesign, unit prices should be set for the work, and procedures for handling the changes should be established. A normal procedure for handling a change order request from a tenant would be for the tenant to go first to the primary contact person—the consultant or architect's representative. Then his request will go through the architectural firm for redesign and to the field for an estimate. The estimate should be presented to the tenant and his approval received in writing at that time.

In some cases, the cost can be determined without preparing detailed plan changes. Often, the change order will involve adding items for which unit prices have already been quoted, so cost determination is simple. In other cases, a simple sketch presented to the contractor is sufficient for him to determine cost. Using a sketch eliminates the preparation of extensive drawings for a change that the tenant may subsequently reject because of cost.

The tenant should be responsible for the cost of any changes in suite layout. At the time he is presented with drawings to sign, he should be made aware that he will be charged with all construction, engineering, and architectural revision time. Some cases should, however, be negotiable, particularly when the hospital is the owner. At times very good reasons may prompt the doctor to change his suite. For example, he may have located an associate whom he is recruiting to practice with him. In such a case, the hospital might not want to make him pay all the change order costs because of the ultimate benefit the hospital will receive from the new physician.

Toward the end of interior construction, a flurry of change orders will be requested as doctors get into their suites and see specifics that need changing—shelving in closets, additional chart racks here or there, additional telephone outlets, and other minor revisions. If the hospital owns the building, it will probably not want these small change orders issued through the contractor, but instead through the hospital's maintenance department. It will be less costly to the tenant and the hospital, and it will prevent overall construction delays to the project. In addition, the hospital will be able to establish good initial relationships with the physician by having its maintenance department available to make the changes at the cost of materials and labor only.

CONSTRUCTION SCHEDULING AND PHASING

The advent of a medical office building project usually produces excitement and interest on the part of the medical staff. This enthusiasm should not be allowed to dissipate by a long, drawn-out construction process. To expedite completion of the project, a number of phases should occur simultaneously.

An average on-campus medical office building of 60,000 square feet can usually be developed, constructed, and occupied within 28 to 30 months. In the first 10 months, the development of the program, preparation of the bid package, bidding, and any necessary approval from planning agencies and the board are completed. The construction sequence will consume the remaining 18 months. If, however, sophisticated hospital functions are included in the building, such as laboratory, radiology, or day surgery, more time may be required.

Significantly, one of the major delaying factors in the construction of an on-campus medical office building is not the contractor's failure to get things done on time, but the owner's inability to make decisions. If construction is to proceed in a timely manner, the owner must be available and ready to make decisions when the decisions are needed, not days or even weeks later.

The actual construction phasing of the project will include a 10-month to 12-month period from the start of construction until the time that final interior plans are absolutely required for the contractor to continue work. At that time the shell and core of the building will be complete and the beginning of interior construction must start. This 10-month to 12-month period is the most valuable time available in marketing the building. The construction process gives the designers time to work with the doctors on developing their custom suite layouts and to prepare final drawings to be issued to the contractor. Undoubtedly, the general contractor and subcontractors will push for drawings as early as possible, which is understandable. They want to plan as far ahead as possible, but this time period is so valuable to the marketing of the building that it needs to be used to its best advantage.

The remaining six to eight months of construction are used for finishing the interior of the building and for tenants to begin moving in. Interior space should be completed in an orderly manner that provides for doctors to be moving in without disturbance from continuing construction. The best procedure is to finish the building a floor at a time, from the top down.

This finishing procedure makes it possible for the building to be occupied a floor at a time over a period of about three to six months, while other floors are being finished. The advantages of this method include the fact that the owner begins collecting some rent earlier in the project; problems with individual suites can be solved more adequately than if everyone were moving in at once; more flexibility is available to physicians who, because of expired leases or other reasons, need to move in by an early date; and traffic flow problems associated with many tenants moving in are spread out and lessened.

Physically speaking, finishing the building from the top down provides a number of advantages. Construction dust and litter are kept below the completed floors so that dirt does not filter down through the building into occupied suites and public areas. Installation of plumbing and other core elements does not have to be done over an occupied suite, which would require removing the ceiling, inconveniencing the tenant, and possibly damaging the suite if an accident were to occur. There is less noise, and construction traffic is minimized on the completed floors.

However, before tenants begin to move in on this basis, proper certificates of occupancy must be obtained and inspections must be made by the code administrators and building officials. In addition, the building owner will want to thoroughly inspect each floor with the contractor before accepting it as ready for occupancy. Any incomplete, unsatisfactory, or damaged items should be carefully noted. Such a procedure eliminates discussion later about whose responsibility such items are—the contractor's or the tenant's. This procedure is especially important when a physician has his own contractor or decorator doing finishing work in his suite. The private contractor or decorator should not be allowed to begin work until the floor or at least the suite has been officially accepted from the general contractor.

MOVING IN TENANTS

The physician's move into the on-campus medical office building is usually the beginning of a closer relationship between him and the hospital, and getting off on the right foot can be important. The hospital, particularly when it is the building owner, needs to anticipate problems and be available to help solve them. In fact, if the hospital can provide one of its maintenance personnel to be available to help the doctors with small problems when they move in, much goodwill can be fostered. This cooperation could mean the difference between a long and friendly relationship and a frustrating one.

Special attention should be given to the building itself during the partial move-in phase. Stairwells must be clean and usable, and at least one elevator needs to be in operation. Ideally, separate elevators should be provided for patients and construction personnel so that the patient elevator can be kept clean. The physicians should be made aware that the heating and air conditioning will be difficult to balance as long as construction continues, but that this will be a temporary problem.

Provisions should be made at the main entrance for patients to come and go easily. If signs are not complete, then the hospital should be prepared to provide temporary graphics to direct patients to the floors where the physicians are located, particularly when all the elevators are not operable. Safety is also important during this transition phase. By using signs, physical barriers, and even locking off floors on elevators, patients should be kept out of construction areas. The hospital should also inspect the building daily to spot hazards or negligence and eliminate them immediately.

When all construction has been completed and tenants have moved in, the hospital can show pride in the building and in the physicians who occupy it by planning an open house. Physicians tend to invest considerable time and money furnishing and decorating their suites. The open house gives them the opportunity to exhibit their new offices to their colleagues and to the public. It also reflects favorably on the hospital and fosters good relationships between hospital management and tenants.

THE BIG PICTURE

The total construction experience of an on-campus medical office building can be either rewarding or frustrating. One key to success is open, continual, and sufficient communication among all design/build team members. Another key is that the hospital must do business with a contractor who is reliable, trustworthy, and honest, and that professionals with experience must be available to supplement the hospital's knowledge and to assist the hospital in making key and timely decisions. If all of these elements can be put together, then a successful construction project is assured.

CHAPTER **17**
Successful On-Campus MOBs in Operation

All the concepts, theories, and guidelines in the world are of little value unless they result in medical office buildings that operate successfully. The following five hospitals represent a broad spectrum of success. They are located in large cities, medium sized cities, and small communities; they have operated medical office buildings for 50 years or just a few years; they used different plans, procedures, and methods; and they all arrived at the same destination—effective on-campus medical office facilities. Here they share some of what they learned, how they planned the building and proceeded with the project, and what their results were.

INSTANT FIVE-STORY BUILDING
Baptist Hospital, Pensacola, Florida
Prepared by
Pat N. Groner, president and chief executive officer
J. Craig Honaman, former assistant director

Baptist Hospital incorporated a physicians' office building into its long-range plans in 1960. At that time, the need was recognized for a facility adjacent to the hospital to provide physicians with office space located near their patients. The overall concept was not new; however, the community situation did not lend itself to immediate implementation of the development of such a building.

Historically, physicians in Pensacola spread their practices between two hospitals and therefore maintained offices at locations convenient to both institutions. This arrangement worked well for the physicians and the hospitals, and adequate office space had been available.

The hospital recognized that expertise was required to survey the community and determine the scope of the project in mind. The hospital engaged a consultant to recommend to the hospital the size of the building needed and a general design for the building itself.

After surveying the community and interviewing a number of interested physicians, the consultants recommended a five-story building with a gross area of 59,000 square feet. With the assistance of a local architect, the building design was established to economize on space and to build in as much flexibility for interior office suites as possible. The consultants were quite accurate in predicting the occupancy rate upon completion, and the hospital was thus able to establish the amount of square footage desired in order to have the building partially occupied at completion, with room to expand.

A fast-track construction mode was selected. Rather than follow the traditional sequence of construction, the hospital selected a contractor to negotiate a guaranteed price. The primary concern of the hospital was that, within the fast-track construction process, a ceiling price was difficult to establish because of the lack of detailed plans and specifications prior to beginning the project. As a result, the hospital negotiated with the contractor a not-to-exceed price figure based on typical floor plans and averages of required fixtures and materials. Much of this information was readily available through the consultants who had extensive experience in suite layouts.

Building a five-story building on a fast-track construction basis required considerable coordination among the consultants, the contractor, the architect, and the owner. Substantial details had to be addressed in a very timely manner. Initially, because of the relatively short time frame that the hospital required all parties to work within, substantial advance commitments were needed to have the work performed. Because of previous experience, the consultant was able to provide enough information for the hospital to proceed with cost estimates. In addition, the use of local contractors and architects contributed substantially to the project's proceeding on schedule.

The result of the project can be summed up as follows:

- The contractor ultimately completed the building from ground level up in less than six months and came in below the guaranteed price, thus saving the hospital in the neighborhood of $25,000.
- The building was occupied on schedule, and the commitment made to the physicians involved was met.
- All parties in the project were paid in a timely manner, and there were no cost overruns. Inflation did not have time to catch up with these suppliers.
- The building was, to the best of our knowledge, completed faster and at a more reasonable cost than any other project of its size in Pensacola.

Operationally, the project has been an outstanding success. The first office building, completed in 1974, was substantially occupied by late summer of 1976, and the hospital proceeded to construct a second building of the same size. The second building was completed in July 1977. Some of the factors that contributed to the success include:

- No lease is required of the physicians. Thirty days notice is asked for. One physician has retired from practice. However, during the life of the project, no physicians have left because of a desire to move.
- The project is operated on a nonprofit basis. The revenues from the project cannot go to subsidize patient care, nor can patient care funds subsidize the office building project.

- Physician occupancy of the office building is contingent on maintaining satisfactory medical staff privileges. Thus, the occupancy of the building is contingent on good quality medical care.
- The hospital is not in the market to sell space, but to provide whatever space is needed. Thus, the physician is not concerned about renting more space than what he may need. In addition, the design of the building is such that maximum effective utilization of square footage is provided.
- The hospital must do a better job of providing services to the tenants than they might otherwise receive in the community.
- The rental rate is an all encompassing rate; the physician does not manage many details such as utilities, housekeeping, and so forth.
- The hospital employed a local contractor and local architect; therefore the physician group felt confident that the major parties involved in the project would stay in the community and would insist on a high-quality project. The consultant contracted with the hospital on a fixed-cost basis, rather than ' on a percentage basis of the project. Consequently, the consultant had no vested interest in selling space.

The impact of the office buildings on the hospital is long term. The space is not intentionally marketed to physicians currently in the community. Many of those physicians have their practices situated at a particular hospital. The office buildings are focused toward the new physician coming into the community who has not established a hospital practice. We found that we have a much younger group of physicians locating in the office buildings than in the surrounding community. Thus, long-range results will occur as the result of the future patients from these physicians, since they will have been in practice much longer than other physicians in the community.

More hospital administration time is directed toward managing the office building and, in some cases, a physician's office practice. This procedure relieves the physician of administrative office responsibilities. This aspect of hospital administration is a new dimension when it pertains to a solo private practitioner and multiple individual physicians.

Generally, the new physicians who have located in the community and rented space in our office building, ultimately have concentrated their patients at our hospital. We assume that if those same physicians had not had office space next to the hospital, those same patients would have been located throughout the community in other hospitals. Thus, although precise numbers cannot be established, we believe that a higher proportion of patients of those physicians use the hospital services than otherwise might have.

Our second office building was completed without any commitments from any physicians for occupancy. In a one-month period after completion, we had commitments from seven physicians. Other commitments were pending. This type of project has been beneficial to the doctors, to the hospital, and to the patients.

SURVIVAL IN THE RURAL NORTHWEST

Community Hospital (now Idaho Falls Consolidated Hospitals, Parkview Facility), Idaho Falls, Idaho
Prepared by
M.J. Foerster, former administrator

The major goal Community Hospital had in developing a medical office building was simple survival. The hospital was operating at 52 percent occupancy and was rapidly going out of business. No multispecialty groups of physicians were located in the community, and the ratio of physicians-to-population was very low.

The hospital had a floor of shelled-in space that was not in use and certainly had no foreseeable need for additional beds. The conversion of this space to doctors' offices seemed to be a reasonable use for the area.

We now have nine physicians in this space, and the success of the program has caused us to find additional space in the hospital to house five other physicians. Having the doctors in the building has certainly contributed to increased patient load (which is now 68 percent); has made it possible for us to recruit physicians into the community, including specialists whom we would probably never have been able to obtain; and last year we were comfortably in the black, instead of experiencing a serious deficit.

Concerning the factors that contributed to the success of the program, it was primarily money. That is to say, if the physician finds that he can use his time more advantageously to increase his income, and if by his using our hospital rather than another hospital, the hospital realizes increased revenue, I would suppose you could say the most significant factor is economic. However, by having the physician close to his patients in the hospital, improved patient care has resulted. It has fostered the development of a multispecialty team approach to patient care. Because of our close-working relationship, it has improved the hospital-physician relationship appreciably.

When we initially started the program, we tried very hard to recruit local physicians into the program, but because of the keen competition between the two hospitals, physicians felt that they could not align themselves with one hospital or the other. Now that the program has been in operation for a few years and the outside physicians have seen the success of the program, I constantly have requests from physicians to move into the hospital. Right now we have no additional space and cannot accommodate them. I must add that the program has been accepted by the local physicians. We have used operating policies similar to those discussed in this book and have found them to be very useful.

The development of this program has been the keystone to the survival of this hospital.

PIONEERS IN PROGRESS
Baptist Memorial Hospital, Memphis, Tennessee
Prepared by
Frank S. Groner, president emeritus
Maurice W. Elliott, vice-president

Baptist Memorial Hospital opened its doors in July 1912 as a 150-bed hospital. In 1928 a wing called the Physicians and Surgeons Building, which was designed to accommodate offices for the hospital's medical staff, was added to the hospital. This was the first hospital-owned and operated office building in the United States, and the success of this venture is best illustrated by the growth of the hospital since that date. Today, Baptist Memorial Hospital, with more than 1,900 beds and 60,000 annual admissions, is the largest private hospital in the country. The development of hospital-owned medical office facilities has kept pace with the hospital's growth.

In 1958 a 10-story office building with approximately 75,000 gross square feet was completed. This building is connected to the hospital by an over-the-street crosswalk.

In 1964 another 10-story physicians' office building with approximately 140,000 gross square feet was opened. This building is connected to the hospital by a tunnel under the street. In that same year the hospital acquired a four-story office building of approximately 25,000 gross square feet, which is located approximately two blocks from the hospital. Because of its remoteness, this office building is operated under a separate for-profit corporation.

In 1975 another 10-story office building of approximately 140,000 gross square feet was developed. It connects to a tunnel leading to the hospital.

A 400-bed satellite hospital was recently built in a suburban area of Memphis. A six-story office building of approximately 81,000 gross square feet was developed as part of this project.

The first floors of all these buildings are occupied by ancillary businesses, which accommodate the medical staff, employees, and patients. The businesses include pharmacies, a blood donor center, an outpatient laboratory, a bank, a surgical supply company, a barber shop, a beauty shop, a cafeteria, an optical dispensary, and hotel facilities.

Baptist Memorial Hospital serves as a referral hospital for a large area of the Mid-South region. Approximately 51 percent of the inpatients are referred from out of town. In order to accommodate outpatients visiting the Medical Center and families of patients from out of town, a 90-room hotel facility occupying three floors was developed as part of the office building completed in 1964.

Of the 394 physicians on the hospital's attending staff, nearly 200 have their offices in the hospital-owned buildings. The office buildings that are physically connected to the hospital are operated under the hospital's not-for-profit corporate charter. The hospital pays property tax on the office buildings and pays unrelated business income tax on some of the ancillary facilities within the buildings. Offices in the buildings are restricted to physicians on the medical staff of the hospital.

From the standpoint of improved patient care, the hospital believes that a sound basis exists for including the office buildings in the not-for-profit corporate structure of the hospital. The closeness of the physician is actually much more important to good patient care than many of the facilities included within the hospital. The hospital operates under the philosophy that the office buildings should not be financially subsidized by the hospital nor should the physicians be exploited or restricted by the hospital. In keeping with this policy, no restrictions are placed on tenants' ability to own x-ray and laboratory facilities within their office suites.

Two basic reasons motivate the hospital to own and operate physicians' office buildings. The primary reason relates to the improvement in patient care that accrues from the proximity of the physician. The physician is more readily available to inpatients and can respond more quickly to emergencies. Our studies have shown that the physicians located in the hospital-owned office buildings provide a significant majority of the consultations rendered to inpatients. Because of the proximity, the physicians are also more readily available to participate in the medical staff education program of the hospital and on the medical staff committees.

The second major motivation in operating physicians' office buildings has to do with the stability and growth these facilities provide for the hospital operation. The physicians in the connecting office buildings admit a proportionately far greater number of patients to the hospital than those who have their offices elsewhere in the community. This close relationship also provides for a more stable occupancy rate year around in that the peaks and valleys in occupancy are less severe. We believe that the physicians whose offices are a part of the hospital complex identify more closely with the hospital and, thus, have more of a feeling of loyalty to the facility and a better understanding of the hospital's operation. This arrangement fosters a good relationship between the medical staff and the hospital, a valuable intangible asset. Also those responsible for the management of the hospital have an opportunity to understand better the problems and needs of the physician. The buildings have also afforded the advantage to the hospital of income produced through office rentals as well as increased use of hospital ancillary services, such as X ray and laboratory, by tenants of the office buildings. Office buildings as part of the hospital complex tend to foster a medical center concept in the mind of the public. Through this arrangement, a complete array of medical specialists are available and referrals among specialists are facilitated.

Through 50 years of experience with hospital-owned medical office buildings, Baptist Memorial Hospital is convinced that the concept is sound and has become an integral part of the modern hospital complex. There is also no doubt that the patient is the primary beneficiary of this development.

'WE SHOULD HAVE BUILT A BIGGER BUILDING'

Anaheim (California) Memorial Hospital
Prepared by
J. W. McAlvin, former executive director
Ronald J. Marott, administrator

The establishment of a medical office building on the campus of Anaheim Memorial Hospital was the result of three years of planning. As a direct result of that planning, the project has been both successful and predictable.

When Anaheim Memorial Hospital was 15 years old, it was mutually agreed by the institution's medical staff and its voluntary board of directors that a medical office structure was necessary for three reasons: to make it possible for members of the medical staff to be physically located near the hospital; to make the practice of medicine easier for physicians; and to provide an enticement for new physicians to come into the area served by the hospital.

Four acres of land adjoining the hospital were acquired. On that land, a seven-story Class A structure was erected, containing a gross of 106,000 square feet, including a full basement. Following two years of construction, the building was opened in January 1975. Total cost of the project was $6.1 million. Half of that cost was financed over 20 years.

The basement and first floor of the structure are primarily devoted to hospital administrative offices, laboratories, classrooms, and computer areas. Within 30 months, the remaining six floors were totally leased. In the 40 available suites, 56 physicians and three nonphysician professionals had located their practices. A waiting list of new tenants as well as those who wanted to increase their existing space had developed.

The hospital administration maintains a landlord-tenant relationship with physicians in the office building. For the most part, month-to-month rental agreements are used. In some instances when extensive internal remodeling was required, annual leases were used. In both cases, office space was rented for 60 cents per square foot per month. This rental figure was based upon a construction cost of $55.00 per square foot, with the structure to be self-liquidating over the 20-year financing term. The hospital's director of engineering acts as manager of the office building, with existing hospital maintenance personnel performing the same functions in the office structure.

Space within the office building is rented to carefully selected medical tenants only. During the planning stages of the facility, the hospital's medical staff formed a committee that established a pattern for the tenant composition. They decided that for the benefit of the surrounding community, tenants should represent a broad spectrum of the medical specialties without regard to the then established medical capabilities of the adjoining hospital. At times, therefore, suites have been empty, even though prospective tenants were on a waiting list. The suite was held vacant because the committee had determined that the physician to occupy that specific suite should be a certain type of specialist, and no such specialist was on the waiting list.

When suites are rented, the tenant is permitted to make any interior design changes necessary for practice. He can bring in outside workmen for the job or use those available through the hospital, at added cost beyond the rent.

Following almost three years of operation of the medical office building, a number of interesting changes have taken place. Anaheim Memorial Hospital is a 240-bed not-for-profit community hospital. Since the medical office building opened, approximately 40 percent of the hospital's patients have come directly from tenant physicians. Some 60 patients per day enter the hospital primarily due to the proximity of their physicians' offices.

For years prior to the opening of the medical office building, Anaheim Memorial Hospital was a general hospital. Since the office structure opened, however, the health care facilities within the hospital are changing to conform to the specific needs of tenants' patients. As a result of the medical office building, the hospital is becoming more specialized.

The medical staff of the hospital is growing steadily, too. A requirement of tenants is that they be on the staff of the hospital. Those physicians who already had staff affiliations before construction of the medical office building and who subsequently became tenants say they have found their practices becoming more efficient. One generalist, for example, moved his practice into a suite having 1,200 square feet. In less than three years he had tripled his space and changed from individual to group practice. He says his relocation to the hospital's medical office building saves him two hours of driving time each day, and his patients who must be hospitalized feel more secure, knowing that their physician's office is only minutes from their bedside.

From the standpoint of the medical profession, new physicians coming right out of school now have a "place to go" within the community, which can provide them with both the offices and the hospital with which to build their practices in a manner that is efficient in terms of both time and money.

Looking back over the success of the project, we have but one comment: "We should have built a bigger building."

TANGIBLE SUCCESS

Methodist Hospital, Jacksonville, Florida
Prepared by
Marcus E. Drewa, president

The decision to construct Medical Center Plaza as the first of two on-campus office buildings of Methodist Hospital, Inc., was foreseen as the initial phase of a larger development venture. The decision was based on the varied advantages that such a facility would offer to the patients of Methodist Hospital, the medical staff, and to the hospital itself.

The proximity of the physician's office to the hospital enables the physician to better utilize his time as well as the service facilities located within the hospital and the office building complex. This closeness provides him with greater ease and convenience in admitting his patients, attending medical meetings, and using the hospital services for outpatient and inpatient emergencies.

The advantages to the patients of Methodist Hospital, Inc., of such a building were outlined in a study conducted by the United States Internal Revenue Service. This report indicated that a physicians' office building located in close proximity to a hospital reduces patient admissions, length of stay, and surgical rates, all of which help to reduce hospital costs to patients. The effect on hospital costs and length of stay, along with more effective use of medical manpower and existing medical facilities, enables the hospital to continue its progress toward serving the total health needs of the community.

In addition to physicians' office space, Medical Center Plaza was designed to house an inpatient and outpatient clinical laboratory, several expanded hospital service departments (oriented primarily toward outpatient treatment), and various commercial shops.

The goal was to construct a building that would summon the attention of the physicians to the convenience and usefulness of locating or relocating their practices within a growing medical complex. Thus with the location of such departments as the clinical laboratory, a complete outpatient surgery department, and other ancillary services within the office building, the individual physician may choose to limit his office staff and reduce the number and types of supplies he purchases. In addition, the proximity of fellow specialists may enhance the practicing physician's delivery of medical care as well as his knowledge of the daily discoveries outside his particular specialty.

Part of the original concept included a belief that the physician alone knows best his needs regarding office equipment and design. Consequently, Medical Center Plaza was designed with the assistance of physicians, translating their desires into office design. The result has been a physicians' office building that ranks among the most modern in existence.

Medical Center Plaza represents the completion of Phase I of the Master Development Plan for Methodist Hospital, Inc. It is the first of two professional office buildings to be constructed as part of the Methodist Medical Center. When completed in the early 1980s, the Medical Center will contain a completely new 300-bed hospital facility and a parking garage, in addition to the twin office buildings. Medical Center Plaza is the location of offices for numerous Jacksonville physicians who serve on the staff of Methodist Hospital. The new building is a vital part of Methodist Hospital, as the building and the hospital are connected by an enclosed corridor that allows for continuous flow between the two facilities.

In the spring of 1977 a study was undertaken to determine what impact the operation of the existing office building had had on the admission and census patterns of Methodist Hospital, Inc. It was also for the purpose of determining a partial rationale for proceeding with the construction of the second planned office complex.

The Study

The first step of the study involved developing a table showing admissions by those physicians or groups with offices in the Medical Center Plaza. This table was developed from a physician index that is kept in the medical records department and that tracks the total admissions per physician for each fiscal year of the hospital's operation.

As a second step, the percentage of occupancy by month, based on discharge days, and the number of admissions per month were tabulated from hospital census statistics for the following years:

Fiscal year 1974 (the year before the opening of the Medical Center Plaza)

Fiscal year 1975 (the year during which the building opened)

Fiscal year 1976 (the first full year of operation since the opening of the building)

The first eight months of fiscal year 1977

Finally, information from these two steps was analyzed in order to develop a comparative look at the admitting patterns of physicians whose offices were located in the office building and those whose offices were located elsewhere.

Results

From 1974 to 1975, a 9.8 percent increase in the percentage of occupancy occurred. (During both years, 164 beds were in service within the hospital itself.) From 1975 to 1976, a 3.4 percent drop in the average percentage of occupancy occurred; however, 26 additional beds were put into operation in 1976. Even with the additional beds put into operation—raising the total from 164 to 190 and representing a 16 percent increase—the percentage of occupancy was higher than the 1974 level, prior to the opening of the office building.

A similar comparison can be seen between 1976 and 1977. The percentage of occupancy remained stable in spite of an increase in beds from 190 to 210.

A net increase of 876, or 13.68 percent, in the number of admissions occurred from 1975 to 1976. Of the 876 additional admissions, 816 were generated by physicians or groups with offices in the Medical Center Plaza. Only 60 additional admissions were generated by the remaining physicians or groups who admit to Methodist Hospital.

A similar pattern occurred during fiscal year 1976 and the first eight months of fiscal year 1977. Admissions increased by 287. Of these admissions, 242 were generated by physicians or groups with offices in the Medical Center Plaza, whereas only 45 were generated by the remaining physicians or groups.

Finally, although the number of physicians and/or groups admitting to Methodist Hospital did, in fact, decrease from 112 in 1975 to 96 in 1977, the number of physicians or groups with offices in the Medical Center Plaza *and* admitting to Methodist Hospital increased from 14 in 1975 to 20 in 1976. Six of these physicians had previously not admitted patients to Methodist Hospital. In addition, the study indicated that those physicians or groups previously admitting to Methodist Hospital continued to do so at a stable rate.

Summary

Concomitant with an increase in bed size from 164 in 1975 to 210 in 1977, a steady increase in the number of admissions occurred and the average percentage of occupancy stabilized. This effect was seen primarily because of the influence of the physicians located within the Medical Center Plaza.

The physicians or groups with offices in the Medical Center Plaza were responsible for generating more than 92 percent of the increases in 1976 and more than 84 percent of the increases in 1977.

The number of admissions generated by all other physicians or groups admitting to Methodist Hospital has remained relatively stable since the opening of the Medical Center Plaza.

The increase in the total number of physicians or groups admitting at Methodist Hospital is indicated by the new physicians who moved into the Medical Center Plaza and who were not previously admitting to the hospital.

The study indicates that, since the opening of the Medical Center Plaza, the major portion of the increase in the number of admissions to Methodist Hospital was generated by physicians or groups with offices in the building. This increase has served to stabilize the average percent of occupancy of the hospital during the time that the hospital was expanding its overall bed capacity. Operation of the professional building has had a tangible impact on the overall operations of Methodist Hospital. With further expansion of Methodist Hospital in the planning stage and near full occupancy of the existing Medical Center Plaza building, the construction of an additional office building is indicated.

Conclusions

APPENDIX A

Sample Letter of Understanding

Dear Doctor(s) _____,

_____Hospital agrees to rent you_____square feet of space in its professional office building at an initial rent of _____per square foot per month, due monthly in advance.

Such space will be fully improved to include standard materials as shown in Exhibit A* attached hereto.

This agreement will continue as long as _____ Hospital remains an accredited general hospital and you are a member of the medical staff of the hospital. This agreement is with you personally and cannot be assigned by you.

The above rent will be adjusted from time to time to compensate for increases and decreases in the operation of the building, to include housekeeping and maintenance costs, taxes, utilities, and labor, because _____ Hospital is providing the operation at cost.

The hospital will obtain fire insurance and extended insurance coverage on the building and public liability coverage for public areas and corridors. As physician tenant, you will be responsible for providing fire and other insurance coverage on the contents of the leased space and for public liability within the leased space.

If this agreement is with more than one physician tenant, notification must be made to the hospital of any change in the group status.

If you agree to all of the foregoing, please sign a copy of this letter at the lower left hand corner and return it to me.

Sincerely,

_____Hospital

By _____

Approved and accepted:

_____M.D.
_____M.D.

---

*Exhibit A would normally consist of an architectural drawing of the finished suite with all detailing of materials indicated.

The forms contained in the appendixes are for the purpose of example and can serve as a convenient reference for legal counsel. The forms should not be used unless they have been reviewed by legal counsel and modified to accommodate specific situations and local law.

APPENDIX **B**

Sample Short-Form Lease

LEASE OF SPACE IN _____HOSPITAL
MEDICAL OFFICE BUILDING

   THIS LEASE of space in the _____Hospital's Medical
Office Building is entered into by and between _____,
hereinafter called ''Hospital,'' and _____,
hereinafter called "Tenant," upon the following terms and conditions.

   1. Only individuals who are eligible for the medical staff of the Hospital and
who regularly admit patients to the Hospital shall be eligible to lease space in
the Medical Office Building. Death, retirement, failure to maintain good standing with the medical staff, or ceasing to actively practice within the leased
space shall result in ineligibility of the Tenant, and the Hospital may terminate
this lease in the manner set out in Item 6 hereof. Any subleases shall be limited
to individuals furnishing medical or paramedical services and shall be subject
to the terms and conditions of this lease, and the Hospital shall have the right to
approve any subleases.

   2. The term of this lease is for five years beginning _____, 19_____.
The Tenant may extend the term for four (4) separate and successive periods of
five (5) years each by giving written notice to the Hospital within six (6) months
prior to the end of the then current lease term, and rental increases during any
succeeding term shall be limited to a maximum of 10 percent of the rent
charged during the immediately preceding term.

> [An initial rental period of five years coupled with four options for
> five years each provides a rather lengthy commitment to the lease.
> Some leases may have shorter initial lease periods, shorter and/or
> fewer renewal options, depending on local circumstance. In ad-
> dition, with current inflation rates, a rent escalator related to in-
> creased operating costs, taxes, insurance, and so forth, might be
> safer than a flat 10 percent ceiling on rental increases.]

   3. The Hospital will obtain fire and extended insurance coverage on the
building and public liability coverage as to public areas and corridors. The
Tenant shall be responsible for providing fire and other insurance coverage on
the contents of the leased space and for public liability coverage within the
leased space. The Hospital shall not be liable for and the Tenant shall indemnify
and defend and hold the Hospital harmless against any loss, damages, attorney's fees, or other expenses resulting from (a) personal injury or property
damage occurring within the leased space, except when proximately caused by

affirmative negligence of the Hospital or its representatives [check local law]; and (b) default by the Tenant in any of the terms and conditions of this lease.

[As indicated within the covenant, the hospital's attorney should localize this aspect of the lease, bringing it into harmony with local laws concerning liability and insurance coverage.]

4. In the event the building is destroyed or the leased space rendered untenantable by fire, earthquake, or other casualty through no fault of the Tenant, then the Tenant shall have the right to terminate this lease if the space cannot be made tenantable within____months and, in any event, rent shall abate during the repair period. [See statute.] The Tenant shall be responsible for obtaining his own business interruption insurance.

[Local statutes should be examined so that the lease will conform to local laws.]

5. The rent shall be $_____for the initial five year term, payable $_____per month, on the _____ of each month, at such place as the Hospital may designate.

[If the hospital has any desire to require a security deposit or to require advance rent, it should be inserted at this point in the lease.]

In the event of the Tenant's default in payment of rent or in the performance of any other condition or agreement herein set out, the Hospital shall have the right to terminate this lease upon giving _____days' notice to the Tenant in writing, mailed or delivered to his last address, and the Tenant shall be obligated to continue paying rent during the time reasonably necessary for the Hospital to relet the space and, thereafter, shall be obligated for the difference between the rent reserved herein and the amount, if any, received under such reletting for the remainder of the term.

7. The Tenant shall not cause or permit damage or injury to the leased space and, upon the expiration or earlier termination of the lease, shall surrender the space in good condition and repair, reasonable wear and tear excepted. The Hospital shall provide routine refurbishing every five (5) years.

8. The leased space is described in Exhibit A,* attached hereto and made a part hereof. The Tenant acknowledges that said space is in good condition and accepts the same "as is."

EXECUTED this_____day of_____, 19____.

_____
Lessor

_____
Tenant

---

*Exhibit A is usually an architectural drawing or floor plan of the leased suite, with all finishes and detailing indicated on the drawing, plus a floor plan of the building indicating where the suite is located.

APPENDIX C

Sample Long-Form Lease

THIS AGREEMENT is made and entered into by and between _____ (hereinafter "Lessor") and _____ (hereinafter "Tenant"), this the _____ day of_____, 19_____.

In consideration of their mutual promises and undertakings as hereinafter set out, the parties agree as follows:

1. *Purpose.* The purpose of this Lease is to provide office space to members of the Medical Staff of_____so that the physician tenants can more readily and efficiently render services to their hospitalized patients. There is no intent in any way to interfere with the physician tenant's independence in the practice of his profession; rather it is intended to establish a mutually congenial relationship between the Tenant and the Lessor and other tenants of the building.

> [Although many leases will not carry this type of "purpose" clause, they often state that the suites are for the practice of medicine only.]

2. *Premises.* The Lessor shall construct an office building in substantial accordance with the plans and specifications that it has developed on its land located _____, and it shall lease to the Tenant the following described premises within said building:

> [If the building is an existing one, the initial statement guaranteeing that the building will be constructed essentially as designed will not be necessary. In addition, in describing the premises being leased by the physician, many leases attach a drawing, rather than a verbal description of the suite. Such a lease might read, "The leased space is described in Exhibit _____, attached hereto and made a part thereof." The exhibit would consist of an architectural drawing of the floor plan of the suite with all finishes—from electrical outlets to toilets—indicated in the drawing. In addition, a floor plan of the building would indicate where the suite was located.]

3. *Term and Commencement.* The term of this Lease is for a period of three years. Renewals, if any, shall be on an annual basis at a rental to be agreed upon. The term, and the rentals accruing hereunder, shall commence on a date specified by the Lessor in a written notice to the Tenant, which written notice shall be given at least sixty (60) days in advance of the completion of the building. Provided, however:

(a) If the Lessor is unable to complete the building for any reason or cause, it shall not be liable to the Tenant. If the Lessor is unable to give possession of the leased premises by the specified date, but is attempting to complete the building, all remedies and rights of both parties shall be suspended during such period; however, if the Lessor is unable to give possession to the Tenant by _____ _____ 19_____, the Tenant shall have the option of cancelling this Lease upon ten (10) days written notice to the Lessor, in which event neither party shall be liable to nor have any further rights against the other.

(b) If the Tenant takes possession and commences use of the leased premises prior to the date specified in the notice, the Tenant's rental obligation will begin on the date possession is so granted and use is commenced.

4. *Rent.* The Tenant shall pay as rental to the Lessor the total sum of $_____, per square foot, per year, for the three-year term, which sum is payable in installments of $_____per month. Each monthly installment shall be due and payable before the 10th day of each month. Any delinquent installment of rent shall bear interest at the rate of 10 percent per annum. It is specifically understood that if the Tenant consists of more than one physician, each shall be jointly, individually, and severally liable for the entire rental obligation.

[Leases vary considerably on the initial term and the renewal options. Whereas the sample lease provides for a relatively short initial term and annual renewal thereafter, some leases might be for five years and contain a specific number of renewal options, each for a specific number of years. Generally, this shorter initial term and annual renewals are more flexible and more desirable. Some leases might also include a limit to the percentage increase in the rent that is allowable at each renewal, but with current inflation rates, that could be risky. A better stipulation would be to relate rental increases to increases in taxes, insurance, and operating costs. Again, this section of the lease is written with some provisions that apply only because the building is yet to be constructed. In this sample, subsection 3(a) would not be necessary in a lease for an existing building.]

5. *Suitability of Premises.* The Tenant's acceptance of the leased premises shall be conclusive evidence that the premises are in good and satisfactory condition. However, a Tenant's entry to the leased premises for the purpose of completing improvements shall not of itself constitute an acceptance of the leased premises.

6. *Lessor's Option in Event of Death, Retirement, Etc.* In the event of the Tenant's death, retirement, failure to maintain good standing with the medical staff, or ceasing to actively practice for a period of six months within the leased premises, the Lessor shall have the option at any time thereafter to terminate this Lease, and the leased premises shall revert to the Lessor notwithstanding that the Tenant may have associates, employees, or nontenant partners who desire to continue to use the leased premises; provided, however, that if the Tenant also consists of more than one physician, the other physician tenant(s) may continue to lease the premises for the remainder of the term.

7. *Nonassignability.* This Lease is not assignable, and the premises cannot be sublet without the prior written consent of the Lessor. This provision also applies to any new members of the Tenant's professional staff, whether partners, associates, or employees. Written consent of the Lessor to a sublease will not

unreasonably be withheld, subject, however, to the understanding that (a) only members of the medical staff may lease or sublease office space and (b) reasonable efforts will be made to sublease the premises to medical staff members who are on the waiting list for office space. If a Tenant incorporates, the corporation may assume the lease with the doctors guaranteeing it.

8. *Floor Weight, Injury to Premises.* The Tenant will not in any manner deface or injure the premises or any part thereof or overload the floors of the leased premises, it being agreed that in no event shall any weight be placed upon the said floors exceeding 50 pounds per square foot of floor space covered without prior written approval of the Lessor.

9. *Renovation, Alterations, Etc.* The Lessor must approve in advance, in writing, any renovations, alterations, or additions to the premises desired by the Tenant, and, unless otherwise agreed in writing, the Tenant shall bear the costs thereof. However, the Lessor's approval of proposed alterations will not be unreasonably withheld.

10. *Name Plates, Locks, Keys, Etc.* Name plates shall be furnished and approved by the Lessor and paid for by the Tenant. The Tenant shall not, without the Lessor's written consent, place additional locks, hooks, or other attachments upon any door or window of the building. The Tenant shall not make nor permit any duplicate keys to be made, it being understood that the Lessor shall furnish all keys to the Tenant at cost. The Tenant shall surrender all keys to the Lessor upon termination of this Lease, and the Lessor will refund to the Tenant the cost thereof.

11. *X-Ray Equipment.* (a) All x-ray equipment that the Tenant plans to install shall first be approved by the Lessor. The Lessor makes no guarantees or representations as to the operations of any x-ray equipment or machine or any other equipment used by the Tenant, and the Tenant assumes the risk of any damage that may result from the operation of or failure to operate any such equipment. The Tenant shall pay for the necessary shielding, electrical connections, and structural support for any x-ray equipment.

(b) In the event the Tenant should use or require the use of x-ray, radium, cobalt, or any other material requiring the use of special devices or equipment, the Tenant agrees to comply with any and all rules and regulations of the Atomic Energy Commission or any other agency having jurisdiction over such materials, and the Tenant agrees to indemnify and hold harmless the Lessor from any and all damages, injuries, and claims of every kind or nature growing out of the handling, use, or possession of such materials and equipment and agrees to be responsible for any and all claims or damages arising from, incident to, or occasioned by the use of such materials and equipment to any and all persons, including the Lessor. This indemnity provision is in addition to and not in limitation of the indemnity agreement in Paragraph 15 hereof.

12. *Additions and Improvements to Remain.* Additions and improvements of a permanent nature made in or upon the leased premises by either the Tenant or the Lessor shall become the property of the Lessor and shall not be removed by the Tenant. The Tenant shall bear the costs of repairs for any damage caused by the removal of any "trade fixtures" or other removable items such as, but not limited to, the removal of wall telephones, carpeting, or equipment.

13. *Personal Property at Tenant's Risk.* The Tenant agrees that all personal property upon the leased premises shall be at the risk of the Tenant, and the Lessor shall not be liable for any damage thereto or for loss or loss of use or theft thereof.

14. *Damage to Person or Property.* (a) Any damage to the leased premises or

to the building or to the property of others, including other Tenants, incident to or resulting from overflows of x-ray developing tanks, sinks, or any other overflows of plumbing fixtures in the leased premises shall be the responsibility of the Tenant. This provision is not intended to charge a Tenant with overflow damage within his leased premises that results from actions of another Tenant or from some action occurring outside the leased premises that causes the overflow. For example, if Tenant A has an overflow because Tenant B's employee caused a stoppage that resulted in water backing up and overflowing in A's premises, then B, not A, would be responsible.

(b) If any property damage to the leased premises, to the building, or to other Tenants shall be occasioned by the acts or activities of or use of the leased premises by the Tenant, the Lessor may at its option repair such damage, and the Tenant agrees to reimburse the Lessor for the costs thereof.

(c) It is further agreed that the Tenant shall bear the risk of any damage to person or property, whether sustained by the Tenant or others, due to the leased premises or any part or appurtenance thereof becoming defective or out of repair or due to any accident in or on the leased premises, and that the Lessor shall not be liable for any act or neglect of any tenant or occupant of the building that results in damage to any person or property.

15. *Indemnification.* The Tenant shall indemnify and save harmless the Lessor from and against any and all claims, expenses (including attorneys' fees), demands, and causes of action of the Tenant, his agents, employees, invitees, patients, or others for injury to person or damage to property of any nature while upon the leased premises or arising from, occasioned by, or incident to the Tenant's use, occupancy, or control of the leased premises. This indemnity and hold harmless agreement shall apply even though the Lessor may be liable for any such damage to person or property, unless such is caused by gross negligence of the Lessor.

The Tenant shall not bear the risk of nor be required to indemnify the Lessor, with respect to injury or damage caused by the Lessor's defective construction of the building itself, including the foundation, outer walls, and roof. It is intended, however, that the Tenant indemnify the Lessor as to injuries and damages occurring within the Tenant's leased premises from all other sources or causes without regard to fault (except Lessor's gross negligence), in order to avoid disputes that might otherwise arise between the parties and result in the parties being at odds with each other. Such risks can be covered under the Tenant's liability insurance policy.

[Some leases actually spell out the amount of insurance to be carried by the Tenant. A typical covenant might read, "The Lessee shall carry public liability and property damage insurance covering any accidents that may occur upon the demised premises in the amount of _____ for any one person, _____ for any one occurrence, and _____ for property damage liability. Such insurance shall carry a clause indemnifying the Lessor against any loss, cost, or damage resulting from any occurrence on the demised premises and providing that such insurance may not be terminated until after the insurer has given the Lessor thirty (30) days notice in writing of its intention to do so."]

16. *Lessor Shall Furnish or Provide:* (a) The Lessor agrees to furnish general housekeeping services, engineering services, elevators to all floors, heat, air

conditioning, utilities, adequate ceiling light fixtures for normal illumination of the leased space, venetian blinds, electric convenience outlets (up to four duplex outlets per room), telephone outlets (up to two per doctor), vinyl asbestos tile floors and painted walls, one standard reception window with shelf, one lavatory in each examining room, built-in double x-ray view box for each physician's consultation room, one compressed air and one vacuum outlet per suite, shelf and rod for coat closets, specimen pass box (if required) at toilets, built-in open shelving in storage closets, and one sink per utility-work area. The Lessor shall also furnish one toilet room per each 600 to 1400 square feet, or two toilet rooms per each 1401 to 2800 square feet, or three toilet rooms per each 2801 to 4000 square feet, or four toilet rooms per each 4001 or more square feet.

The Lessor further agrees to maintain the common areas; extend its paging system into the corridors of the building; to provide a parking space for each physician tenant in the medical staff parking lot or other special area as may be designated, but in no case will more than one space be provided; and to post on the directory of the building one name to be designated by each physician tenant. Employees of the Tenant may be allowed to use parking lots maintained for Lessor's employees, if space is available, but the Lessor is not obligated to provide such parking.

The space of a Tenant who has continuously leased for five (5) years shall be eligible for repainting without cost to the Tenant, and if repainting is desired sooner, the cost will be ratably apportioned between the Tenant and the Lessor.

The Tenant shall make his own arrangements with the telephone company for telephone service; however, the Lessor can provide the Tenant with a telephone line from the Lessor's system for which the Tenant will be changed at the rate established by the Lessor from time to time. This service is available only as an addition to a system subscribed to by the Tenant from the telephone company. The telephone number for the line from the Lessor's system is not to be listed in the public telephone directory. This practice is controlled by the _____General Subscriber's Tarriff.

> [The list of suite finishes and building services provided may vary considerably from one project to the next. This list, however, is certainly representative of how this section of the lease might be handled. In addition, parking provisions will certainly vary according to locality. In some leases a site plan may be attached as an exhibit, with specific parking areas designated for physicians, employees, and patients. Some leases provide free parking for patients; others do not. Whatever the parking provisions, they should be spelled out clearly.]

(b) *Tenant Shall Furnish or Be Financially Responsible for:* delivery service for mail and x-ray films, transporting of patients, x-ray equipment and the installation thereof, floor drains and the installation thereof, case work, intercom system, interior locks, carpeting, wall coverings, and drapes.

(c) *The Lessor Shall Not Be Liable for:* damages by abatement of rent, or otherwise, for failure to furnish or delay in furnishing elevator service, heat, air-conditioning, electric current, janitor service, or utilities, including water, when such failure to furnish or delay in furnishing is occasioned by needful repairs, renewals, or improvements, or in whole or in part by any strike or other labor disturbance, demonstration, or by any accident or casualty whatever, or by the act, neglect, or default of the Tenant or other parties, or by any cause or causes beyond the reasonable control of the Lessor; nor shall the Lessor be liable for any act or default not authorized by the Lessor of the janitors or other employees of the Lessor; and such failure, delay, or default in furnishing elevator service, heat, air conditioning, electric current, janitor service, or water, or any unauthorized act or default of the janitors or employees shall not be considered or construed as an actual or constructive eviction of the Tenant, nor shall it in any way operate to release the Tenant from the prompt and punctual payment of rent and the performance of each and all the other covenants herein contained that are to be performed by the Tenant. The rent shall, however, abate in the event the premises are rendered untenantable by fire or other casualty not the fault of the Tenant, until the premises are substantially restored to their former condition. See Paragraph 18.

(d) All other or extra work, equipment, refinements, or facilities required by the Tenant shall be paid for by the Tenant but shall be performed or furnished by the Lessor at actual cost to it and may be billed or invoiced to the Tenant.

(e) It is further understood and agreed between the parties that any charges against the Tenant by the Lessor for supplies, services, or work done on the premises by order of the Tenant or otherwise accruing under this Lease Agreement shall be considered as rent due and shall be included in any lien for rent due and unpaid. This provision is not intended to charge the Tenant with any costs that are the responsibility of the Lessor under Paragraph 16(a).

17. *Default and Option to Terminate.* If default shall at any time be made by the Tenant in the payment of the rent or in any other covenants herein provided to be kept, observed, and performed by the Tenant or if the leasehold interest shall be levied on under execution or if the Tenant shall be declared bankrupt or insolvent according to law or if any assignment of the Tenant's property shall be made for the benefit of creditors, then and in any of said cases the Lessor may, at its option, at once and without notice to the Tenant or any other person, terminate this Lease.

18. *Destruction or Damage to Building.* If without the Tenant's fault: (a) The building is destroyed by fire or other casualty, this lease shall immediately terminate; (b) the building is so damaged as to render the leased premises untenantable and repairs cannot be completed within 180 days, either party may terminate this Lease on 30 days' written notice, and the Tenant shall pay rent up to the date of such damage. If the premises can be so repaired within 180 days, the rent shall abate during the repair period with respect to such portions of the leased premises that are untenantable, and the amount of abatement in rent shall be apportioned on a square foot basis during the repair period, provided the damage was not the fault of the Tenant.

19. *Tenant's Obligation After Termination.* Upon termination of this Lease for any reason, the Tenant shall be obligated to immediately surrender the premises to the Lessor in as good a condition as when the Lease commenced, reasonable wear excepted. The Tenant shall also be obligated to remove from the leased premises his effects immediately after any such termination. Following termination, the Lessor shall have the right to reenter the premises and retake possession thereof and remove the effects therein without liability for trespass or damages, and the Lessor may at its option store any property removed at the Tenant's expense.

20. *Payment after Termination.* No receipt of monies by the Lessor after termination of this Lease in any manner or after giving of any termination notice shall reinstate or continue or extend the term of this Lease or affect any notice given to the Tenant prior to the receipt of such money.

21. *Enforcement of Obligations and Lien.* The Tenant agrees to pay all attorneys' fees and expenses incurred by the Lessor in enforcing any of the obligations of the Tenant under this Lease or incident to any litigation or negotiation in which the Lessor shall, without its fault, become involved through or on account of this Lease. The Lessor shall also have and is hereby granted a first lien upon the leasehold and the Tenant's property within the leased premises for the payment of all rent and other sums that may become due hereunder.

22. *No animals (except guide dogs), bicycles, or other vehicles* (except those designed for medical conditions and usage and approved by the Lessor) shall be allowed in the premises, and the Tenant shall cooperate with the Lessor in enforcing this provision.

23. *The Tenant will not permit obstruction* of the sidewalks, corridors, elevators, or stairways, nor permit the use thereof except for the purposes for which the same were constructed, without the express consent of the Lessor.

24. *Canvassing, soliciting, and peddling* in the building is prohibited, and the Tenant shall cooperate to prevent the same.

25. *Transport of Patients from Hospital.* In order to minimize risks incident to transporting of patients, the Tenant agrees not to cause hospitalized patients to be transported to a Tenant's office or elsewhere for treatments, X rays, laboratory, or other tests that can be satisfactorily provided without the necessity of transporting the patient from the hospital. In the event the Tenant deems it necessary to transport the patient to his office or elsewhere, the said transfer shall be at the sole risk of the Tenant, who shall be solely responsible for providing the means and personnel therefor, for obtaining the informed consent of the patient thereto, for assisting the Lessor in obtaining from the patient a release and waiver of any cause of action for injury or damage that may result from any cause whatsoever incident to the patient's transportation, and the Tenant shall indemnify and hold harmless the Lessor from and against any cause of action the patient may have incident thereto.

26. *The entire agreement* between the parties is set out herein, and no other agreements, representations, or warranties, expressed or implied, have been made.

27. *This Lease Agreement shall be binding* upon the respective parties, their heirs, personal representatives, successors, and assigns.

28. *Waiver of Subrogation.* The Lessor and the Tenant each hereby release and waive all right of recovery against each other, irrespective of any carelessness or negligency, for any loss or damage sustained to the property of the other, to the extent such loss or damage is covered under the terms and provisions of any policy or policies of insurance in force at the time of such loss, and the Lessor and the Tenant, to the extent the same shall not invalidate such policy or policies, each agree not to assign any subrogation rights against the other to any such insurer. The Lessor shall provide and pay for all hazard insurance desired to cover the building, including the leased premises, and the Tenant shall provide and pay for all hazard insurance desired to cover the Tenant's leasehold improvements, trade fixtures, equipment, and property of every kind. This release and waiver of subrogation shall not be inoperative by reason of indemnity provisions of Paragraph 15 of this Lease, and neither the provisions of this Paragraph nor of Paragraph 15 shall relieve either party of their respective undertakings pursuant to the indemnity provisions of Paragraph 15 of this Lease.

IN WITNESS WHEREOF the parties have executed this Agreement as of the date first above set out.

_____Hospital

_____

LESSOR

_____

_____

_____

_____

TENANT

GUARANTEE

If Tenant is a professional corporation, the Lease and the Tenant's obligations are guaranteed by:

_____

_____

_____

_____

This particular lease, based on one written for use at Baptist Memorial Hospital's (Memphis) newest office building, is quite thorough and understandable. Only two covenants that appear frequently in hospital-owned medical office building leases are not included. The first is a covenant stating that a waiver or indulgence of any breach of the lease does not imply any waiver of rights in the future. This covenent might cover payment of rent only or it might be so stated to include any aspect of the lease. The primary reason for including such a covenant within a lease is so that the hospital can deal flexibly with its physician tenants without endangering its rights to enforce the lease at any point in the future. The second is a covenant that guarantees the tenant "quiet, peaceful, and uninterrupted possession" of the premises as long as he keeps all the covenants of the lease.

APPENDIX D

Sample Commercial Lease

1. *Parties.* THIS LEASE AGREEMENT, made and entered into on this the ____ day of_____, 19_____, by and between _____, of _____, party of the first part, hereinafter called "Lessor," and _____, party of the second part, hereinafter called "Lessee."

2. *Consideration.* WITNESSETH: That each of the aforesaid parties acknowledges the receipt of a valuable consideration from the other, and that they and each of them act herein in further consideration of the engagements of the other, as herein stated.

3. *Premises.* That Lessor has and does hereby grant, demise, and lease unto the Lessee the premises situated in the City of _____, County of _____, and State of _____, more particularly described in Exhibit A, attached hereto, and made a part hereof as fully and particularly as if set out verbatim herein.

> [As with a physician tenant's lease, exhibit A would consist of a floor plan of the building indicating the location of the leased space and a specific architectural drawing of the leased space showing all finishes to be included.]

This lease is made subject to those liens, easements, encumbrances, and exceptions listed on the attached Exhibit A, and also subject to all zoning ordinances and laws affecting the demised premises.

4. *Term.* TO HAVE AND TO HOLD the premises described in Exhibit A, attached hereto, unto the Lessee for a period of ten (10) years, hereinafter referred to as the "Primary Term," commencing on___, 19___, and ending on___, 19___.

> [The term of a commercial lease is almost always longer than that for the physician tenant. An initial lease of five years would usually be the minimum. Because the commercial tenant normally has to make many expensive leasehold improvements on the premises in order to conduct his business, he will insist on a fairly lengthy initial lease term.]

5. *Options to Renew.* In consideration of the Lessee entering into this lease agreement for the Primary Term, and provided that the Lessee at the time of the notice of the exercise of the respective options hereinafter granted, and at the time of the commencement of the respective renewal terms hereinafter granted, is not in default under the terms of this lease, the Lessor grants to the Lessee the following options to renew and extend this lease, each of such extensions to be upon the same terms and conditions as with respect to the Primary Term.

(a) The Lessor grants to the Lessee an option to extend this lease for an additional term (hereinafter called the "First Extended Term") of five (5) years from the date of the expiration of the Primary Term; and in the event that the Lessee shall elect to exercise the option herein granted to extend this lease for the First Extended Term as herein provided, the Lessee shall so notify the Lessor in writing of his election not less than three (3) months prior to the expiration of the Primary Term.

(b) If the Lessee shall have availed himself of that first option to extend, as set forth in subparagraph (a) above, the Lessor grants to the Lessee an additional option to extend this lease for two (2) additional separate terms of five (5) years each from the date of the expiration of the First Extended Term; and in the event that the Lessee shall elect to exercise the options herein granted to extend this lease for such additional terms as herein provided, the Lessee shall notify the Lessor in writing of his election not less than three (3) months prior to the expiration of the First Extended Term or any subsequent extended term.

(c) Notwithstanding the foregoing provisions, the Lessor shall have the right to purchase from Lessee the leasehold interest and pharmacy business, as set out in paragraph 5.

[Renewal options may differ in number and length; nonetheless, in a commercial lease the tenant will usually insist on a fairly lengthy period being available in some manner. The provision for the hospital to have the right to purchase the pharmacy is probably somewhat unusual, but protects the hospital's interest and options.]

6. (a) *Rental.* The Lessee covenants and agrees to pay to Lessor, as rental for the aforesaid premises during the Primary Term, _____per square foot per year or _____percent of Lessee's annual gross sales, whichever is greater. Such rental shall be due and payable on the 10th day of each month in an amount representing one-twelfth (1/12) of the rental due on a square foot basis. If the gross sales provision is greater than the square foot rental, then in such event the difference in rental shall be paid by the Lessee to the Lessor within thirty (30) days after the anniversary date of this lease.

(b) Included in such rental shall be all utilities (except telephone) and housekeeping and maintenance, which shall be paid by Lessor.

[The provision of housekeeping services may well be omitted from the lease for security reasons, or the housekeeping service may be provided during business hours only.]

(c) All rentals or other payments due under this lease shall be payable to the order of _____, at _____, unless the Lessee be otherwise notified in writing.

(d) If the expenses for maintaining and operating the Building during the calendar year beginning January 1, _____, or during any calendar year thereafter exceed the expenses for maintaining and operating the building during the calendar year beginning January 1, _____, then the Lessee shall pay to the Lessor as additional rent (over and above the base rent, but to be offset by the gross sales provision) the portion of such excess attributable to the Premises, such additional rent to be paid in twelve (12) equal monthly installments commencing March 1 of the calendar year immediately succeeding the calendar year in which such excess occurs; provided, however, that any such additional rent shall not be due and payable beyond the term of this lease or renewal thereof. On or before February 15, _____, and on or before February 15 of each calendar year thereafter, the Lessor shall furnish to the Lessee a written statement showing the computation of such excess, if any, for the preceding calendar year and showing the amount of additional rent for which the Lessee shall be obligated under this paragraph.

7. *Quiet Possession.* The Lessor hereby covenants that if the Lessee shall keep and perform all of the covenants of this lease on the part of the Lessee to be performed, the Lessor will guarantee to the Lessee the quiet, peaceful, and uninterrupted possession of the said premises, except as against taking by public authority under power of eminent domain.

8. *Use of Premises.* The Lessee shall use and occupy the premises only for the purpose of operating a retail professional pharmacy, offering drugs and nondrug items usually handled in a retail professional pharmacy. When there is a question involved in the selling of duplicate items by Lessees, there will be a meeting by the Lessees involved and the Lessor to seek agreement on the adding or deleting of competitive items. In case the Lessees cannot come to an agreement, then the Lessor will make binding decisions that the Lessees must abide by.

LESSEE FURTHER COVENANTS:

9. *Lawful and Moral Purposes.* That the premises and all buildings and improvements thereon shall during the term of this lease be used only and exclusively for lawful and moral purposes, and no part of the premises or improvements thereon shall be used in any manner whatsoever for any purposes in violation of the laws of the United States, the State of_____ _____, or the ordinances and laws of the City of _____.

10. *Protection From Violations.* To save and hold the Lessor harmless from violations of the laws of the United States, of the State of _____, and the ordinances and laws of the City of _____.

11. *Waste.* Not to commit or permit to be committed any waste of utilities or systems.

12. *Obstruction.* Not to commit or permit obstruction of the sidewalks, corridors, elevators, or stairways, nor permit the use thereof except for the purpose for which same were constructed, without the express consent of the Lessor.

13. *Nuisances.* Not to create or allow any nuisance to exist on said premises, and to abate any nuisance that may arise promptly and free of expense to Lessor.

14. *Going Business.* That, following completion of construction of the new buildings and improvements that the Lessee contemplates constructing upon the leased property, the Lessee shall thereafter maintain a going business on the premises throughout the Primary Term and any extension thereof.

15. *Costs of Collection.* In the event that either party hereto defaults in the payment or performance of any of the terms, covenants, agreements, or conditions contained in this lease and the other party places the enforcement thereof in the hands of an attorney or files suit upon the same, the defaulting party agrees to pay to the other party a reasonable attorney's fee and the costs of the enforcement.

16. *Insolvency of Lessee.* In the event that (a) The Lessee shall become insolvent (as that term is defined in the_____Uniform Commercial Code) or bankrupt, or

(b) The Lessee shall file in any court, pursuant to any statute, either of the United States or any state, a petition in bankruptcy or insolvency, or for the appointment of a receiver or trustee of all or a portion of the Lessee's property; or

(c) There shall be filed against the Lessee, in any court pursuant to any statute, either of the United States or of any state, a petition in bankruptcy or insolvency, or for the appointment of a receiver or trustee of all or a portion of the property of the Lessee, and such petition shall not be dismissed within sixty (60) days from the date of the filing thereof; or

(d) Lessee shall make a partial or general assignment for the benefit of creditors, then and in any such event the Lessor may, at the Lessor's option, terminate this lease upon five (5) days' notice in advance.

17. *Damage, Accidents, etc.* To keep and hold the Lessor harmless from any liability, cost, or expense of any nature for loss or damages to persons, property, or things, both real or asserted, arising from any cause or causes in or connected with or about, or by virtue of the use of, the leased premises (excepting any loss, injuries, damages, expenses, or costs occasioned by the negligence of the Lessor, its agents, servants, or employees, for which the Lessor will indemnify and hold the Lessee harmless).

18. *Tax Increases.* In addition to the rental hereinbefore provided to be paid, the Lessee further covenants and agrees to pay its pro rata portion of all lawful increases after _____ in State, County, City, and other governmental, educational, or improvement district real estate ad valorem taxes, assessments, and charges that may be assessed or otherwise imposed upon the leased premises or upon any buildings or improvements thereon, within thirty (30) days after the same shall become due and payable.

19. *Insurance.* (a) Throughout the term of this lease, the Lessee shall keep the leased property insured, at Lessee's sole cost and expense, against claims for personal injury or property damage under a policy or policies of general public liability insurance, with limits of at least $ _____ for bodily injury and $_____ for property damage.

(b) However, the Lessor shall keep the leased premises insured against loss or damage by fire and such other risks as may be included in the broadest form of extended coverage insurance from time to time available, and in any event in an amount that is not less than ninety percent (90%) of the actual replacement cost of such leased premises.

20. *Damage or Destruction, etc.* In the event of destruction of or damage to the leased premises by fire, windstorm, or any other casualty, the Lessor shall have ninety (90) days in which to rebuild and restore the premises to its previous condition, and during such period that the premises are untenantable by the Lessee, the rental shall be abated in full. In the event that the premises are not or cannot be restored or rebuilt by the Lessor within the ninety (90) day period, then the Lessee shall have the right to terminate this lease without any further liability thereunder, or to await restoration or rebuilding, at the Lessee's option.

21. *Assignment and Subletting.* The Lessee shall not, either voluntarily or by operation of law, assign, transfer, mortgage, or otherwise encumber this lease or sublet the premises or permit any part thereof to be used or occupied by anyone other than the Lessee or the Lessee's employees, without the prior written consent of Lessor in each instance.

22. *Alterations.* The Lessee shall not, without the prior written consent of the Lessor make any alterations to or removals from the leased premises, if such alterations or removals, without repair or replacement by the Lessee, would materially decrease the value of the Lessor's reversionary interest in the leased premises.

23. *Delivery at End of Lease.* Upon the expiration of the term of this lease, the Lessee will deliver unto the Lessor the possession of said leased premises,

cleared of all persons, goods, and things not properly belonging to the same, and in as good order and condition as the same were received, ordinary wear and tear excepted, and no demand for such delivery shall be necessary; provided, however, the Lessees shall have the right to remove its trade fixtures, movable equipment, furnishings, and signs.

24. *Right of Entry, etc.* The Lessor reserves the right during the term of this lease to enter said premises at reasonable hours to show the same to other persons who may be interested in renting or buying the property, and for the purpose of inspecting the premises and to make such repairs as the Lessor may deem necessary for the protection and preservation of the leased premises and any buildings and improvements thereon.

25. *Waiver of Breach.* No failure by the Lessor to insist upon the strict performance of any term or condition of this lease, or to exercise any right or remedy available on a breach thereof, and no acceptance of full or partial rent during the continuance of any such breach, shall constitute a waiver of any such breach or of any such term or condition. No term or condition of this lease required to be performed by the Lessee, and no breach thereof, shall be waived, altered, or modified, except by a written instrument executed by the Lessor. No waiver of any breach shall be taken to constitute a waiver of any other breach or of a subsequent breach of the same covenant, and each term or condition shall continue in full force and effect with respect to any other then existing or subsequent breach thereof.

26. *Renewal.* No renewal of this lease will be binding on either party unless it be in writing and signed by the Lessor and the Lessee; except and unless the Lessee shall give the Lessor notice of its election to renew and extend this lease for either of the Extended Terms (as provided in paragraph 5 hereof), which notice must be signed only by the Lessee.

27. *Notices.* All notices to be given hereunder shall be in writing and shall be delivered in person or mailed, by registered or certified mail, return receipt requested; the time of any notice shall begin with the date of delivery, if in person, or upon the date of mailing, if mailed. Notices shall be addressed and mailed or delivered to the following addresses:

> IF TO THE LESSOR:
> Copy To:
> IF TO THE LESSEE:
> Copy to:

or to such other address or addresses as either party may designate to the other, by notice in writing, given as above provided.

28. *Binding Upon Successors in Interest.* It is hereby covenanted and agreed between the parties hereto that all covenants, conditions, agreements, and undertakings in this lease contained shall be binding upon and shall inure to the benefit of the respective heirs, administrators, executors, successors, and assigns of the parties hereto, the same as if they were in every case named and expressed.

29. *Contract.* This lease is a _____ contract and all the terms and conditions and provisions thereof shall be governed by the laws of the State of _____.

30. *Commission.* Each party covenants with and represents to the other that no real estate commission is owed to any party in connection with the negotiation and execution of this lease.

31. *Entire Agreement.* This lease contains all of the agreements and conditions made between the parties hereto and no representations or statements

claimed to have been made and not herein contained shall vary or modify this agreement in any way whatsoever.

32. *Short Form Lease.* The parties agree that they will enter into a short form memorandum of this lease for recordation, in order that it shall not be necessary that the entire lease be recorded. Such short form memorandum lease shall, *inter alia,* set forth the exact beginning and ending dates of the Primary Term and the existence of the options to renew and extend the lease for the Extended Terms, but no reference in said memorandum of lease shall be made to the rental to be paid by the Lessee to the Lessor.

[This covenant is a means for providing privacy for both the Lessor and the Lessee. By agreeing to file a short form lease, the parties prevent all the details of the lease from becoming a part of public record. Such a procedure would be desirable if either party did not want competitors or others to know the details of their agreement.]

33. *Condemnation.* If the whole of the premises shall be condemned or taken either permanently or temporarily for any public or quasi-public use or purpose, under any statute or by right of eminent domain, or by private purchase in lieu thereof, then in that event, the term of this lease shall cease and terminate from the date of title vesting in such proceeding or purchase, and the Lessee shall have no claim against the Lessor for the value of any unexpired term of said lease and shall release unto the Lessor any such claim it may have against the condemnor. In the event a portion only of the premises or a portion of the Building containing same shall be so taken (even though the premises may not have been affected by the taking of some other portion of the Building containing same), the Lessor or the Lessee may elect to terminate this lease from the date of title vesting in such proceeding or purchase, or the Lessor may elect to repair and restore, at its own expense, the portion not taken and thereafter the rent shall be reduced proportionately to the portion of the premises taken.

34. *Trade Fixtures, Movable Equipment, Furnishings, and Signs.* All trade fixtures, movable equipment, furnishings, and signs, installed on the leased property by the Lessee for the conduct of the business of the Lessee, shall remain the property of the Lessee; and the same may be removed by the Lessee upon the expiration of the term of this lease, or any extension thereof, provided that any damage caused by such removal shall be repaired by the Lessee at its expense and the premises left in good condition, ordinary wear and tear excepted.

[Most leases also carry exact provisions about what types of signs can be used by a commercial establishment and where they can be placed. For example, most businesses will want large exterior signs; however, for tax and esthetic reasons the hospital will usually not allow them. The placement of signs outside the building implies the solicitation of business from outside the building, and that implication can jeopardize the tax exempt status of the building. Consequently, most leases either prohibit the use of signs on the exterior of the building or require the approval of the hospital for any sign to be placed outside.]

35. *Purchase of Pharmacy.* The Lessor shall have the option to purchase from the Lessee the pharmacy business conducted by the Lessee in the premises and the Lessee's leasehold interest in the premises. Such option may

be exercised by the Lessor by written notice to the Lessee within thirty (30) days of the Lessee's notice to the Lessor of its intention to extend the Lease, pursuant to paragraph 5(b), past the First Extended Term. The purchase price of the pharmacy business and leasehold interest shall be as mutually agreed upon between the parties, or if they are unable to agree upon a price, then the option price shall be established as follows: the Lessor and the Lessee shall each, within fifteen (15) days of the notice of exercise by the Lessor, appoint an arbitrator and the two arbitrators shall choose a third arbitrator. The three arbitrators shall meet and by majority decision establish the purchase price, and shall in writing report such purchase price to the Lessor and the Lessee within thirty (30) days after their appointment. The purchase pursuant to the purchase price shall be closed within fifteen (15) days after receipt of such notice. The purchase price shall be payable in cash in full at the time of the exercise. In the event that the Lessor exercises its right to purchase pursuant to this paragraph, the Lessor agrees to operate the pharmacy on its own behalf and not to release the pharmacy or premises or to allow any person, firm, or entity to manage or operate the pharmacy for a period of five (5) years from the date of purchase by the Lessor.

[This covenant also is rather unusual, but provides a means for the hospital to buy back the pharmacy if it so chooses.]

36. *Arbitration.* In the event the Lessor has any complaint about the Lessee's use and operation of the premises that cannot be resolved with the Lessee, then in such event the parties agree to appoint an arbitration committee consisting of a doctor, a pharmacist, and a third member selected by the two arbitrators so chosen. The three arbitrators shall meet and by majority decision, which shall be binding on both parties hereto, decide the matter or matters in controversy.

IN WITNESS WHEREOF, the Lessor and the Lessee have executed this Lease Agreement on the day and year first above written.

By _____
Title: _____
                    LESSOR
By _____
Title: _____
                    LESSEE

Although this lease covers most of the important covenants, some areas are not mentioned; for example, parking. The omission of parking from commercial leases is typical, for the lessor assumes the customers of the commercial establishments are patients already visiting the building or the hospital. Generally, parking is not made a covenant within the lease unless some type of validation parking is to be provided, and most medical office buildings do not validate parking. Frequently, commercial establishments will demand reserved parking for their customers. It should be avoided. Not only does it irritate patients and employees, but it implies the solicitation of business from outside the building.

Another area covered rather thoroughly in the physician's lease that is not mentioned in detail in a commercial lease relates to the lessor-provided suite finishes and services. The commercial lease mentions only the provision of utilities, housekeeping, and maintenance. More commonly, the lease would also include an itemized list of physical facilities or finishes provided by the landlord. Typical examples would be a specified type of ceiling, basic wiring with a specified number of electrical outlets, so many feet of glass store front and/or dry wall partitions, front and rear doors and hardware to conform to the other commercial spaces, adequate heating and air-conditioning, and perhaps even some plumbing, including a toilet and a sink. This covenant would vary widely, but some finishing provisions are usually included in the lease.

Limitations on the weight that can be placed on the floor are not included in this lease because in this particular building all commercial establishments were located on grade, where overloading of floors was not a problem. Most commercial establishments are located on grade, but if they are not, some provision would probably need to be included concerning weight.

One other covenant not included in this lease is the statement that acceptance of the leased premises would be evidence of the premises' good and satisfactory condition. In many states, that covenant is assumed by law; however, inclusion of that covenant would not be a mistake.

Finally, many commercial leases might go into more details on liability, indemnity, and insurance coverage. Much would depend on the relationship between the lessor and the lessee and on local laws and statutes.

Index